To Be a Slave in Brazil

To Be a Slave in Brazil

1550–1888

KATIA M. DE QUEIRÓS MATTOSO

translated by Arthur Goldhammer

Foreword by Stuart Schwartz

Rutgers University Press *New Brunswick, New Jersey*

Library of Congress Cataloging-in-Publication Data

Mattoso, Katia M. de Queirós.
To be a slave in Brazil, 1550–1888.

Translation of: Etre esclave au Brésil: XVIe–XIXe.
Bibliography: p.
Includes index.
1. Slavery—Brazil—History.   2. Slave–trade—Brazil—
History.   I. Title
HT1126.M3713   1986   306'.362'0981   85–27760
ISBN 0–8135–1154–2

CONTENTS

FOREWORD

All the slaveholding colonial powers and the independent states of the Americas where slavery persisted confronted in the nineteenth century a series of profound moral, philosophical, social, and economic dilemmas around the question of manumission. In each colony and metropolis and in each nation a literature specific to that place developed on the issue of freedom and abolition, seeking to defend or attack slavery in the peculiar context of its place and time. One need only mention the work of the Cuban Jose Antonio Saco, the Brazilian Perdigão Malheiro, and the North American George Fitzhugh as examples of this development. But even in its origins the study of slavery in the Americas often had a comparative perspective. The work of Saco and Perdigão Malheiro was certainly proof of that. British parlimentary committees on the slave trade and emancipation in the West Indies often heard testimony on conditions in other slaveholding societies. Those with experience in other slaveholding regimes sometimes wrote in detail about observed similarities and differences. And information on the progress of slavery and abolition was anxiously passed among opponents and advocates from one colony or nation to another. Nor were the slaves themselves unaware of the condition of their fellows in other places. The news of the Haitian rebellion spread rapidly and with obvious effects among slave communities from Carolina to Venezuela and Brazil. The international marketplace and common concerns made the slave systems of the Atlantic world a unity in the nineteenth century, and probably before that, which contemporaries, both slave and free, often recognized.

For this reason it is somewhat curious that after emancipation the comparative perspective was often forgotten or ignored. The best scholars of slavery such as W. E. B. Dubois or U. B. Phillips gave some attention to slavery in a broader perspective, but in general the study of slavery in the first half of the twentieth century was increasingly parochial and overwhelmingly concerned with the impact of slavery on national development and on national character. Only with the publication in 1947 of Frank Tannenbaum's *Slave and Citizen* did the comparative approach to slavery in the Americas really return as a legitimate and useful method for study. Tannenbaum, greatly influenced by Latin American social scientists of the 1930s and 1940s, especially the Brazilian Gilberto Freyre and the Cuban Fernando Ortiz, contrasted the slave systems of Protestant North America and Catholic Latin America. Implicitly, he saw the differences in contemporary race relations in the United States and Latin America as a direct result of the differences in the two systems of slavery. Whatever the validity of Tannenbaum's thesis, the effect of his book was to stimulate a reexamination not only of the comparative perspective, but of the existing assumptions and the level of knowledge about North American, West Indian, and Latin American slavery per se. We need not review here the considerable debate that developed between those who followed Tannenbaum's lead or shared his assumptions and found startling contrasts between slavery in the United States and Latin America and the various critics who attacked these assumptions, or the scholarship on which they rested, and saw instead disheartening similarities in the slave systems. It was a long and often heated debate and it continues today. Right or wrong, after Tannenbaum's slim volume it was difficult to propose a generalization about slavery in any one region without at least an implicit comparison to other American slaveholding societies. This alone made his book an important milestone.

While anglophone historians responded to Tannenbaum's challenging formulation of the problem, Latin American scholars responded to the internal intellectual and sociopolitical dynamics of their own societies. Many North American comparative historians beginning with Tannenbaum had turned to Brazil as an obvious point of comparison. There the work of Gilberto Freyre, especially *Casa Grande e senzala* (1933), which emphasized the integration of Indian and African elements in Brazilian life, had dominated both popular and academic thinking about slavery and race relations. But, in the turbulent 1950s and 1960s, Freyre's views were coming under increasing critical scrutiny by a new generation of Brazilian sociologists and historians, mostly from São Paulo and often writing from a Marxist perspective, who began to reexamine the history of slavery in their country. The work of these scholars—Octavio Ianni, Fernando Henrique Cardoso, Florestan Fernandes, and Emilia Viotti da Costa— presented Brazilian slavery as a far less benign institution than had been previously thought, and it threw into question some basic assumptions of those who like Freyre and Tannenbaum emphasized the dissimilarities between the slave systems and the subsequent race relations in the United States and Brazil. While the work of this newer generation of Brazilian scholars concentrated on southern Brazil and the nineteenth century, it had a solid documentary and theoretical foundation and thus provided a new point of departure for the study of slavery in Brazil. The principle concern of the "São Paulo school" was not so much the slaves themselves as the impact of slavery on the economic development of Brazil, and while historians of the skill and perception of Viotti da Costa gave considerable attention to slave life and conditions, the main thrust of these studies lay in another direction. The Portuguese language is far more subtle in this regard than English for there are a number of terms to describe what in English we usually refer to as "slavery." The São Paulo school was interested in what was called *escravismo* or the slave system, its economic ramifications, and its effects on the subsequent development of Brazil and the position of blacks in Brazilian society. It was less concerned with an older line of inquiry, mostly associated with anthropologists and folklorists in Brazil, which had been preoccupied with the ethnic origins, religions, cultures, and life of slaves, or *escravidão*, what we might call the inner aspects of slavery. Freyre's work, in fact, had been much influenced by this tradition and although his comprehensive reading led him to a concern with broader social and economic issues, he was essentially discussing aspects of slavery and general social patterns which were not the primary focus of the São Paulo school; so at times criticism of him was misplaced. Still, the essential contribution of the new scholarship on Brazilian slavery was to reexamine the whole question of slavery in a far more critical perspective and with a more rigorous methodology and to frame the issue in the broadest terms. It made the economic and systemic effects of slavery on Brazilian history the central question of historical study in the following decades.

Here once again scholarship in North America, Latin America, and Europe began to converge. Historians and social scientists writing from a directly comparative perspective such as C. R. Boxer, Herbert Klein, Stanley Elkins, Marvin Harris, David Brion Davis, and Carl Degler stimulated continual reexamination fo the various slave regimes in works that made it clear that the evidence itself often allowed for widely different interpretations dependent as much on methodology, ideology, and supposition as on the historical record. But works of direct comparison were only one stimulus to a renewed interest in the comparative study of slavery.

General issues had to be confronted comparatively. The development of historical demography, the study of *mentalité*, and studies of the international traffic in slaves had obvious implications for all the slaveholding regions. In the United States the work of Albert Raboteau on slave religion, Herbert Gutman on the slave family, John Blassingame on the slave community, Eugene Genovese on slave life and culture, resistance, and planter ideology, Robert Fogel and Stanley Engerman on demography, productivity, and other such questions all reflected an implicit comparative viewpoint at least and raised comparative questions in the minds of Latin American and Latin Americanist historians. In the United States, the issues of slave life and culture and slavery as an economic system were fusing into a broader and more complex field of study. A comparative perspective had enriched the study of slavery in the United States and as this field developed rapidly in the 1960s and 1970s it stimulated Latin Americans to address similar issues, although often from a different ideological perspective than their anglophone colleagues. Brazilian scholars remained interested in broad economic and theoretical aspects of slavery as a system but there was also a renewed concern with the social aspects of slavery and slave society. Important new studies were done on the economics and demography of slavery, on the ideology of the slave system, on the process of manumission and the role of free blacks in Brazilian society, on slave religiosity, on slave resistence, and on slavery's impact on regional development. The historiography of Brazilian slavery was undergoing a rapid change that reflected a growing integration of the study of *escravismo* and *escravidão*.

In this exciting new development of slave studies in Brazil, few have played a more important role in bringing attention to the social aspects of slavery and slave society than Katia Mattoso. Born in Greece, educated in Switzerland and France, and greatly influenced by her wide reading in contemporary French and North American historical scholarship, she has brought to Brazil—where she has lived for some twenty years—a cosmopolitan and eclectic approach to the study of slavery. Her writing has always been marked by its attention to and imaginative handling of primary sources, and she and her students in Bahia have gathered and used materials long unknown or ignored. Her own monographic work on wages and prices, manumission, epidemics, and the role of free people of color in Brazilian society has been continually innovative and is consistently characterized by a solid documentary base, but it has never been separated from a concern with larger questions and a desire to synthesize. These qualities are best displayed in her excellent study of the city of Salvador in the nineteenth century (*Bahia: A cidade do Salvador e seu mercado no século xix* [São Paulo, 1978]) which integrated the results of many of her monographs. Her studies have been mostly regional, concerned with Bahia where she has long resided, but her impact by example, lecturing, and writing has been felt all over Brazil as well as in France and the United States where she has also taught.

To Be a Slave in Brazil, published originally in French in 1979 and in Portuguese in 1982, is a most welcome addition to the works on Brazilian slavery available to English-speaking readers. Written without scholarly footnotes for a general readership, it is a deceptively simple book direct in its presentation, lacing a specialized jargon, and organized in an imaginative and interesting way. But it also is a volume that reflects some of the most recent and innovative research on the question of slavery (much of it Mattoso's own). Putting aside the somewhat arid debate over the feudal or capitalist nature of the "slave mode of production" and the political aspects of the movement for abolition—questions that have been the focus of much Brazilian writing on slavery—*To Be a Slave in Brazil* presents an overview of Brazilian slavery which reflects the trend toward study of the slave community, religion, the family, and other features of the internal aspects of slavery. By studying in detail the manumission process and the position of free people of color in Brazilian society, it also seeks to understand slavery as part of a broader social and economic system. The author's work does all this based on a thorough familiarity with the existing literature and in some cases with the use of heretofore unused primary sources. Here for the reader is reflected the impact on Brazilian scholarship of the newer studies of slavery done in the United States and Europe. But in its analysis of manumission and slave life and culture the book suggests areas that students of slavery in the United States might find worthy of more attention. It is a book that will interest anyone who wishes to understand American slavery in the fullest sense, and it should be especially welcome for the manner in which it summarizes recent Brazilian scholarship. Controversies abound in the study of Brazilian slavery, and not every scholar will agree with all of the author's conclusions, but there are few books that summarize our knowledge of Brazilian slavery better than this one. English-speaking students of slavery will want to consult *To Be a Slave in Bra-*

zil when they seek to understand Brazil, and this book should establish Katia Mattoso's reputation in the anglophone world as a leading scholar of Brazilian slavery.

Over the years, in the heat of Bahia and the cold of Minnesota, I have had many occasions to discuss, debate, and collaborate with Katia Mattoso on historical issues, especially on those concerned with slavery and with our beloved Bahia. She has always brought to these exchanges the same clarity, frankness, and perception that she consistently demonstrates in her scholarship. It is a pleasure, therefore, to present this book to the English-reading public and to continue my association with one of Brazil's most distinguished contemporary historians.

Stuart B. Schwartz

University of Minnesota

In my introduction to the original French edition I may not have adequately stressed the severity of the constraints imposed by the publisher: within the space of 320 pages, without notes, I had to give an overview of three centuries of Brazilian slavery. I was therefore forced to make choices, guided in part by the work of Brazilian and foreign historians and sociologists and in part by my own research.

Brazilian historiography in the twentieth century has been dominated by two major schools. The earlier of these, strongly influenced by physical and cultural anthropology, attempted to show that the slave system in Brazil was milder than slave systems in other countries, especially the United States, thanks to the development of a true racial democracy that made social relations under slavery less harsh than they otherwise would have been. Typified by the work of Gilberto Freyre and such American sociologists and anthropologists as F. Tannenbaum and D. Pierson, this school fostered numerous studies, the results of which, published in the 1960s and subsequently, frequently ran counter to the positions taken by earlier writers. Among the more notable of recent writers in this tradition are C. Boxer, S. Stein, T. de Azevedo, R. Bastide, F. H. Cardoso, F. Fernandes, O. Ianni, E. Viotti da Costa, and others, whose work is valuable for shedding new light on the role of African cultures and religions in shaping Brazilian society and above all for posing the question of the relationship of rulers to ruled in a system whose economic character was undeniable. This new direction of research into Brazilian slavery ultimately gave rise to a new school of thought, whose followers studied slavery as an economic system. From the 1970s on many papers have been published concerning slave demographics, the slave trade and its disappearance, the abolition of slavery, and above all the political economy of slavery, focusing on such questions as the nature of slavery as a mode of production, its effects on economic development, and its impact on industrialization (see the bibliography at the end of the present work). While shedding fresh light on the slave system, however, this new line of research has left a fundamental problem still shrouded in shadow: namely, that of the social relations among the various economic actors—free men and slaves, free men and freed slaves, freed slaves and slaves.

Here, my own research suggested an avenue to explore. From the outset I was motivated by the belief that social relations in all societies are established upon a contractual basis and hence cannot be reduced to a simple relationship of ruler to ruled. Even in a slave society, I felt, social relations are conditioned by the nature of economic activity, by the relative number of slaves and freed slaves compared with the population as a whole, and by the percentage of the free population consisting of people of color. These basic conditions, I believed, could not have remained constant over three centuries of slavery or over the whole range of a country as vast and varied as Brazil. With these hypotheses in mind, it was tempting to explore a new avenue of research, following the example of my own previous work on Bahia. While this work focused primarily on the nineteenth century, it enabled me to show the specific determinants of social relations under slavery in the Bahia region and to interpret the results in light of what general information we have about other regions of the country. To have focused so closely on Bahia may perhaps place this book in the category of a monograph. But as Jean Meuvret says, "the monograph, no matter how broad or narrow, which explores, with massive documentation, the concrete complexities of specific historical periods, is absolutely essential to ensure the validity of subsequent work. Economic history may seek to be global at the summit provided that it is total at the base."[1] I hope that Meuvret's invitation is widely heeded, for not until we have assembled many more monographs based on solid research can we hope to achieve a true overview of the social history of slavery.

For the convenience of my English readers, I have added a brief bibliography of unpublished theses and works on Brazilian slavery published after 1979.

Katia M. de Queirós Mattoso

Paris
May 1985

[1]Jean Meuvret, *Etudes d'histoire économique* (Paris: Armand Colin, 1971), p. 312.

To Be a Slave in Brazil

BRAZILIAN EMPIRE (1882–1889)

INTRODUCTION

Presumptuous as it may sound, my purpose in writing this book was to discover what life was really like for the slaves in Brazil. This was a presumptuous project for several reasons. First, the masses of slaves toiled in obscurity and left no records of their thoughts or feelings. Their ways of thinking were not the same as ours, and I found that an effort of empathy was necessary before I could really begin to understand the workings of their minds, before I could hope to avoid the twin dangers of treating actual human beings either as an anonymous collective "labor force" or as sources for an anthology of biographical sketches—with the result, in either case, of reducing those men and women once again to slavery.

It was also presumptuous of me to attempt to treat so vast a subject for so vast a country over so lengthy a period. The book spans more than three centuries starting with the "discovery" of Brazil by Pedro Alvares Cabral in 1500, three centuries that saw dramatic changes in a country almost twenty times the size of France. To make matters even worse, the slave "class" in Brazil was neither well defined nor clearly distinguished from other social groups. Who would be so bold as to link together as members of a single social class the African toiling over the red earth of the cane-growing regions and the half-breed drover accompanying his herd and his heavily laden mules down the trails from the plateaus to the slaughter-houses of the city and the warehouses of the ports? What differences and similarities might we expect to find between the attitudes of, say, a slave whose job was to search for gold and another employed as an itinerant merchant, or between a recently emancipated slave who, unable to compete as a coffee grower, was expelled from his land and a sailor who, having gained his freedom, somehow amassed a fortune?

This book is addressed to an audience of general readers. I have therefore felt free to dispense with the usual scholarly apparatus of extensive footnotes and bibliography. The reader who wishes to begin in the middle—to start with, say, Chapter 3—may feel free to do so. Perhaps, his curiosity aroused, he will then wish to turn back to the more austere pages that recount, with a minimum of statistical detail, the sordid tale of the way in which shrewd slave traffickers and dealers profited from the purchase and sale of a commodity that unlike other commodities thought and suffered, a commodity that, wrenched from its native soil, needed very special conditions in order to survive and to bear its finest fruit—which is nothing less than today's Brazil.

Presumptuous as this work may be, it is nevertheless the product of mature research. Some earlier writers have formed an almost idyllic view of Brazilian slavery, while others have been harsh judges indeed of the slave system. To sort out these contrasting views it was necessary to sift through the existing literature as well as to seek out new sources of information. Insofar as possible I have also tried, quite consciously, to share the point of view of the black community. In short, this book is the product of both scholarly research and personal sympathy. Its title, *To Be a Slave in Brazil*, is not intended as a rhetorical flourish. Rather, it signals my intention to adopt the standpoint of the slaves themselves. It also reflects my wish to trace the various stages in the lives of slaves as individuals and of the slave group as a community.

What were those stages? To begin with there was the phase of depersonalization, loss of individuality, which came when African captives— bought, sold, mortgaged, rented, and bequeathed, deprived of dialogue with their captors and of the ability to express their own will— became beasts of burden, beasts that some doubted, despite the teachings of the Church, to be possessed of souls. Then, slowly and with great difficulty, slaves gradually adapted—some more, some less successfully—to the demands of the new society, a society with a unique dual structure in which black and white communities coexisted side by side. Brazilian society bears little resemblance even to its slave-holding neighbors, the Antilles and the Southern United States.

I have attempted to examine the thinking and attitudes of these new men, both African slaves and creoles, or slaves born in Brazil, as well as freed men of every sort and color. Many worked the earth. It was to provide agricultural labor that the profitable slave traffic first developed. But we know more about urban slaves than about their brothers, the field hands, because the government, with its interminable regulations, its police crackdowns, and its red tape of licenses, registrations, taxes, and notarized documents, kept closer watch on the former. It should not be forgotten, however, that town and country were intimately related in seventeenth-, eighteenth-, and even nineteenth-century Brazil. Geographically, it would have been difficult to say where the one left off and the other began; economically, town and country lived in symbiosis. A constant traffic of horses, mules, palanquins, and pedestrians ceaselessly moved back and forth from town to countryside, countryside to town. The cities were in fact gardens, urbanized fields.

In undertaking this new interpretation of the slaves' world I have drawn on voluminous, if rather fragmentary, sources. The documentation concerning the nineteenth century is certainly more abundant than that for earlier periods, although we have no slave reminiscences or memoirs of the sort relatively common in North America. But in addition to such familiar sources as official documents and accounts by contemporary witnesses, both Brazilian and foreign, we have been able to exploit a whole new range of materials: wills, estate inventories, emancipation papers, court documents, and archives of the police and of lay and religious organizations, as well as the precious oral traditions of certain present-day "Afro-Brazilian" communities.

My heart and my passport both tell me that I am a citizen of the Brazilian state of Bahia. Is my account perhaps overly Bahian in its outlook? If so, the fault may lie in part with the fact that much of the work on these new sources has been done in Salvador under the combined auspices of the National Council for Scientific and Technological Development (C.N.Pq) and the Society for the Study of Negro Culture in Brazil (S.E.C.N.E.B.). The first of these organizations has, for the past two years, funded the work of a group of historians who have enthusiastically taken up work begun ten years ago by unpaid researchers. And the second organization has, for some five years now, funded research by ethnographers, anthropologists, sociologists, artists, and historians associated in one way or another with the religious community of Axe Opo Afonja. This book draws heavily on their work. With such help I have tried to rescue from three centuries of anonymity and forced labor some three and a half million slaves, men and women who may now take their place not as mere agents of the will of their masters but as worthy and sentient human beings in their own right, whose suffering and toil have fertilized the soil of Brazil.

Katia M. de Queirós Mattoso

Salvador da Bahia de Todos os Santos
July 1978

PART 1

To Be Sold into Slavery

ONE

To Be Sold into Slavery in Africa

WHERE THE CAPTIVES WERE FOUND

Are South America and Africa really, as some geohistorians believe, mere vestiges of an immense prehistoric continent known as Gondwania? Be that as it may, the two continents resemble each other quite closely, ancient plains patchily overlain by layers of sedimentary rock, here thrust high above the flatlands, there eroded or deeply fissured. Like South America, Africa is huge, an immense territory concentrated in tropical or equatorial latitudes, traversed by great rivers of astonishing length, subject to extremes of climate, and covered by a natural vegetation of forests and savanna. To go from the stately forests that flank the Zambesi or Niger rivers in Africa to the tropical forests lining the São Francisco River in Brazil is to find what seems to be a familiar climate and vegetation in a remote and hostile place. On both continents the air is humid, the forest dark, and the soil dry. But similar as the natural environments of the two continents may be, the same cannot be said of the peoples and civilizations that inhabited them at the beginning of the sixteenth century. The native inhabitants of South America were quickly subdued by white invaders. In Africa, however, a diversity of peoples continued to live in independence: black "melano-Africans"; tall, slender, very dark, dolichocephalic Sudanese; smaller, lighter-skinned, less dolichocephalic Guineans; stocky, brown-skinned Congolese; rather tall, fine-featured Zambesians; and graceful Nilotics, along with Peuls, Negrillos, Berbers, and Moors.

The black Africa with which we are concerned here was as unknown to Europeans in the sixteenth century as the New World that fired the imagination and inspired the ambition of white conquerors. At various places along the hostile African coast men bent on acquiring wealth and power no sooner established settlements than they began to look inland for sources of supply. Each new port or beachhead was at first isolated in the midst of mysterious and hostile territory. Everyone knows how the white man came to settle the coasts of Africa and South America and how, as farmland was cleared in South America and ports were developed in Africa, the Atlantic came to be less and less an obstacle for European sailors, who reunited what the pre-Cambrian chaos had torn asunder, establishing a profitable traffic in slaves upon which New World development became increasingly dependent. Brazil's almost unoccupied and easily conquered territory tempted white men with the promise of wealth and glory. By contrast, black Africa, with its many tribes and kingdoms, was a populous region and apparently rather poor in precious metals, hence not an attractive prospect for conquest or colonization. Gradually, as Africa's other natural resources—gold, spices, ivory—were depleted, the black man became the prime resource, a unique commodity, unlike any other, the continent's life blood of labor, which the slave traders drained away and transported to the New World. In this way black Africa was grafted onto the native stock—white and red—of South America.

Transatlantic exploration was mainly the work of the Iberian nations. Impelled by the avidity of merchants and the desire for knowledge of the wider world, the Spanish and the Portuguese developed the arts of navigation in the fourteenth and fifteenth centuries: under Alfonso V (the Wise) astronomical tables were prepared; the stern rudder was developed; and a new type of ship, the caravel, capable of lengthy, rapid ocean crossings, was designed and built. Portugal was driven to expand across the seas by excess population, shortages of wheat, fish, and spices, and the impossibility of taking territory from its powerful neighbor, Castille. Trade was hampered by lack of precious metals, and the need for slaves grew with the establishment of sugar mills in the south, in Algarva and Madeira, as well as in the Azores and on the islands of Cape Verde, São Thomé, and Principe. Sugar growers in Brazil drew on this fifteenth-century experience with cane cultivation in the Atlantic islands. On the oceans Castilian and Lusitanian caravels competed; the Moors, finally driven from the Iberian peninsula, were pursued beyond Gibraltar by Spaniards and Portuguese, who thereby discovered, often to their misfortune, the coasts of Africa and especially the gold mines of Guinea. Cape Bojador was rounded in 1434, and Portuguese sailors began their methodical exploration of the African coast. As the coasts and winding rivers were explored, it became clear that the continent contained not only jungle and desert but also heavily traveled trade routes. The mouth of the Senegal and the islands of Cape Verde off the coasts were reached in 1444–1445, and the first regular commercial contacts with the interior of Mali began at about the same time. In 1471 the islands of São Thomé and Principe came under Portuguese control, making possible more extensive exploration of the powerful African kingdoms of Benin and the Congo. In 1482 construction began on the mainland, at São Jorge de Mina, of a Portuguese fort. In less than one century, thanks to tireless efforts, to expedition after expedition, Europeans thus methodically dispelled the terrors of the unknown and ultimately, in 1497 and in the person of Vasco da Gama, rounded the Cape of Good Hope—aptly named, for it opened a new route, a royal route, to the East Indies. This ocean route supplanted the land routes across the Sahara which had brought power to the old empires of Ghana and Mali and wealth to the ivory, gold, and spice traders of Timbuktu and Djenne. In 1500 there were no more than 25,000 slaves in the Old World. Interest in the slave trade did not really develop until the discoverers of the New World, disappointed at not having found the fabulous riches described by travelers to the Orient, realized that these vast new territories called for new modes of exploitation. The American lands discovered by the sailors who followed in the wake of Christopher Columbus were inhabited by peoples that found themselves unequal to the European invaders, even when, as was the case in the islands of Spanish America, their numbers were relatively large. In Brazil, where the Portuguese Pedro Alvares Cabral landed, in 1500, south of the present site of Salvador da Bahia de Todos os Santos, the indigenous population consisted of a small number of Indians, who lived essentially by hunting, gathering, and fishing and who were soon decimated by war and disease. A nomadic people used to long journeys, the Indians did not adapt well to being forced to work as sedentary agricultural laborers. At this stage, Brazil, like the Caribbean islands, offered little in the way of readily consumable or marketable riches to Europeans who had come so far in search of quick and easy profit: no gold, no precious stones, no spices, only immense, virgin lands to be cleared for farming or forests to be exploited for the Campeachy or Brazil wood so prized in Europe. Explorers who did not wish to see their careers promptly terminated were obliged to earn substantial profits for those who had financed their explorations. Nor were the explorers themselves indifferent to profit. In a world still relatively backward technologically, the question of how best to exploit the new territories took a relatively simple form: an abundant source of labor had to be found quickly. That the need for such labor was indeed acute is made clear by the fact that the first black slaves arrived in Spanish America in 1502, opening the era of colonialism and its attendant slave trade. Very quickly the slave trade came to be closely associated with the growing of sugar cane, a crop that was soon widely cultivated in tropical regions of the New World and that required year-round labor by many hands. Thus colonial Brazil in its early years, years of scarce labor and absence of precious metals and before the introduction of livestock and draft animals, was a country strictly dependent on a one-crop economy. And that crop imposed stringent requirements: Because sugar cane depletes the soil quite quickly unless it is fertilized, new land had to be cleared constantly, and a steady supply of skilled workers able to work under Brazilian conditions had to be secured.

Between 1502 and 1860 more than 9,500,000 Africans were brought to the Americas, with Brazil the largest importer of black men. The slave trade reached a peak in the eighteenth century, during which colonial America imported 6,200,000 slaves. All the great modern powers were involved, each dominating the slave traffic in turn. As the mining of precious metals ceased to be the major economic activity (as in the early Spanish colonies in Central America, for example), the amount of slave trade grew along with the size of the colonies. From the earliest days of the colonial period, the Dutch, the French, and the English attempted to assert their control over African slave markets. Since the slave trade yielded huge profits, expansion was rapid, all the more so because the demand for labor grew steadily. No country shrank from this profitable line of business; indeed, in keeping with the spirit of this imperialist age, each sought to monopolize the entire traffic for itself.

Throughout the sixteenth century slaving was a Portuguese monopoly. The West African port of Arguin sent Portugal a thousand slaves a year during the latter half of the fifteenth century. The Cape Verde Islands, where sugar plantations developed after 1460, became a center of slave trade for the whole section of coast between Senegal and Sherbro Island (in present-day Sierra Leone). The importance of Cape Verde did not begin to decline until the middle of the sixteenth century, when English and French traffickers first set up operations in Gambia. Besides Arguin and Cape Verde there was a Portuguese fort at São Jorge de Mina (1482), but in 1637 the Dutch dislodged the Portuguese not only from São Jorge but from all their other strongholds along this section of coast. Although the Portuguese from then on held no territory in this part of Africa, they continued to be a commercial presence, because Brazilian tobacco was one of the principal commodities exchanged for slaves. The Dutch authorized the Portuguese to trade in the ports of Popo, Ouidah, Jacquin, and Apa provided that each ship unload one-tenth of its cargo of tobacco at São Jorge. The French, the English, and the Portuguese all built forts at Ouidah, side by side, starting in 1721. The island of São Thomé, located just south of the equator, was the first major Portuguese slave distribution center. Slaves were brought to the island from the mainland. Later, Angola became the central distribution point—an Angola enlarged in 1665 by the annexation of a large part of the former kingdom of the Congo, which had previously enjoyed political and administrative autonomy under Portuguese protection. Between 1650 and 1750 two black kingdoms, Angola in the north and Benguela, four hundred kilometers farther to the south, prospered as a result of their participation in the shipment of slaves to Brazil.

For the Portuguese in Africa trading did not mean ruling or colonizing. By the end of the eighteenth century the Portuguese empire in Africa was reduced to Guinea, apart from a major fortress at Ouidah and trading posts in Mozambique, key stations on the route to the Indies but isolated and difficult to defend, especially since they were also coveted by the Dutch, the French, and the English. Portuguese commerce later diversified as the Dutch took over much of the old Portuguese monopoly, establishing their first fortress on the African coast at Nassau (in present-day Ghana) in 1611. The Dutch West India Company, established in 1621, was granted a twenty-four-year monopoly on trade and navigation along the west coast of Africa from the Tropic of Cancer to the Cape of Good Hope, a coast occupied in part by the Portuguese. The Dutch took the offensive on both sides of the Atlantic, attacking Portuguese possessions in both the New World (where they seized control of the rich sugar-growing region of Pernambuco from 1630 to 1648) and Africa. Finally it seemed that the Dutch had succeeded in closing the loop: now sugar producers themselves, they were also in a position to supply the labor required by the cane plantations. But this situation did not last long, for in 1648 Holland was forced to restore Pernambuco to Portugal, along with Angola and São Thomé. But the Dutch held on to their conquests on the Gold Coast and turned to growing sugar in the Antilles using techniques learned in Brazil, thereby breaking the Portuguese monopoly on sugar. Not germane to our subject here is the fate of the Dutch West India Company, which was dissolved, replaced by another company, then dissolved again over the course of the seventeenth and eighteenth centuries. Whereas the colonization of southern and southeastern Africa was carried out by European farmers and breeders who paved the way for the East India Company, however, the colonization of black West Africa was undertaken for the purpose of promoting the slave trade. What is more, the Dutch, owing to their experience as a seafaring and trading nation, were able to profit greatly from that trade. In the race to rule the seas and, with them, commerce and the slave trade, the other European powers were late to arrive on the scene, but when they did arrive competed successfully with the early leaders. The Royal African Company of England extended its influence along the coast of Guinea, present-day Ghana, and Dahomey, and by the eighteenth century 70 percent of the slaves destined for the Antilles and North America were carried by British slavers. One hundred and one slave ships were registered at the port of Liverpool. Paradoxically, however, it was in England, a country made wealthy by its trafficking in slaves, that the antislavery movement first developed in the nineteenth century.

The French were also fairly successful in establishing slave depots in Senegal, on the isle of Gorée off the Ivory Coast, and in Dahomey. After 1814 they were left only with their bases in Senegal and the Bourbon Island on the route to the Orient.

Only those colonial powers that possessed their own outlets for exported African labor thrived in the slave trade. Witness, for example, the modest role played by Denmark and Sweden in this traffic. Such countries were simply not equipped to compete with the colonial monopolies.

For Portugal Brazil was a safe market, always in need of more slaves, though it is true that early in the seventeenth century the Portuguese were still supplying slaves to Spain, which had found the Indians unsuited ot the work of timbering and cane growing. Sudanese and Bantus came to Brazil in four great waves. The first, or Guinean, wave came in the sixteenth century from parts of Africa north of the equator, bringing Wolofs, Mandingos, Songhais, Mossis, Hausas, and Kamite Peuls to Brazilian shores. In the early seventeenth century a second wave of imports coincided with a "slave shortage" in Brazil due to the Dutch-Portuguese wars. This second wave brought Bantus, regarded as excellent farmers, to Brazil from equatorial and central Africa by way of Angola and the Congo. It was always Portuguese policy to mix Africans of different ethnic groups in order to prevent concentrations of slaves with similar origins on a single plantation. In the war waged to win Pernambuco back from the Dutch there were black regiments made up of troops of a variety of ethnic backgrounds: Minas, Ardas, Angolans, and creoles. What is more, the waves referred to above were not sharply distinguished; slaves continued to arrive from areas associated with earlier waves of immigration. Guineans are still coming to Brazil, and, according to a tradition that is difficult to verify, Bahians have always preferred to import Sudanese and Pernambucans, Bantus, while Rio de Janeirans liked both. Blacks from Mozambique also came to Brazil, especially during the period when the Dutch occupied Angola.

The eighteenth century saw a third wave of the slave trade, which brought Sudanese from the Mina Coast, and then, in mid-century, a fourth wave which drew slaves primarily from the vicinity of the Bay of Benin. After 1830, when England imposed restrictions on the slave traffic, an illicit trade began to develop. Slaves came to Brazil in the nineteenth century from many different places, although Angola and Mozambique, then Portuguese colonies, were by far the major sources of supply.

It was the growing of sugar cane in Pernambuco, Bahia, and Rio de Janeiro that made it necessary to import slaves in the sixteenth and seventeenth centuries, and it was the mining of gold that heightened the demand for slaves in the eighteenth century. Even at mid-century, however, when gold extraction was at its peak, 40 percent of all newly imported slaves were still destined for employment in agriculture. The mines, though nearly as desperate for labor as the cane plantations, received only 20 percent of arriving slaves. The rest went to cotton and rice plantations, to spice picking, or to work as domestic servants, hired laborers, and artisans. In the nineteenth century, coffee, the new king of Brazilian agriculture, would help to keep slave trading, illegal after 1830, a profitable activity until well beyond the 1850s.

Thus for three long centuries, during which the influx of slaves from Africa never slackened, the slave trade brought together blacks from different ethnic groups, tribes, and clans. African nations were politically, socially, and economically complex. Before we can understand what people were sold into slavery and forced to make the great journey into the unknown, we must delve a little into the diversity of Africa itself. The slavers' human cargo passed from hand to hand; it was bought, sold, and resold as it moved along well-established trade channels, governed by an established system of social relations, customs, practices, regulations, and risks. To understand the slave, we must not only investigate the work he did and the masters he served in Brazil but also the way in which he became a captive and the people who profited from his purchase and sale.

THE DESTRUCTION OF OLD AFRICAN SOCIAL STRUCTURES

The black slave, who from the sixteenth to the nineteenth century became a commodity without which Brazil could not survive, did not come from an amorphous continent, a place with no culture, traditions, or history of its own. Notwithstanding ignorant remarks by certain European contemporaries, for whom what was different was necessarily inferior, the African captive whose fate was to assist in the development of America possessed a personality and a history all his own. Animists, Muslims, and Christians from the Dark Continent fought for their beliefs, and religion and politics often mingled in complex ways. Africans knew many large, centralized empires whose influence and authority went unchallenged, tribal confederations, kingdoms more or less recognized by their neighbors, and caravan cities along trade routes to rich markets for gold, spices, ivory, salt, and slaves. The warriors, fishermen, shepherds, merchants, and farmers of Africa entered into shifting alliances and engaged in bitter struggles that cannot be explored here. Broadly speaking, however, the Europeans of the early sixteenth century encountered two quite different types of African civilization: the Sudanese along the northwestern coast and the Bantu farther south and extending all the way to East Africa. Each of these regions was inhabited by a variety of ethnic groups, which differed in physical aspect, language, and religion. Linguistic similarities are less clear-cut in the Sudanic group than in the Bantu, but related families of languages were common: Wolof in the area of Senegal, Lambara and Mandingo in western Sudan, the More of the Mossis and Hausa in northern Nigeria and Niger, and even Kanouri in Chadian Sudan, not to mention the Agni-Baoulé languages of the Ivory Coast, Fon of Dahomey, and Douala of Cameroon. Well before the European attempts at colonization, technically fairly advanced civilizations developed in a number of regions. Extensive cultivation was practiced with the hoe, as well as intensive cultivation near dwellings. Property in land was unknown, but the arts of working with iron, gold, bronze, and copper were practiced, often by artisans who combined skill with a little sorcery and medicine. Pottery, often by women, weaving, and timbering supplied local needs as well as remote markets, where trade was conducted mainly in the form of barter, though cowries (shells from the Indian Ocean) were used as money.

Slavery existed in these highly stratified societies, but it was widely practiced only in Benin and in the Sudan-Sahel region. In any case, "captives" were integrated into the family and could not be sold. This slavery was quasi-patriarchal, and there was no trade in slaves. In Dahomey the children of slaves were born free and treated as members of the master's family. It was not until fairly late, under foreign influence and the pressure of external markets, that slavery and the slave trade spread, with sale of slaves becoming the more or less immediate goal. Only then did an African form of slavery come into being, through and for the slave trade, which required the constant infusion of fresh blood. The trade brought slavery to many forest peoples and numerous communities on the coast. Here slaves were at first the common property of a family. The personal slave was a rather late development. "Captives" never lost their personalities. Even if the master reserved the right to choose slaves as needed for his personal service, these captives retained their economic autonomy and ethnic personality. They were simply required to pay tribute, dues, and various forms of labor service to the master. In the Sahel the proportion of slaves may have been as high as 30 to 50 percent of the population. Free men entitled to own slaves were sometimes subject to the same obligations as their slaves, including payment of taxes or dues and performance of labor services for the king or aristocratic families; this was the case among the Fons, the Wolofs, and the Peuls of Dahomey.

In Senegal and Nigeria artisans formed endogamous castes of fixed hierarchical rank. Among the Peuls, for example, ironsmiths were at the bottom of the social scale, more scorned than serfs or slaves, and scarcely less than the *laobe*, or artisans working in wood; above them were weavers, cobblers, and finally witch doctors. In the space of three generations the slave became a serf: First he was a captive to be sold; then his child became a captive in the master's house, where he was fed, clothed, and required to perform five days of labor per week; and finally, in the third generation, the slave became a *rimaïbe*, who tended his own enclosed plot and owed the master only three days of labor each week.

Aristocrats were either born into noble families of the tribe or elevated to aristocratic status by grace of the sovereign. Only the royal clan was a true "blood nobility" (*noblesse de race*). In Dahomey, on the eve of the colonial conquest, the royal clan numbered some twelve thousand individuals. Aristocrats generally served as warriors and state administrators; the crucial functions of state were discharged not by the king but by this administrative apparatus, of which the king was merely the chief or symbol. The apparatus consisted of innumerable ministers, dignitaries, functionaries, and professional soldiers. The European intervention of the fifteenth and sixteenth centuries, conducted almost exclusively through the slave trade, did not fail to exert a strong influence on the evolution of society in states whose governmental apparatus was highly developed. The function of the state was to collect tributes and dues and see to their distribution. The lure of profit drew most states into the business of capturing and selling slaves. For this they required powerful armies equipped with modern weaponry. The most profitable ventures came to be associated with war and man hunting, and this in turn explains why political instability became endemic in this part of the world from the seventeenth century on. Empires and kingdoms that predated the arrival of the Europeans vanished and were replaced by new states, many of them founded by adventurers: for example, Dahomey, born of and sustained by the slave trade. These new states were organized along territorial lines, which gradually replaced the ancient communal organization of the earlier kingdoms. Successive invasions ultimately led to mixing of different ethnic groups, and community structures often lost their designation and meaning. Only the extended family and the village retained their former unity, until finally the family structure itself disintegrated and the status of women declined almost to a par with slaves. Yet even though women could be bought and sold, they enjoyed an autonomy and individuality unmatched in ancient Europe. In the communal system of organization, the division of labor was based primarily on sex and occasionally also on age. In any case, the extended family was often a veritable community composed of a wife or wives, children, parents, and cousins. Hausa children referred to their father's brothers as "father" and to their mother's sisters as "mother." Whether or not the matrilinear clan predated the patrilinear is still a matter of controversy among ethnographers. One thing is certain: the extended family, which endured until the first stages of colonization, disappeared with the rise of large territorial states, states whose structures were in many cases tailored to suit the requirements of the slave trade. A case in point was the Congo, whose development was hastened by the arrival of the Portuguese. The kingdom flourished from 1506, when its king converted to Christianity, until 1665. The kingdom of Loango, north of the Congo River, became an important slave supplier in the early eighteenth century and is said to have provided a sixth of all slaves exported from Africa, while remaining free of European influence and preserving its own customs and divine kingship. The kingdom of Angola, which was occupied by the Portuguese in the final third of the sixteenth century, was the heir of the ancient kingdom of Dongo. Whereas the Congo was able to remain independent, Angola, conquered by force, succumbed to fairly efficient Portuguese administration and became the major supplier of black men for the Brazilian trade. As for the kingdom of Benguela, where the Portuguese in 1617 established the port of São Filipe de Benguela, there was no real penetration of the interior until the end of the eighteenth century. But in 1685 the Portuguese took the rather rare step of setting up a post at Caconda, two hundred kilometers from the coast and in the center of a region inhabited by a large, homogeneous ethnic group, the Ovimbundu, a warlike people divided into hostile principalities. Finally, the Bantu lands, which included Mozambique and the Monomotapas, maintained close commercial ties with the Indies and Asia via Arab and Persian traders.

All of these kingdoms, with their often unstable institutions, had long histories of struggle and warfare, which at times impeded the slave trade but at other times provided traders with new sources of captives. In any case, it is certain that the arrival in Africa of powerful European nations, well armed and avid for profit, helped to exacerbate rivalries and foment tribal warfare. Even more important, the European presence dealt a severe blow to existing social structures and cultural traditions and caused some to disintegrate.

What about religion? Was its evolution also influenced by ongoing social and political transformations? Black Africa, with its diversity of languages, ethnic groups, and social systems, was also diverse in religion. Except for Islam and Christianity, African religions were variants of animism. Religion was a form of social organization that permeated all aspects of daily life. Animistic religions are characterized by totemism and ancestor worship. Totemism stems from dietary taboos applied to certain animals or plants. The totem is not altogether divine. It is rather a symbol of clan and community solidarity, although not the object of any specific cult. In contrast, ancestor worship was everywhere a vital tradition. As practiced by the family head, its purpose was to maintain harmony between the community of the living and that of the dead. It was often found together with agrarian myths and worship of the soil or water: African religions did not oppose the natural to the supernatural world. They embodied a dialectical logic, embracing struggle and the unity of opposites. Long regarded as polytheistic, they are more properly viewed in a monotheistic context. Of religions born outside Africa, only Islam established itself on a firm and durable footing prior to the colonialist era. In the old kingdoms of Ghana, Mali, and Bornou it was the predominant religion, especially in urbanized areas, where its development was linked to commercial prosperity. Except in Bornou, however, Islam often remained a state religion, practiced by the dominant social classes. In order to penetrate more deeply into the social structure, it had to contend with numerous animist counteroffensives, for animism remained a vital tradition despite the social and political transformations brought on by the slave trade and the new structures imposed on Africa as a result.

THE ORGANIZATION OF THE SLAVE TRADE IN THE PORTUGUESE EMPIRE: COMMERCIAL OPERATIONS

By the time the African slave trade had been organized on a fairly extensive scale, the practice of hunting and capturing men for sale as slaves had almost disappeared. Europeans purchased slaves from African kings and merchants. Accordingly, from the early part of the sixteenth century, when the traffic in blacks began to increase, European slave traders concentrated mainly on the Gold Coast, where it was easiest to find Africans accustomed to European merchandise: fabrics, hardware of various kinds, alcoholic beverages, and above all firearms were highly prized and much in demand, indeed necessities. Guinean merchants, accustomed to trading gold for European knickknacks, naturally turned to supplying slaves when the demand increased.

At first the trade was rather disorganized, but by 1650 it had become a major enterprise involving the new kingdoms around the Gulf of Guinea; these kingdoms, which ranged over the interior, slowly moved their centers away from the coasts. New slave markets were established farther to the south, in the Congo, Angola, Benguela, even as far away as the East African coast. The Europeans limited themselves to establishing depots, warehouses, and fortresses along the coasts of territories that were left to the control of local African states, such as the Yoruba empire of Oyo, the empire of the Ashanti, and the kingdom of Dahomey. These kingdoms quite predictably became increasingly warlike; their power was based on military might, and they needed weapons. The centers of power moved inland in order to secure a monopoly on the profitable trade in slaves. As we saw earlier, the Portuguese managed to convert the king and leading families of the Congo to Catholicism. But by 1575, owing to the increased demand for slaves for Brazil, the Portuguese changed their policy and lost interest in fostering a Christian state in Africa. It was as a conquistador that Paulo Dias de Novais was sent to the Congo, and missionaries gave way to soldiers sent to conquer Angola, which in the seventeenth and eighteenth centuries became the center of the Brazilian slave trade. The slave trade in Guinea did not lead to devastation or catastrophic depopulation; indeed, it increased the wealth of the more advanced Guinean communities at the expense of weaker ones. By contrast, in Angola, as well as in East Africa later on, the slave trade quickly brought disaster in its wake, turning the country into a veritable desert: major population shifts deprived the region of manpower while enriching the black and white merchants who sold laborers to rapidly growing Brazil. The depletion of manpower in those areas of Africa affected by the Portuguese trade—Angola, the Congo, lower Zambesi, Monomotapa—was not compensated by the trade's one positive contribution, the introduction (by the Portuguese in the sixteenth century) of new crops, such as maize and manioc, which provided coastal dwellers with a better-balanced diet, thus stabilizing the population. But this single contribution could hardly make up for the sterilizing effects of the slave trade, which halted the social, economic, and cultural development of black Africa. There can be no doubt that the chiefs of the coastal tribes bear a heavy responsibility in this pillage. European traffickers were clever enough to take advantage of the situation and to assist in the development of a well-oiled machine whose purpose was to transform the African captive into the Brazilian slave, with handsome profits for everyone involved in the process.

Slaves were "recruited" for the trade in a variety of ways. It was customary to dispose of village hotheads, men who had broken the laws of the community by stealing or committing adultery, by selling them into slavery. Children, regarded in hard times as idle mouths to feed, and debtors were also sold, as were the losers in fratricidal wars waged between half brothers vying for their late father's crown. Thus slaves stemmed from all social categories—an important point to bear in mind. In addition, during periods of famine, common enough in the Sahel and the Gold Coast which often suffered from prolonged periods of drought or heavy rains, entire families sometimes sold themselves into slavery so as not to die of hunger. But in the seventeenth and eighteenth centuries, wars—military campaigns undertaken to conquer not land but men—remained the major source of new slaves. Such wars also proved to be an excellent way for the chiefs of coastal tribes to get rid of the energetic and hence dangerous young men of hostile inland tribes.

Captives destined for eventual sale were brought to the coast. Traditional African chieftains sometimes used these prisoners as money to pay the taxes or tribute they owed to Portuguese colonizers. But usually it was without obligation, and solely in pursuit of profit, that the African chieftain personally led his slaves to the European port to be sold to the slave dealers. Sometimes he dealt through intermediaries, usually half-breeds but commonly enough blacks, who took it upon themselves to lead the captives from the interior to the port cities. These agents were known as *tangomau* in Guinea and as *pombeiro* or *lançado* in Angola. Unlike the pombeiro, the lançado resided in the court of a native king or chieftain. He was generally white or mulatto, and his job was to sell the king's (or local chieftain's) slaves. Sometimes the lançado resold his slaves to the pombeiro instead of selling them directly to Europeans in the ports. Thus the organization of the trade was very flexible yet efficient and highly structured, with official intermediaries supplying the traffickers; the system was well adapted to the requirements of European merchants.

There were three ways of organizing slave commerce in the Portuguese empire: slave trading as private enterprise on a large or small scale, slave trading in conjunction with other commercial activities carried on by large trading companies, and slave trading under the terms of a form of commercial contract that Iberians called the *assiento*. Remember that from 1580 to 1640 the Portuguese and Spanish crowns were combined. The combined kingdom granted the assiento first to the Portuguese, then to the Dutch, then to the French, and finally to the English. The assiento was a farm on licenses to export slaves from African ports, fees for which were paid to a *contratador*, who could be a person or corporation. The contratador who received the assiento obtained a virtual monopoly on the slave trade in a particular area: Guinea, Angola, Cape Verde, or all three combined. In return, he agreed to provide to the colonies a specified number of slaves on terms set forth in his contract. The *contratador* was not required to do the work himself, however. He issued licenses (*avenças*) to individuals who then outfitted ships for use as slavers. The assiento was used mainly in Spanish colonies. Until 1640, metropolitan Portugal does not seem to have been unduly concerned about the supply of slaves to its Brazilian colony, and none of the assientos signed before that date was valid for the Portuguese possessions. The first written contract of which we have knowledge dates from 1587; it granted the contratadores Pedro de Sevilla and Antonio Mendes de Lamego a monopoly on barter for slaves (*resgate*) in Angola and its dependencies in the Congo and Benguela. But the Portuguese who had settled in Brazil took it upon themselves as early as 1559 to furnish their Brazilian estates with a supply of black manpower. Bahia, with its port Salvador, and Pernambuco, with its port Recife, became, thanks to their merchants, major centers for the importation of slaves, indispensable for the economic development of the sugar-producing hinterland. This take-over of the slave trade by private enterprise was the first break in the monopoly, and the history of the slave traffic in Brazil would thereafter be one of constant struggle between private initiative and the Portuguese trading companies that were established, with a fair amount of success, from the second half of the seventeenth century on. Significantly, it was dynamic and adaptable private entrepreneurs who helped to establish direct commercial ties between Brazil and Africa, thus eliminating the European leg in the classic triangular trade. This was a crucial development, and it explains why state trading companies and private traders fought bitterly throughout the seventeenth and eighteenth centuries. In theory, in order to trade directly with Africa one required a special license generally issued by the Portuguese monarch, who was thus forced to arbitrate between competitors both holding privileges he himself had granted. This competition for licenses and royal grants of privilege ultimately led, in the eighteenth century, to institutionalization of the private slave trade and to authorization of trading companies with headquarters in Brazil.

The first trading company for Brazil, which was established in 1647 and whose legal existence came to an end in 1720, held a monopoly on wine, olive oil, wheat flour, and cod but took no interest in the slave trade. It was in 1662 that Pascoal Ferreira Jansen and his associates obtained a contract for the states of Grão Para and Maranhão, which obliged them to import 10,000 blacks at the rate of 500 per year. The privilege was withdrawn at the end of three years because no slave had yet arrived in Maranhão. In any case, the number of slaves imported into Maranhão in this period was very small, and those that were imported were brought in under licenses granted to individuals: 145 in 1692, 145 in 1693, 218 in 1698, 200 in 1702, 200 in 1708, 150 in 1718 and 1721—far below the anticipated 500 per year. The assiento was a mere fiction. Similarly, the

Royal Company for Guinea and the Indies, which Dom Pedro II would be forced to liquidate in 1706, played at most a limited role in Brazil. The effort of supplying slaves to Brazil was left to private initiative.

The discovery of gold and the exploitation of gold mines as early as the late seventeenth century would increase the demand for black manpower, but Portuguese policy was slow to adjust; indeed, the Portuguese government did not change its methods until the mining activity that had brought about the changes was already on the wane! In fact, it was not until the second half of the eighteenth century, at the behest of the Marquis of Pombal, that the companies of Grão Para e Maranhão (1755) and of Permanbuco and Paraíba (1759) were founded. In theory they enjoyed the privilege of the slave trade over the entire coast of Guinea and Angola. For the first time the import of slaves to Brazil was clearly stated among the companies' aims. The range of these two companies' activities was relatively limited, however: they affected only the northern and northeastern portions of Brazil and did not touch the captaincies of Bahia, Rio de Janeiro, or Minas Gerais, which were the three greatest slave consumers of the time. These two companies, whose avowed goal was to cut out the wholesale merchants of Bahia and Pernambuco, did not fully achieve their aim. In effect, metropolitan Portugal, which unlike its Dutch, French, English, and even Danish and Swedish competitors showed little interest in establishing slave-trading monopolies, was responsible for the development of strong, direct commercial ties between Brazil and Africa. Thus the success of the private sector was due in part to the attitude of the mother country, but in part, too, to Brazil's capacity to produce merchandise that was easily sold and much in demand on the African barter markets. Brazilian tobacco, sugar, and spirits were exchanged directly by traders from Bahia, Pernambuco, and Rio for the slaves needed to produce them.

Colonial merchants thus established themselves solidly in the African ports where the slave trade was carried on. From the end of the seventeenth century tobacco played a very important role, as it was in demand not only by natives but also by Europeans engaged in the trade along the African coast. In 1699 a royal *alvara* authorized direct trade, and a very simple mechanism was established, whereby ships arrived on the coast of Guinea and the Congo loaded with Brazilian goods and exchanged their cargo for gold, ivory, wax, and above all blacks. Part of the cargo went to Europeans in exchange for goods from Europe. The Portuguese in the Americas sold tobacco to their European competitors in exchange for fabric, for example. Then the fabric might also be used to barter for slaves.

These practices, which show how well the whole system was adapted to the needs of local commerce, explain why the Dutch, who had seized São Jorge del Mina in 1637, were able to persuade the Portuguese to leave 10 percent of their cargo of tobacco whenever they came to the fort in search of African merchandise. Later, it was to avoid payment of this duty, which was deemed an outrageous tribute, that the Portuguese crown created, in 1723 at the behest of a Frenchman named Jean Donsaint, the Company of the African Coast, or Corsico, from the name of the Gabonese port where its headquarters were located. The Corsico was granted, for a period of fifteen years, the privilege of sending four ships from that port to Brazil; these ships were to be laden with captives and other African cargo, to be exchanged in Brazil for gold and other colonial cargo. But this company lasted only a short time, and by 1737 Jean Donsaint was in a Portuguese prison. We have no idea how many blacks he managed to transport to Brazil during his company's brief existence.

In the same period, Bahia, a major tobacco producer, attempted to improve its relations with Guinea but encountered strong competition from non-Portuguese Europeans. On the Guinean coast, which the Bahians called the Mina Coast, they set out to build a Portuguese fort in the famous port of Ouidah, in the kingdom of Dahomey. The garrison of the new fort was under the command of the viceroy who resided in Bahia, and Bahian merchants bore all costs of its upkeep. The founding of this fortress inaugurated the "Mina Coast era" in the Brazilian slave trade, an era that did not end until the abolition of the trade in 1850. Starting in 1730, moreover, the Portuguese, afraid that Bahians would monopolize the trade throughout the region, required that a license be obtained from the viceroy in Bahia or Pernambuco for each ship that departed for the coast of Africa. The obvious intent of this measure was to place Pernambuco in competition with Salvador, to break the stranglehold of that proud Bahian city. But licenses were issued in such a haphazard way that the price of slaves did not drop but steadily rose, owing to a mechanism that we shall have to explore in some detail. In any case, by the end of the 1730s the traffic in slaves between Africa and Brazil was still a problem for the administration. Wenceslau Pereira da Silva, general superintendent for gold and president of the Bahian Chamber of Inspection, an agency set up to m6nitor the quality of goods produced and exported by Bahia, indicated in a report to the government in Portugal that the only way to deal with the shortage and high price of slaves was to set up a company modeled on those established by other European states for their trade in slaves. In other words, the center of activity should be moved from the colony to the mother country. The point was to pattern the Brazilian trade after European models and eliminate its novel features. Dom João V in Lisbon, whose chief concern was to make his court the rival in luxury and sumptuousness of Louis XIV's, emptied his treasury, whose main source of revenue was the wealth of Brazil. The Treaty of Methuen (1703) between Portugal and England established a system favorable to the latter country, whereby the English received Brazilian gold and Portuguese wine in exchange for supplying Portugal with needed goods.

Since creating a company to exercise a monopoly in the slave trade was a long-term project, the Portuguese government turned in the meantime to a temporary system: twenty-four ships, fitted out in Bahia and Pernambuco and sailing every three months in groups of three would make the journey from Brazil to the Mina Coast to pick up slaves. But this provisional measure became permanent, since the projected company never got off the ground. Bahia and Pernambuco continued as rivals within the framework of this system, with Lisbon as arbiter; and the capricious, not to say incoherent, actions of the Lisbon government favored first one, then the other. In 1746, for example, Bahia was favored when the order of rounds was changed, starting from the Brazilian ports. Then in 1751 and again in 1756 the metropolitan government attempted to redress the balance in favor of Pernambuco shippers: each shipping company was allowed to send only one ship whose tonnage could not exceed that necessary to transport three thousand rolls of tobacco. But these efforts proved vain, so that in the same year, 1756, the twenty-four-vessel privilege was abolished and free navigation restored, thus renewing unbridled competition among Portuguese traders in the African markets. The Bahia shippers, already stronger than their Pernambucan competitors, adapted more rapidly to the new situation. The shippers of Recife were slowly squeezed out, especially after 1759, when the Pernambuco and Paraiba Trading Company was established, with headquarters in Lisbon. The price of a slave, which had been 7–10 rolls of tobacco, increased to 15–20 rolls, and virtually all traffic was handled by the fifty Bahian vessels that sailed between Brazil and West Africa. Some forty corvettes and *sumacas* sailed toward the Mina Coast, and ten others toward Angola, which remained the principal supplier of slaves to the captaincies of the south: Rio de Janeiro, Minas Gerais, São Paulo. Rio became a major slave-importing port. Between 1701 and 1800, 70 percent of imported slaves came from Angola; Phillip Curtin estimates their number at 1,414,500. During the same period, 611,000 slaves were imported from other parts of western Africa. This important Angolan traffic was carried on without intervention by companies holding royal privileges; the central government had no effective means of regulating the trade. The explanation for all this is clear: the Portuguese who had been firmly entrenched in Angola since the end of the sixteenth century were in control of the market and suffered very little from competition with other European nations. The slave trade could be entrusted, with perfect quietude, to private hands.

Although we have a fairly good idea of the structure of the slave trade during the late eighteenth and early nineteenth century, our information for the sixteenth and seventeenth centuries is not so good. As with the Guinean coast in the same period, the *assientistas* (of whom there were only seventeen for Angola and eleven for Cape Verde) played only a minor role in the Angolan slave trade, which was also left to private initiative with more or less government regulation at different times. The alvara of 1758 declared the slave trade between Angola and all Brazilian ports to be free. Any loaded ship could leave port and set sail for Brazil, whereas in 1755, as we saw earlier, Lisbon had included Angola in the domain reserved for the new companies of Grão Para e Maranhão and Pernambuco and Paraíba! In 1770 free trade in slaves was officially reestablished, and the privileged companies disappeared from the scene after playing a role whose importance is difficult to evaluate. Yet it is certain that that role was far less important than that played by private traders: the slave trade was quite tempting to anyone with sufficient capital and products to sell, for a ship's cargo could always be advantageously traded for black manpower in Africa, and the slaves obtained could be readily sold in Brazil. What drove the slavers? A spirit of enterprise, a liking for risk, or virtually assured profits? The question should really be asked later, after we have examined in greater detail a system that worked fairly efficiently in spite of a meddlesome government slow to react to crises, competition, and needs of the market. That the system worked as well as it did is a tribute to the imagination and organizational skills of wholesalers, merchants, and traders always ready to respond to market forces, indeed to create those forces when they could and to expand their area of operation. Slavers were generally fitted out in European ports or even in Brazil itself, in such major slave-importing centers as Bahia, Pernambuco, and Rio. The local naval authorities then issued a "passport" indicating the ship's tonnage and transport capacity.

Until 1800 the principal African port used by these traders was São

Paulo da Loanda, with later competition from Benguela and Cabinda da Loango. After 1815, when under English pressure slave trading was declared illegal north of the Equator, and especially after 1830, when it became completely illicit, the Brazilian slave trade would shift toward East Africa, which had previously furnished only insignificant numbers of blacks from Mozambique. In the nineteenth century East Africa would supply 75 percent of the slaves imported to Brazil, compared with only 3 percent for the period 1790–1811. In that period a galley could transport nearly 400 adults and 100 or so children. Generally the captives belonged to many different owners, each possessing only a few slaves; often the captain was among the slave owners. We know the story of one galley, the Santo Antonio, Santa Ana, and Almas, which left Loanda on 26 October 1727 with 385 adults and 77 children belonging to 99 different owners. In this case it seems that the captain and the Angolan merchants who were his partners were representatives of the Bahian merchants and planters who owned the ship. It is difficult to know, however, whether this voyage was typical of the eighteenth-century slave trade in general. It is certain, though, that merchants established in Loanda generally each sent one or two slaves per ship and retained ownership of those slaves until they found buyers in Brazil. Certain slave traders were also established in Rio or Bahia, with correspondents in Portugal who participated indirectly in the traffic. Bahian merchants supplied Loandan residents with European food and other merchandise, thus avoiding the long and perilous journey from Portugal to Angola and substituting the two-stage itinerary Lisbon-Brazil, Brazil-Angola.

In the nineteenth century this pattern was appreciably modified: Brazilian merchants imported on their own account captives handed over to them by Angolan merchants. The captive became the property of a Brazilian even before leaving the African port to which he had been brought. We know the names of some one hundred Rio merchants in the period 1825–1830, ten of whom received 40 percent of the slaves imported. Merchants tended to specialize in a particular region of supply, and only four received captives from both Mozambique and West Africa. In any case, all the merchants, whether African or Brazilian, great or small, had to work within the economic and political constraints outlined above.

In addition to these general constraints, there were also local ones. What was the day-to-day nature of the slave trade on the African coast for the host of agents and suppliers who dealt in precious living merchandise? The time has come to describe the face-to-face dealings between buyers and sellers. For such dealings were the first link in a long chain, even if the captives being sold had little inkling of what lay in store.

The slave trade was essentially based on barter. The vats, cowries, and zimbos that natives used among themselves as money and that Europeans used in the early days of the trade played a dwindling role and eventually fell into disuse. The unit of barter was quite varied: "packs," "packets," "bars," and other units generally contained powder, weapons, fabrics, hardware, and trinkets if the ship came from Europe. If it came from a Brazilian port, it usually carried, in varying proportions, tobacco, sugar, manioc flour, and spirits. As mentioned earlier, tobacco became a prized item among both Europeans and blacks. In any case, no ship ever carried just slaves. Vessels had to carry basic food supplies for the crew for both the voyage out and often the return voyage as well, since many needed supplies could not be obtained along the African coast. The ships engaged in the slave trade were equipped with immense cauldrons for cooking the captives' food. Barrels of water also occupied a great deal of space. The equipment of a slaver included irons for securing slaves and stockades for keeping them confined. We know very little about the voyages between Lisbon and Africa in the sixteenth and seventeenth centuries, but we are well informed about those that departed from Nantes in the eighteenth century. The passage from Nantes to Angola normally took around two months, though six-month voyages were not unusual. Proceeding from port to port, via Madeira or Tenerife in the Canary Islands or Gorée, ships reached the coast of Africa. Ships sailing from Brazil could make ports in the Congo, Angola, Benguela, and Mozambique without any stops.

Portuguese navigators found varied opportunities along the four to five thousand miles of African coastline. On the coast of Guinea, that is, between the mouth of the Senegal and Orange rivers, the Portuguese had to compete with other Europeans. What is more, all the installations necessary for the slave trade had to be authorized by local kings and chieftains, who generally offered wholesalers long-term leases on port and market facilities. Foreigners paid landing fees and other duties and also made personal gifts to kings, dignitaries, and chieftains, gifts that quickly became compulsory. Together, these dues, gifts, and so on were referred to as "customs." Add to this the fees that might have to be paid to brokers. In the eighteenth century these intermediaries played an important, indeed an indispensable, role. Called *tangomaus* by the Portuguese, they conducted the inland resgate and led their charges to the coast. Colorful, courageous characters, true adventurers little inclined to associate with their tamer compatriots, these agents were widely accused of blasphemy and dissolute ways.

Despite the existence of these brokers and of rudimentary treaties fixing the "customs," relations between Europeans and natives were not always peaceful. Native clients could turn into enemies and attack European buildings, forcing the personnel to take to the bush, where they were sometimes massacred or abandoned. Or apparently peaceful Portuguese merchants could turn into aggressors and fill out an incomplete cargo by "impressment," that is, by forcing free blacks seized close to the coast to embark for America. Still, there were numerous brokers available to meet the merchants' demands. Some lived in the ports, such as Annamambou or Ouidah. These were generally Europeans, who also served the traders as interpreters and procurers. Others were blacks chosen by their masters to act as official intermediaries. All these brokers were entrepreneurs in the end, dealers in men, and ships' captains often entrusted them with trade goods even before they delivered their captives.

The situation was a little simpler in territories belonging to Portugal. In the sixteenth and seventeenth centuries slaves were "discovered" by pombeiros. These were blacks or mulattoes, themselves slaves of white planters, who assigned them to go inland to buy slaves. The word pombeiro derives from the word for "carrier pigeon": like the bird, they carried messages and then returned faithfully to the nest from which they had been released. In native languages the pombeiros were referred to as "hawkers." The two interpretations of their role are both apt. These slave procurers seem to have vanished in the seventeenth century. Care must be taken to distinguish them from the lançados, whites or mulattoes who lived in the courts of native rulers, or *sovas*. There they lived in huts just like the villagers, but without any protection, entirely dependent on the good will of the sovas. They took it upon themselves to sell the sovas' slaves and were thus stationed at the very source of the slave trade.

As one moves forward into the eighteenth and nineteenth centuries, the number of ports of embarkation with permanent, fixed, and well-organized slave depots increases. The various fees and customs paid to native rulers along the Guinean coast are now replaced by exit duties paid to the government of Portugal. We shall see, in fact, how native populations were totally denied any share in the profits of slavery. When brokers brought in only two or three slaves at a time, slavers were obliged to collect their cargo at various ports along the coast, a process that could take months. This was an old system, but not very practical, since captives had to be maintained for long periods while awaiting the ocean crossing. Some slavers fitted out their steerage for this purpose, but this raised many problems of space, because merchandise had to be unloaded as new slaves were taken on board. More commonly, slaves were held on shore, in a *coral* surrounded by pickets to prevent escape and ward off attacks. This system, too, had its disadvantages, because ships often moved long distances, more than two hundred leagues, which meant that the center of operations also had to be shifted constantly, with additional fees and customs paid at each new anchorage, thus reducing the profits of the voyage. Thus all slavers tried to avoid the collection process. The Portuguese, who had anchorages of their own in the Congo, Angola, Benguela, and Mozambique, were more successful at this than other Europeans, particularly after the end of the sixteenth century.

Thus the "fixed depot" system was in widest use: under this system, employees were permanently stationed at depots at certain points along the coast. They had plenty of time to gather up large numbers of captives to be delivered in groups to the slavers. This profitable method of operation became possible in Ouidah, for example, when Bahians set up depots there and a fort was built in the 1720s. Captives were assembled near the point of embarkation in wooden or stone barracks, many of which can still be visited today. Many came from far away, some from very long distances indeed. They often served as porters, carrying merchandise and supplies along the inland trails. In the depots the captives were specially cared for prior to embarkation. They were well fed and given palm oil to grease their skin. The sick were treated and isolated from the rest. If embarkation was delayed, captives worked the land to grow food needed for their upkeep. In a variant of this system, captives were held not on land but on a large ship permanently anchored in the port. The Portuguese used this method, which made the slave depot less vulnerable to attack, in Angola.

Regardless of the system used, it was always difficult to predict how long it would take for a slaver to complete its cargo, and the mortality rate was high among both captives and crew. Sailors were well aware of the dangers that awaited them along the African coast. It has been calculated that the death rate was higher among the crew of English slavers than among the captives, who after all constituted a precious cargo that had to be delivered in the best possible condition to the American market. Profits from slave trafficking varied widely, and merchants sought to multiply the number of voyages as much as possible.

THE PERILS AND RISKS OF THE SLAVE TRADE

Coastal searches, fixed depots, apparently friendly relations with local natives, the presence of large numbers of dependable procurers and intermediaries, and all the well-oiled machinery for procuring and shipping slaves often concealed the many serious difficulties that made the slave trade a highly risky business, particularly in areas where Europeans lacked a firm foothold.

Sometimes native rulers were enticed into marauding, as in 1580 in Angola, when the local king managed to massacre thirty Portuguese and all their Christian slaves and then attacked the ten or twelve ships moored in the harbor in order to lay hands on the cargo he craved, some twenty thousand crusados worth of merchandise. Or a chieftain might wish to replenish his own stock of captives at little cost to himself, or to resell his prisoners to other slavers. This situation was quite common in areas where the slave trade was unregulated. Or again, a chief dissatisfied with the merchandise received in exchange for his captives might wish to take his vengeance. Merchants were also affected by wars in Europe; each country tried to use local rivalries and pent-up jealousies to its own advantage against the enemy of the moment. These ever-present dangers were aggravated by the fear of rebellion among the captives, much more common and terrifying on shore than on board ship, since the captives knew perfectly well that they did not know how to sail the vessels that were taking them to Brazil. Imagine the threat posed by the confinement in a small space of large numbers of strong men whose only thought was to regain their liberty, to flee. This situation explains why slavers took such care in guarding their prisoners: captives were segregated by sex and hotheads were kept in irons. Precautions were redoubled as the date of departure approached, since preparations could hardly be kept secret from the captives. The longer they were held in port, the greater the risk. As was mentioned earlier, the wait was inevitably fairly lengthy. It depended on how far a ship had to sail to meet its quota and above all on internal African struggles: political struggles, social struggles, struggles for survival during famine in drought-ridden areas. In any case, it does not seem possible to assert that the chronological development of the slave trade followed a geographic progression, that is, that the coast was the first area whose slave supply was depleted, followed by areas farther inland. Combinations of circumstances led to the capture of prisoners, so that at different times the markets were supplied with blacks from the interior and blacks from the coast. Only Angola, which was depopulated early and with great rapidity, may have been an exception to this rule. One factor never influenced the time it took to embark slaves, however: demand from the other side of the Atlantic, which increased steadily throughout the slave-trading period.

To be sure, European wars frequently disrupted the trade, but as the business became more and more highly structured, capture and storage of slaves came to be less and less governed by local circumstances, and the length of wait in the ports tended to increase, especially where Europeans had permanent installations. There was of course seasonal variation: the number of captives was higher during the southern summer, when trading activities were most intense, and lower during the winter. Such epidemics as smallpox, which frequently cut down large numbers of captives, also depleted the slave reserves. Traders generally preferred to embark captives who had been held for a long period, who were thus "prepared," and who also posed the greatest threat of revolt. But if demand was high, slavers did not hesitate to take on newly arrived captives, who were less fit for the hardships of a long and difficult voyage. Wrenched out of their families, communities, clans, and tribes, wrested from their familiar spiritual, cultural, and physical surroundings, captive blacks were treated by their European captors as a human herd in transit; their legal status was ambiguous, because they would not really become slaves until they had been sold once more.

But were the captives really unorganized? To be sure, their first reactions were stupor and fear, prostration, dread, and horror before the unknown, in the face of harsh discipline and much that was strange. But gradually, painfully, they learned of the existence of a different and peculiar world. Used to living in an organized social framework that had become incorporated into the structure of their personalities, captives found themselves almost anonymous, lost in a mass in which one was distinguished from another only by sex, age, physical appearance, and behavior in the face of the unknown. The new masters were studied and their gestures examined. There was both active and passive resistance. Captives quickly learned that survival was the most important thing, and the desire to commit suicide or rebel was gradually overcome, in appearance at any rate, by European-imposed discipline.

Religion and surveillance were the best ways of taming the captive. Camps were always provided with an effective police force, assisted by informers. Above all, traders agreed on the value of Christianity, with its promise of a better world on the other side of the Atlantic. Indeed, the Portuguese prohibited the embarkation of unbaptized slaves. Group baptisms were held, in which the entire ceremony involved having a priest give each captive a Christian name while placing a bit of salt on his tongue. Upon arrival at a Brazilian port or plantation, these baptismal rites were often repeated, for it was well known that harried captains frequently took on unbaptized blacks. A resolution of 1620 even ordered that chaplains be taken on board to catechize the blacks during the crossing. It hardly needs saying that these orders remained futile and that blacks who left Africa as "pagans" arrived as pagans in Brazil, even in the nineteenth century. In any case, when baptisms were held, the priest's interpreter spoke words similar to these, which date from the seventeenth century: "Know that you are now children of God. You are leaving for the lands of the Portuguese, where you will learn the substance of the holy faith. Think no more of your native lands, and eat no dogs, rats, or horses. Be happy."

Content or not, believing or not, the day of departure always came too quickly for the African facing the unknown prepared for him by his Portuguese masters. Sold once and destined to be sold again, he was compelled to embark upon a lengthy voyage.

TWO

In Brazil: Merchandise like Any Other

FROM CAPTIVITY TO SLAVERY: A ONE-WAY JOURNEY

The imminence of departure was heralded by the preparation of the transport ship. In the seventeenth century it was quite difficult to maintain vessels that rarely returned to Lisbon. In 1622, for example, the governor of
São Thomé explained to the king that of four ships dispatched in resgate,
two were lost and two others delayed because of poor mending and
caulking. São Thomé had no real caulker or carpenter but "only a few Negroes who take the place of one." By contrast, Brazilian slave ports were
well equipped. But the merchants of Bahia and Pernambuco, intent on
quick profits, often turned their ships around without adequate inspection. This situation continued into the eighteenth and nineteenth centuries, because reconditioning a ship required not just necessary repairs but
cleaning the hull and checking the condition of the holds, irons, rails and
stanchions, and rigging. Occasionally a worn anchor or mast had to
be replaced.

Then the supplies were brought on board: the indispensable fresh water
was carried in "pipes"—one pipe contained five to six hundred liters, and
at least twenty-five were required for every hundred captives. But many
captains, eager to save space, sought to cut down on the amount of water
loaded. The ship's carpenter-cooper was responsible for checking the condition of the barrels: a shortage of water was worse than a shortage of
food. Besides the pipes of water, the ship took on wood for heating the
stew of rice, dried vegetables, and manioc that was fed to the captives. A
Portuguese law of 1684 required that captives be given three meals a day
together with a *canada* (2.662 liters) of water. The law also required load-
ing of medications needed for care of the sick and stipulated that a chap-

lain be taken along to say the mass. Violations of this law were to be punished, in theory, by a fine of two thousand crusados plus twice the value of the captives transported, together with ten years' exile. Food for the crew consisted mainly of flour, biscuits, fowl, and fruits, mainly bananas and lemons, which were necessary to counter the danger of scurvy.

The ship's surgeon then checked the health of all captives, who were marked with an iron on the shoulder, thigh, or chest, a scene which, though often described by authors intent on showing how the slave was robbed of his human dignity, was but one stage in the lengthy process of enslavement. Once on board, captives were placed in irons until the coast of Africa was out of sight. The promiscuity and horror of this imprisonment have also been described in terms to wrench the heart of any sensitive reader, and it is indeed true that the conditions in which captives were confined were frightful. But one should be careful not to generalize, for the treatment of prisoners varied from ship to ship, as did the degree of discomfort, hunger, thirst, and filth. The number of captives carried by a ship of course depended on the capacity of the vessel. For the sixteenth and seventeenth century we have little information about the types of ships used in the slave trade, their tonnage, transport capacity, frequency of voyages, and age and sex of slaves transported, nor do we know anything about the economic organization of this traffic. In this period Dutch slavers ran from 450 to 1,000 tons, but Portuguese ships were apparently smaller, better organized, and cleaner (which is not to say that they were clean). The Portuguese carried 500 captives on one caravel, whereas the Dutch put only 300 on a large vessel. A small Portuguese brigantine could carry up to 200 slaves, a large vessel up to 700.

It took thirty-five days to sail from Angola to Pernambuco, forty to Bahia, fifty to Rio de Janeiro. But if the winds died and the ship in full canvas was caught in the silence of the equatorial calms, who knows how many anxious days the sailors, themselves prisoners and sharing their captives' hunger, spent scanning the heavens and the endless ocean? We hear of crossings that lasted three, four, or even five months, by which time food had run short and tempers were stretched to the breaking point. Even if the crossing was smooth and quick, without major problems, it was horribly painful for the captives. Brother Carli describes one ship loaded with 670 captives in the following terms. "Men were piled in the bottom of the hold, chained for fear that they would rise up and kill all the whites aboard. Women were held in the second steerage compartment, and those who were pregnant were grouped in the rear cabin. Children were crowded into the first steerage like herring in a barrel. If they tried to sleep, they fell on top of one another. There were bilges for natural needs, but since many were afraid of losing their place they relieved themselves wherever they happened to be, especially the men who were cruelly cramped. The heat and stench became unbearable."

This concise, dry, eyewitness account is more eloquent than any bombastic commentary. Equally eloquent are the vain attempts of the Portuguese Crown to regulate the trade: the law of 1684, for example, required that the number of Negroes embarked not exceed five to seven "head" for every two tons of ship's weight, and that ships must be equipped with portholes so that the captives could breathe. The regulation added that the upper portions of the vessel could carry an additional five "little heads" (that is, children) per ton. The regulations were easily evaded: slave traders listed as children young blacks who had reached adult height.

Who died during the long forced voyage? In these conditions the mortality rate was high. Life was hard for the ship's crew as well as the slaves. It has been suggested that the latter suffered an average mortality of 15 to 20 percent. In fact, there are virtually no quantitative studies, and we have little accurate information to go on. From isolated cases we can, however, establish orders of magnitude for the sixteenth and seventeenth centuries; for the eighteenth and nineteenth centuries there are some excellent studies, but they are limited to a few years' duration. In 1569 Frei Tomé de Macedo mentioned one ship that carried 500 captives. In one night it lost 120 of them, or 20.4 percent of the cargo. In 1625, the governor of Angola, João Correa de Souza sent five slavers to Brazil, for which we have the following figures:

Number of captives	Number who died	Percentage who died
195	85	44.4
220	126	57.2
357	157	43.9
142	51	35.2
297	163	54.8

Thus, in a total cargo of 1,211 captives, only 628 survived the crossing (49.2 percent). And 68 more died immediately after the landing. Of the 195 "pieces" on the first vessel, we are told that 110 survived, 25 of them elderly, sick black men, 55 elderly black women, and 30 youths and children. Were such high mortality rates common? Was this disastrous voyage typical? It is hard to say, for we know nothing about the tonnage of the five vessels, the composition of the cargo by age and sex, the duration of the voyage, the health conditions on board, or the state of health of the captives when they boarded. The oldest and youngest passengers in any case seem to have weathered the crossing best, which suggests that death struck mainly young adults! Great caution is therefore advisable in dealing with these reports. Other reports of other crossings give very different indications. Most historians who have attempted to separate true from false in these accounts today agree that the average mortality rate was 15 to 20 percent. We hear of one ship in which only two captives died in the crossing. In any case, a mortality rate in excess of 20 percent would have made it very difficult for most ships to have turned a profit.

We are much better informed for the eighteenth and nineteenth centuries, thanks to recent work by Pierre Verger and Herbert Klein. Their answers to questions about the organization, pace, direction, and volume of the slave trade have shed new light on certain fundamental aspects of the subject. But their research is limited in space and time: it covers no more than a twenty-year period and is limited to Angola, Benin, and Mozambique. Still, this work is invaluable and useful.

Angola, as we have seen, continued to be the principal supplier of slaves to Brazil in the eighteenth century. Between 1723 and 1771, 51 percent of imports from Angola went mainly to Rio de Janeiro, compared to 27.3 percent to Bahia, 18.2 percent to Pernambuco, and a modest .2 percent to Santos. During the period when the slave trade was supposed to be controlled by the Maranhão e Para Company, these would-be monopolies accounted for just 2.2 percent of the traffic! Once the privileges and monopolies were abolished, Pernambuco, Maranhão, and Para saw their share in the trade increase: in the years 1812, 1815, 1817, and 1822–1826 they received 37 percent of the blacks imported. In this same period, the figure for Rio increased to 54 percent, while that for Bahia declined to 6 percent. The reason for this was that Bahia drew its supplies mainly from the Mina Coast, and for it Angola was only a secondary source at this time.

The eighteenth century was the age of heavy galleys and maneuverable corvettes. Eighteen different kinds of vessels have been counted that plied the Atlantic in the slave trade. Fifty-five percent of these were galleys and corvettes, though at the end of the century there was a sharp increase in the number of brigantines sailing form the port of Rio. The bulk of the traffic moved between July and November, and as in the previous century voyages to Rio took 35–40 days from Angola and 50–70 days from

Mozambique, assuming that no major difficulty cropped up during the crossing. But the number of voyages made by each vessel varied: it appears that ships belonging to the monopoly companies made fewer crossings than those belonging to free merchants. Herbert Klein gives the following figures:

between 1790 and 1811, 43 vessels belong to independent merchants made 195 voyages in 32 years, or 4 voyages per ship;
25 other vessels made 125 voyages in 27 years, or five per ship;
for the company of Grão Para e Maranhão, the average was two voyages per ship, and for the company of Pernambuco and Paraíba it was 3 voyages;
after the abolition of the companies' privilege, in the period 1723–1728, the free merchants with 61 vessels made 118 voyages, or 1.9 voyages per ship, and for 1762–1767 with 63 vessels they made 140 voyages, or 2.2 voyages per ship.

It is relatively easy to explain these differences. The monopolistic companies were obliged to import a fixed number of captives, set by the terms of their contract. The free merchants were motivated by nothing other than profit. Furthermore, the capacity of vessels varied. Free traders could carry an average of 420 captives per vessel (their vessels ranged from 120 to 168 tons), whereas the company of Pernambuco and Paraíba carried an average of 397 captives per ship and that of Grão Para e Maranhão, 160, owing to regulations imposed by the law of 1684, which, as was mentioned earlier, limited the number of "head" on board to 2.5–3.5 per ton, depending on the fitting of the ship.

Slavers always carried more men than women: the ratio was generally about two men for each woman. We know almost nothing about the age of the captives. No tax was paid on nurslings, and small children went for half the normal tax. Thus it was tempting for slave traders to say that older children and even adolescents were younger than they actually were, or even to leave them out of the passenger list altogether. In letters of manumission and wills left by Africans in Brazil, most former slaves maintain that they came to Brazil when still very young. Thus the number of children listed as passengers on slave ships was probably much smaller than the number actually carried. In any case the number must not have been very large: between 1734 and 1769, children officially accounted for 6 percent of the 156,638 captives exported from the port of Luanda. They accounted for 3.1 percent of the captives exported through the port of Benguela between 1758 and 1784, compared with 8–13 percent of Dutch cargoes during the eighteenth century. At the destination, Rio de Janeiro on the other side of the Atlantic, the number of captive children officially disembarked fell to .5 percent of the total imported between 1795 and 1811! Was this due to extremely high mortality during the crossing? Apparently not, for during the same period we know from reliable data that the mortality rate was 6.2 percent for children and 9.5 percent for adults. It seems that children were quite simply not counted as part of the ship's cargo because they could not be sold or were difficult to sell. The question of why seems difficult to answer. Let me suggest, at any rate, that the child was not immediately productive; indeed, on the contrary, he or she was a burden. What is more, the child mortality rate was high in Brazil, so that there was a great risk of seeing one's investment disappear.

By contrast, the adult mortality rate of 9.5 percent during the crossing, calculated by Klein, agrees quite well with the figure of 10 percent calculated by Goulart. The most lethal voyages were thus undertaken during autumn and winter. Since the total mortality rate, from the time of capture until the day of sale in Brazil, was around 15–20 percent, more than half the losses in human lives occurred during the crossing itself, which seems fairly plausible. This figure represents, in any case, an improvement of 10 percent over the previous two centuries. The improvement was only by comparison with earlier years, since the mortality rate was still quite high, especially when compared with mortality rates in European countries during the same period: for England and Wales between 1780 and 1810, the mortality rate ranged from 2.3 to 2.8 percent. For France from 1770 to 1790 it varied from 2.7 percent to 4.4 percent. But figures for stable populations, during a period in which the great killer epidemics had disappeared, cannot really be compared with figures for the herd of uprooted captives who were packed on board the slave ships. During the seventeenth century, France, too, experienced mortality rates as high as 25.3 percent during periods of crisis, compared with a normal mortality rate for the same period that fluctuated around 3.4 percent.

During the nineteenth century the mortality rate during passage improved somewhat. It declined from the previous 9.5 percent to about 7.1 percent during the period 1825–1830, even though these were difficult years for the slave trade, which since 1815 had become illegal north of the equator.

All these averages, whatever they may have been, must not be allowed to obscure the realities, the extreme, indeed exceptional, cases. Mortality rates of more than 20 percent were not rare (they occurred on 5.6 percent of the ships leaving Angola and Mozambique for Rio de Janeiro). During the eighteenth and nineteenth centuries it was mainly galleys, corvettes, and brigantines that confronted the dangers of the Brazilian trade, and they were usually overloaded. The average number of captives carried per voyage from the ports of the Congo (Malembo, Cabinda, the Zaire River) to Rio was 359.1. For Angola (Ambriz, Loanda, Benguela) the figure was 407.9. Even more crowded were slavers sailing from far-off Lourenço Marques Inhanbanes, Quelimane, and Mozambique, which carried an average of 558.9 captives per vessel; the reason for this overcrowding was that these longer voyages were expensive. By carrying more captives, ship-owners could keep profit margins as high as those obtained by ships sailing from East African ports. Higher-than-average mortality rates can be explained by any number of causes, which in extreme cases combined to produce the catastrophic voyages of which slave traders have left accounts. These may of course be exaggerated, for in magnifying their losses traders may have been trying to avoid various taxes or duties. Among the leading causes of mortality, the length of the voyage and the port of origin of the captives seem to have been the most important factors. If the voyage was prolonged beyond a certain length, mortality increased. The threshhold was fifty days for West African sailings, seventy days for East African. Beyond that time, lack of food and above all lack of water made survival difficult above decks as well as below. The supplies taken on board, in amounts based on the length of an "ideal" voyage, represented a heavy investment by ships' captains, who tried to take as little as possible with them. When rations had to be reduced, obviously those of the captives were reduced more than those of the crew. Exceptionally bad weather or pursuit by pirates could force a ship off its normal course and thus dangerously prolong the length of the crossing. In the nineteenth century, when most European nations declared all traffic in slaves to be illegal, slave traders attempted to use smaller, faster, more maneuverable vessels, but this forced them to crowd a part of their human cargo onto the open decks, which considerably complicated the manipulation of the sails. We learn as much from the account of a man named Hill, who served as chaplain on board the slave ship *Progresso*. He reports that the ship lost fifty of its captives in one day. They had been carried on the deck, but a storm arose that forced the captain to order the sails attached. The captives crowded on the deck made this impossible, and they had to be sent below, into a hold too small to hold such a crowd.

On board the slaver, the captive was a man exposed to every kind of risk and defenseless against death. His diet changed suddenly. He lacked physical exercise, even when he was forced to walk or dance on deck during the crossing. The promiscuity of the holds was unbearable. Fear and despair rent his heart. Shipboard hygiene was generally poor. To be sure, the captive washed daily and was supposed to clean his "quarters." But he passed his nights in horribly crowded steerage, where the air was barely breathable. During the day he was somewhat freer to move about, but his movements were closely watched and depended on the weather, the size of the cargo, and above all on the crew's assessment of the captives' mood, for rebellion and mutiny were a constant worry. In fact, we know of no case of slave mutiny on board a Brazilian slaver; if any attempts were made, they were apparently quickly and easily put down. The one exception to this statement dates from 1823. It involves the fantastic story of a slave ship carrying black Macuas to the port of Bahia. Rebellion is said to have broken out on the high seas, instigated by a black *ladino* (one who already spoke Portuguese) by the name of José Toto or José Pato. José had told the blacks that they would be eaten by the whites once they reached land. The blacks rose, we are told, killed the whites, and managed to reach Bahia, a feat made possible by the presence on board of several slave sailors who knew a little bit about navigation. In any case, the atmosphere on board a slaver was one of suspicion and hostility. It was a hermetic universe divided into two parts, and tension was constant. For the crew the voyage was long. How much longer was it for the captive, clamped in irons and knowing that he was on a one-way journey, where each passing hour took him farther and farther from his native country until he was delivered, bound hand and foot, to a strange and brutal oppressor.

FROM THE SIXTEENTH TO THE NINETEENTH CENTURY: THE ATLANTIC TRADE AND THE INTERIOR TRADE

Between the second half of the sixteenth century and 1850, when the Brazilian slave trade was finally abolished, the number of captives introduced into Brazil has been put at 3.5–3.6 million. Though based on incomplete data, this figure is now accepted by all researchers who have worked on the problem. In other words, Brazil imported 38 percent of all slaves brought from Africa to the New World.

During the second half of the sixteenth and all of the seventeenth century northeastern Brazil specialized in growing cane sugar for export. To that end Bahia and Pernambuco imported 30,000 Africans from the Guinean coast in the final decades of the sixteenth century. But by the beginning of the next century barely 15,000 remained. The seventeenth century was chiefly a period of sugar growing, even though Portugal lost its monopoly on sugar sales in the 1670s owing to strong competition from the Dutch, French, and English established in the Antilles. The Brazilian sugar industry expanded steadily, with a consequent increased demand for manpower. When the native Indians proved unsuitable for sedentary labor, the volume of the African trade had to be increased. This was the heyday of the slave trade, as 500,000–550,000 slaves from the Guinean coast and especially Angola were imported, mainly prior to 1640, by traders who were often themselves landowners and planters. Most of these slaves were absorbed by the sugar plantations of Bahia and Pernambuco, with comparatively few going to the markets of Para or Maranhão in the north and Rio de Janeiro in the south.

In the late seventeenth century the discovery of gold in the province of Minas Gerais created a new demand for labor and tripled the volume of the slave trade. It has been calculated that 1,700,000 blacks were imported, 1,140,000 of them from Angola and the rest from the Mina Coast. We do not know how this new contingent of slaves was divided among the captaincies of the colony. Two-thirds apparently went inland and populated Minas Gerais, Mato Grosso, and Goiàs, where the discovery of diamond deposits further increased the demand for slaves. Imports continued to flow through the traditional ports of the northeast such as Bahia and Pernambuco, the queens of the slave trade. But Rio de Janeiro, which became the capital of the country in 1763, saw its role grow and its importance increase. The gold and diamond rush slowed after 1760. Slave labor then flowed mainly into the coastal area, where sugar production found its second wind, with periods of glory such as that stretching from 1787 to 1817–1820; fresh land was even cleared in the captaincy of São Paulo. New agricultural activities, such as the growing of subsistence crops, further increased the need for slave labor, which became so indispensable that the volume of trade remained steady and even increased in the 1820s when coffee became king in the provinces of central and southern Brazil. The coffee industry alone swallowed up almost all of the 1,350,000 slaves imported from the Mina Coast, the Congo, Angola, and Mozambique. Of those 1,350,000 captives, 570,000 were imported via the port of Rio, by far the most important point of entry, compared with 220,000 via Bahia, 150,000 via Pernambuco, and 40,000 via Maranhão.

The volume of the slave trade thus closely followed the demand for labor. If that volume increased steadily, the reason was that new activities created fresh demands for labor as older industries became less starved for new workers. Gold replaced sugar in the eighteenth century, then coffee supplanted gold in the nineteenth. The demand for labor increased constantly, but its qualitative nature changed, and the structure of the slave trade changed with it in order to adapt to the new manpower requirements.

As inland regions developed and became populated, the coastal zones lost their monopoly on economic power. At the same time, the slave trade, once limited to port-to-port traffic, expanded to involve land routes as well. This was a fundamental change, which transformed the market for slaves. Hence only a detailed chronological study can hope to capture the evolution of a system that remained flexible enough to accommodate to changing requirements.

In the sixteenth and seventeenth centuries, then, the slave trade was port-to-port. Traffickers who had obtained their avenças (export licenses) were obliged to bring captives to the port designated in the license documents. These ports were of course located where there was a real demand for slaves, that is, in the market towns of agricultural regions where sugar cane was grown on a large scale for export to steadily growing foreign markets. These market towns were found in the north (Grão Para and Maranhão), the northeast (Pernambuco and Bahia), and farther south (Rio de Janeiro). We know little about the structure of this early slave traffic, but it seems to have been based on one of two models. Either the African slave was brought in by a slaver and sold on behalf of a third party who financed and organized the African expedition, or the black was imported directly by landowners who as far back as 1558 had obtained the right to secure their own labor supply, provided that no one owner import more than 120 captives annually. This was a fairly large number, and in any case compliance must not have been easy to monitor. We do not know the number of slave-importing landowners. But we do know that at least until the restoration of the Portuguese monarchy in 1640, the activities of production and sale were not separate. The same person produced a crop and then sold it. A merchant class did not develop until later. Thus the plantation owner himself had to assume all the risks of directly importing slave labor.

Still, even if a grower imported his full quota of 120 captives annually for a number of years, it is hard to see how, if the grower owned just two or three sugar mills with 80–100 slaves each, all the slaves imported were absorbed, especially since the replacement rate for plantation slaves in this period was about 6.27 percent per year. It therefore seems reasonable to assume that slave-importing growers disposed of most of their authorized allotment on local markets, thereby supplying slaves to *senhores de engenho* who lacked the capital required to participate directly in the trade. Hence it was the slave trade itself which, from the second half of the seventeenth century on, helped to differentiate a class of landowners from a class of merchants.

It was characteristic of the sixteenth and seventeenth centuries that slave markets located in the ports served a relatively small region of the hinterland, really the outskirts of the port cities themselves, where the growing of sugar cane reigned supreme. In the port cities, where freshly disembarked captives still breathed the salt air of the voyage, slaves were sold privately between individuals as well as at auction. In either case the buyer entered into direct contact with the seller, and no intermediary was necessary. The circuit was relatively short, since captives were generally purchased for immediate use and not for purposes of speculation. Each producer bought only enough hands to meet the needs of his plantation. Alongside these markets for selling slaves, there quickly developed a market for *renting* slave labor on a temporary basis. During the sixteenth and seventeenth centuries slave rental was still found only in the larger coastal cities; it made sense only in highly urbanized areas. Pyrard de Laval, who visited Bahia at the beginning of the seventeenth century, has this to say: "There is not a single Portuguese, however poor, man or woman, who does not possess two or three slaves, slaves who earn their masters' living by working a certain number of hours every day and generating sufficient profit to sustain their owners." The slaves were generally artisans whose place in the labor market was similar to that of free men: they hired themselves out, negotiated contracts with their employers, and received money for their work, a percentage of which went to their masters.

The discovery of gold and diamond deposits in the interior of Brazil, especially in Minas Gerais, led to considerable changes in the structure of the slave trade, extending it far beyond the port of entry. *Tratantes* was the term for the merchant-miners whose principal role was to serve as intermediaries between the large importers on the coast and the consumers of slave labor in the mining regions. The commercial organization of the trade, already complicated by the emergence of this new group of merchants, was further complicated by the development of speculation in slaves, the immediate consequence of which was a sharp rise in the price of slave labor. The price increase encouraged the development of a new, internal market for slaves.

What historians customarily call the "gold cycle" in the Brazilian economy began in 1693. This was the year in which the sugar-based economy experienced its first major slump. As a result, sugar dealers in Bahia and Rio were forced to seek new commercial contracts in the hope of surviving the crisis. Moreover, these merchants were the only ones with sufficient experience to cope with the new labor-market problems and the vast distances between the coastal markets and the new consumers of slave labor. It was at this point that Brazilian commerce was reorganized and Salvador and Rio de Janeiro developed into the major markets supplying the vast inland plantations with food, tools, fabrics, and above all slaves, as precious a commodity as the gold for which they were traded. This conjunctural shift in the Brazilian economy was mainly of a qualitative nature, however; the economy was still based on the production of primary products for export, such as gold, diamonds, sugar, and tobacco. To be sure, sugar production ceased to increase, but tobacco production did rise and tobacco was used to buy slaves in Africa. In any case, the sugar plantations were no longer the only consumer of slave labor. The dynamic new gold-mining sector required enormous numbers of slaves, at a time when the mother country, Portugal, remained divided and uncertain over the issues of supplying Brazil with slave manpower. Lisbon sometimes favored the large monopolistic trading companies and sometimes inclined toward free trade in slaves. Its policy shifts were often clumsy, but ultimately it decided in favor of free trade and established new commercial structures better adapted to the increased demand and the needs of the mother country as well as Brazil. What were those structures?

To begin with, the merchant class diversified: alongside the great wholesalers, who imported food and manufactured goods from Lisbon and Porto and slaves from Africa and exported sugar, tobacco, and gold, there emerged a new category of middle-level merchants who dealt exclusively in slaves and directly with West Africa. In addition, there was a fair number of small merchants (*tratantes* in Portuguese) who were generally mere agents of the large wholesalers but who sometimes made purchases with their own capital. The way the system worked is best illustrated by example. The following anecdotes are based on the records of the Inquisition, which tried a number of Bahia merchants on the charge of being "new Christians."

In 1726 the wholesaler Diogo de Avila Henriques was arrested. The inventory of his property shows the diversity of his commercial contacts: he exported hides and imported other goods through his agents in Porto. He also seems to have had correspondents on the Mina Coast who sold fabric, tobacco, manioc flour, and spirits there and purchased black captives to be sold on the markets of Minas Gerais. Diogo de Avila Henriques also maintained good commercial relations with Rio de Janeiro. His cousins Gaspar Henriques and Diogo d'Avila were also his partners. The former sold merchandise and slaves in Minas and Rio de Janeiro, as did the latter, though he sometimes joined in partnership not with his cousin Diogo de Aliva Henriques but rather with one Guilherme Belar Campanha to sell slaves, not for *reis* but for gold pieces-of-eight, as was customary in the mining areas. What we see here, then, is a complete commercial network, involving both large and small merchants. Gaspar Henriques and Diogo d'Avila worked on a percentage basis (8 percent of the profits) for their cousin Diogo de Avila Henriques. By contrast, the tratante Antonio Roiz Garcia, who was arrested in 1733, seems to have worked for himself alone, selling slaves, horses, and other merchandise in the *sertão*, or hinterland. Pedro Nunes de Miranda, a new Christian merchant established in Bahia and arrested in 1731, dealt in slaves directly with the Mina Coast and owned a *fazenda* on which he grew corn, no doubt used to feed the imported slaves.

As we just saw, the increase in the demand for labor also led to the development of an internal slave traffic and a major shift in manpower from agricultural to gold-producing areas. This shift, hastened by the rise of speculation, was the consequence of the collapse of the sugar economy. The return on the investment in slave labor for sugar production was low and threatened to fall sharply, so that it became tempting for slave owners to sell their slaves to mine owners hungry for labor. But didn't this move away from sugar by plantation and mill owners threaten to deal a blow to the agricultural economy from which it would never recover? Antonil, writing in 1711, was well aware of this possibility when he said that "the best mines in Brazil" were its fields of cane and tobacco, and that "gold mines are false wealth." This prediction proved true; indeed, the internal traffic in slaves reversed its direction in the last quarter of the eighteenth century, when gold production fell, leaving an excess labor supply that would quickly be shifted toward the coastal regions in which agricultural activity was again on the upswing, as well as toward the São Paulo region and other areas of the interior, where the farming of subsistence crops and new cane fields developed rapidly. Thus it was again the farming interests that put the captive labor force to work and determined its disposition in a continent increasingly susceptible to the vagaries of supply and demand.

Landowners, and later also owners of mines that had become unprofitable, often traveled personally to areas where the demand for slaves was high to sell their unneeded workers. But it was easier and more attractive to use the services of agents who went from engenho to engenho to recruit workers in areas hit by crisis. These agents would travel thousands of kilometers to reach markets where new buyers awaited them. Their troops of slaves resembled the herds of cattle and mules that the sertão raised for the large cities, and they followed the same routes. But because the former were herds of men and women rather than animals, they eventually became, in the nineteenth century, an object of interest not only to economic actors and speculators but also to government regulators—a political football.

The laws governing the slave trade, some of them enforced, some not, many of them circumvented or flouted, grew in number during the nineteenth century and gradually altered in important ways the structures we have just described, particularly in the ports of entry. The trans-Atlantic slave trade between Brazil and Africa ran afoul of measures intended to make it illegal. Between 1815 and 1830, slave trafficking remained legal, but only south of the equator. Between 1831 and 1851 it went underground and was finally outlawed by a ministerial decree signed by Eusebio de Queiros Coutinho Mattoso da Camara on 28 September 1850. It hardly needs emphasizing that slavers tried by every possible means to evade the English ships that watched the coast and were the principal enforcers of the laws against slave trafficking. Vessels departing to pick up slaves were issued passports to imaginary destinations or, prior to 1830, to ports south of the equator when their real destination lay in the northern hemisphere. Double passports and flags of convenience were also used. It was easy, once on the high seas, to take down the Brazilian flag and run up a Portuguese, Spanish, or American flag instead. The captain could also

declare his ship to be "in distress" or "in ballast" and say that it risked going down with all hands unless it could make land at some slave port.

The new restrictions also led increasingly to concealment of vessels' sizes
and capacities. William Pennell, the English consul in Bahia, communicated to the Foreign Office on 16 June 1827 that "the Brazilian brig Felli-
cidade arrived on the ninth from Lisbon, drawing 144 tons. It departed
for Cabinda, regauged locally at 202 tons, and on the same day, the ninth
of June, received passport number 18 allowing it to import 505 slaves
from Cabinda." Thus there was no want of complicity between merchants
and the authorities, both intent on securing the benefits of a profitable
trade. Still another example: on 18 June 1827 the commissioners of the
mixed tribunal of Sierra Leone reported the case of the *Créola*, which
though measured for 214 slaves, carried 308, or seven slaves for every two
tons of ship's weight. Between 1815 and 1830 an average 7,023 captives
per year were imported through the port of Bahia alone. For the peak
years 1826–1830 we have the following figures:

Years	Number of captives
1826	7,858
1827	10,186
1828	8,127
1829	12,808
1830	6,425

Subsequently, the traffic stagnated during the first years of clandestinity,
then picked up again after 1835. For the port of Bahia, for example, the
peak came in the years 1846–1850:

Years	Number of captives[a]	Number of captives[b]
1840	1,675	1,413
1841	1,410	1,470
1842	2,360	2,520
1843	3,004	3,111
1844	6,201	6,501
1845	5,582	5,582
1846	7,824	7,354
1847	11,769	10,064
1848	7,383	7,299

Years	Number of captives[a]	Number of captives[b]
1849	8,401	8,081
1850	9,102	9,451
1851	785	—
Total	65,506	64,946

[a]Pierre Verger, *Flux et reflux de la traite des nègres* (Pan's 1968), p. 666.
[b]Leslie Bethell, *The Abolition of the Brazilian Slave Trade* (Cambridge, 1970).

If we now compare the annual averages for numbers of captives imported (5,454 and 5,904 respectively) with the annual averages for the periods of totally free trade (1801–1815) or of trade limited to the southern hemisphere (1815–1830), we find that the differences are not so large as we might have supposed:

Years	Annual averages (number of captives)
1801–1810	7,500–7,700
1801–1815	5,500–5,700
1815–1830	6,196–7,023
1840–1851	5,454–5,904

This suggests that the average level of importation held steady, despite the new restrictions. We also need to know whether this level satisfied the demand for slaves. To be sure, until 1830 captives were unloaded in the same ports as before, ports specializing in the import of black manpower. But after 1830, these ports were replaced by unofficial ports of debarkation, clandestine anchorages in out-of-the-way inlets near large ports. Today in Pernambuco, Bahia, and Rio one still finds sheltered, out-of-the-way beaches near the old official ports, beaches that were used for unloading slaves, almost always with the active connivance of local authorities eager to maintain the slave traffic. This clandestine trafficking has left many traces in local place names: for example, one Bahian beach frequently used for unloading slaves was baptized the *"praia do chega nego,"* the beach where the Negro arrives. Today one can still see the remains of the old slave depot, built of stone, in which arriving captives were held. The building furnishes striking proof of the Bahian authorities' tolerance of these unofficial ports of debarkation, this one obviously built to last. But usually the buildings were temporary, hastily constructed of light wood and easy to destroy at the first sign of trouble. Clandestine ports were more readily identified by the presence of large stores of food, barrels of water, and cauldrons for cooking rations for illegally entered slaves shipped either directly from Africa or indirectly via some northeast Brazilian port.

The African who disembarked, usually at night in a small boat to the sound of the muffled voices of men hoping to keep their activities secret, must have been quite puzzled about his peculiar destiny. Even if the authorities closed their eyes to the illegal goings-on in the clandestine ports, newly arrived captives obviously could not be sold openly. To sell their cargo the slavers resorted to various subterfuges, such as selling small lots put out to "board" with major slaveholders. When a slave died at a large sugar mill, the master seldom notified the appropriate authorities. Thus it was easy to replace deceased slaves with new arrivals. This was an advantage for the slave trader able to hide his merchandise, as well as for the planter, who received new workers on a trial basis. After testing them on the job, he had the pick of the lot for himself. Only a short while before, landowner and slave trader had been one and the same person. In any case, planters and traders worked hand in hand to accustom stunned arrivals to their new homes. Captives must have been quite mystified and frightened by what they saw when they emerged from the hold or steerage of their rolling, pitching vessel and stepped onto a fine, sandy beach hidden at the end of a small bay.

New arrivals were also included in lots sold in the western regions (Rio de Janeiro) and to the south (especially in the area around São Paulo), when the internal trade (with its long journeys on foot) underwent a vast expansion after 1850, spurred by the rise of coffee growing. Merchants eager to move their lots of slaves quickly to the interior and to the state of São Paulo made use of the brand-new railroads. This traffic did not come to an end until after the 1870s, when local governments imposed duties that reduced the profits considerably.

Thus in the nineteenth century, as in the eighteenth, new economic interests were responsible for the shifting about of large contingents of slaves. Many came from the provinces of northern and northeastern Brazil, which experienced a deep depression, especially after 1850. They moved through the ports of Rio de Janeiro and Santos. Between 1852 and 1870 5,000–6,000 slaves were involved in this transfer each year. Between

TABLE 1.
Free and Slave Population of Brazil
1823 and 1872

Province	1823			1872		
	Freemen	Slaves	Total	Freemen	Slaves	Total
Corte				226,033	48,939	274,972
Minas Gerais	425,000	215,000	640,000	1,669,276	370,459	2,039,735
Rio de Janeiro	301,099	150,549	451,648	490,087	292,637	782,724
São Paulo	259,000	21,000	280,000	680,742	156,612	837,354
Espírito Santo	60,000	60,000	120,000	59,478	22,659	82,137
Bahia	434,464	237,458	671,922	1,211,792	167,824	1,379,616
Pernambuco	330,000	150,000	480,000	752,511	89,028	841,539
Sergipe	88,000	32,000	120,000	153,620	22,623	176,243
Alagoas	90,000	40,000	130,000	312,268	35,741	348,009
Parahyba	102,407	20,000	122,407	354,700	21,526	376,226
Rio Grande do N.	56,677	14,376	71,053	220,959	13,020	233,979
Amazonas				56,631	979	57,610
Para	88,000	40,000	128,000	247,779	27,458	275,237
Paranhão	67,704	97,132	164,836	284,101	74,939	359,040
Piauhy	80,000	10,000	90,000	178,427	23,795	202,222
Ceará	180,000	20,000	200,000	689,773	31,913	721,686
Parana				116,162	10,560	126,722
Santa Catarina	47,500	2,500	50,000	144,818	14,984	159,802
Rio Grande do S.	142,500	7,500	150,000	367,022	67,791	434,813
Goiás	37,000	24,000	61,000	149,743	10,652	160,395
Matto Grosso	24,000	6,000	30,000	53,750	6,667	60,417
Total	2,813,351	1,147,515	3,960,866	8,419,672	1,510,806	9,930,478

Source: Oliveira Vianna, "Resumo histórico dos inquéritos censitários realizados no Brasil", pp. 404–405, 414, *in* S. J. Stein Vassouras, *A Brazilian Coffee County 1850–1890: The roles of Planter and Slave in Changing Plantation Society* (New York: Atheneum, 1974), p. 296.

1872 and 1876 the port of Rio de Janeiro alone received 25,711 slaves from the north and northeast. Other slaves were moved along overland routes; we have no information about the volume of this traffic. Regions such as Minas Gerais which had formerly been consumers of labor and were located near the new coffee-producing centers lost many of their slaves to Rio and São Paulo.

Between 1850 and 1888 the volume of the internal slave trade seems to have attained an average level of 5,500 slaves moved each year, which would give a total of 209,000 for the period. The sugar-growing regions would then have lost 100,000–200,000 slaves: this figure seems plausible, given the fact that the economic crisis was most strongly felt in the northeast. Table 2 gives an idea of these transfers.

Thus the salient features of the nineteenth-century slave trade are these: slave trading became illegal after 1830, and there was a massive transfer of slave manpower from economically depressed regions of the north and northeast to new centers of development in southern and central sections. The internal slave trade first developed in the eighteenth century. Its character was closely tied to the economic situation. In reality, throughout the three centuries during which Brazil developed with and by means of slave labor, the slave trade, whether trans-Atlantic or internal, sustained a similar set of practices and customs. Slave traders were quick to invent efficient and presumably profitable methods for transforming the captive into a slave or the agricultural laborer into a miner. Debarkation, fattening for market, and sale were the first steps in the fate of the black man, no matter who he was or where he came from.

TABLE 2.

Brazilian Slave Population Compared to Total Population, by Region
1819 and 1872

Region	Total Population		Slave Population		Percentage of Slave Population	
	1819	1872	1819	1872	1819	1872
North	143,251	332,847	39,040	28,437	27.3	8.5
Northeast	1,112,703	3,082,701	367,520	289,962	33.0	9.4
East	1,807,638	4,735,427	508,351	925,141	28.1	19.5
South	433,976	1,558,691	125,283	249,947	28.9	16.0
Centerwest	100,564	220,812	40,980	17,319	40.7	7.8
Total	3,598,132	9,930,478	1,081,174	1,510,806	30.0	15.0

Source: Thomas E. Skidmore, *Preto no Branco. Raça e nacionalidade no pensamento brasileiro* (Rio de Janeiro, Paz e Terra, 1976), p. 57.

DEBARKATION AND FATTENING FOR MARKET

Whether he arrived from some remote port after a month or two or even longer at sea or was shifted about in a dangerous and sometimes clandestine coastal trade, the captive generally left the ship in an easily imaginable state of physical and moral exhaustion. If he came from across the ocean he had suffered the psychic trauma of capture and the long marches required in some cases to reach the slave ports. He had been placed in irons and often been forced to wait long periods for the arrival of the *tumbeiros*. Imprisoned on board ship, he had experienced the ups and downs of a hard passage only to be disembarked, more dead than alive, in strange and hostile territory. The slave who came from less far away did not necessarily suffer less, for he may have been forced to leave friends and relatives behind and to abandon a way of life to which he had become more or less accustomed, only to be chained up and dragged off once again to face an unknown future, in a state of anguish equaled only by the physical exhaustion that surely followed his forced voyage, with its accompanying promiscuity, hunger, and brutality. But for his new master—a temporary master to be sure, and in fact more owner than master—he represented a major investment of capital on which it was natural to seek the greatest possible return. Slaves therefore had to be shown to prospective buyers in the best possible physical and even moral condition, because buyer and seller would inevitably bargain, and bargain hard, over the price, which could hinge on the health of the merchandise. Thus prior to sale the captive was always well cared for and fed. he was rubbed down with palm oil to hide any wounds he might have, conceal skin diseases, and above all to give his black body that luster which was always taken as a sign of vigor. Teeth and gums were often rubbed with astringent roots, which gave the mouth a healthy appearance. Exercises helped to overcome the stiff joints and muscular atrophy brought on by long voyages in uncomfortable positions, and in quarters so cramped that the captive often had to sleep on his side.

In the early days of the trade, in the sixteenth and seventeenth centuries, when the Brazilian ports of entry were still modest villages with plenty of open space on their outskirts, newly arrived captives were held in open barracks whose roofs afforded the only protection against the winds and rains so common in the tropics. But as the trade developed in the second half of the seventeenth century, and as the outskirts of the cities became more and more urbanized, it became necessary to establish permanent slave depots, sometimes even whole districts, whose purpose was to house new arrivals: a good example is the commercial parish of Pila in Salvador (Bahia) in the eighteenth and nineteenth centuries.

We do not know the precise capacity of these depots. Let me suggest, as a hypothesis, that they could hold 400–500 slaves, a number equivalent to the average cargo of a slave ship. Actually, to be unloaded into a depot or warehouse was a privilege reserved for captives arriving in well-established ports. In other ports of entry there were no permanent shelters, and the slave market was an open-air affair, exposed to the elements. Sometimes slaves were sold in the streets and squares; local merchants displayed their human wares at the doors of their shops and sold them at auction to the highest bidder. A German traveler by the name of Freyreiss, who visited Bahia in the middle of the nineteenth century, has left this description of a slave market and depot: "The slaves, packed by the hundreds into a sort of hut, are scantily clad, wearing a bit of cloth or wool around the stomach. As a matter of hygiene their heads have been shaved. Thus, naked and shorn, seated on the ground, looking curiously at passersby, they are not much different in appearance from macaque monkeys. . . . Some arrive from Africa branded with hot irons like animals."

Little remains today of these slave market depots. Urbanization, abetted by guilty consciences, has destroyed these vestiges of the past. In Olinda, Recife's sister city in the state of Pernambuco, however, an old slave market still stands with its original structure almost intact. It is a large rectangle enclosing a square. On two sides slave depots form the walls of the enormous stone building. The façades are protected by a beautiful arcaded gallery. The depots had only one gate, which served as both door and window and which was the main source of ventilation; at night it was securely locked for obvious security reasons. Small openings in the tops of the walls allowed just enough air to enter for the captives to breathe at night. The central square was naturally the marketplace where auctions were held, but in its center was a pillory, still standing today, which could be used to tie and whip slaves from the city sent for punishment, thereby inspiring fear and terror in the minds of the new arrivals. Thus the market, for all its harmonious proportions, was a place to sell and discipline slaves; for the new arrival it was a horrible ghetto, a sordid place in which he was isolated, put on display, palpated, and sold.

It is clear that permanent depots were established in the major ports of entry. With the development of an internal slave traffic, traders began to build lodgings on the major roads which could be used as way stations and rest stops for slaves to be sold in nearby cities: some were final stopping places, physical conditioning stations, around which developed small villages that eventually grew into fairly large towns. Later, when the now illegal slave trade became too difficult and too dangerous to practice on land, the slave ship itself was used as warehouse and marketplace. Buyers—in these circumstances almost always intermediaries—came on board to make their transactions, and "the merchandise" was unloaded furtively at night, at some secure site safe from prying eyes. In all these market depots, whatever their nature or location, Africans were cared for, groomed, and well fed, by force if necessary. Dried meat and fish, manioc flour, and bananas and oranges were supposed to restore their health and appearance. The important thing was to avoid death and disease and obtain the best possible price.

THREE

To Be Valuable Merchandise

How Slaves Were Sold

Public auction and private sale were the two systems of selling slaves used throughout Brazil's three-hundred-year history of slave labor.

Auctions were used chiefly with captives newly arrived in Brazil. They were generally held in the ports of entry, starting ten to fifteen days after the unloading of cargo and lasting until all the Africans on board had been sold, which could take quite some time. When the demand for labor was high, sellers took advantage of the situation by putting hard-to-sell captives on the block first. The best of the lot were saved until last. Three examples, selected from the few pieces of relatively detailed information we have, will illustrate this technique, which was well established and advantageous to shrewd dealers and sharp buyers.

There is a surviving *certidão*, or record, of an auction sale held in 1612, involving seven of a lot of ten captives brought in from Angola. The three others died during the crossing. The seven survivors sold for 28,000 reis apiece, or 196,000 reis for the lot. The shipper, who was selling the slaves on behalf of a third party, received from the ship owner as reimbursement for the transport of the three deceased captives 7,200 reis, to be paid in Angola in fabric (48 *panos* at 200 reis each, or 9,600 reis in all, less a discount of 2,400 reis). Thus the seller received a total of 196,000 from the auction plus 7,200 reis, or 203,200 reis in all. What were his outlays? To begin with, a duty of 40,000 reis, or 4,000 per head, dead or alive), plus 1,000 reis in costs for the five days prior to the sale, plus the cost of transport of 9,600 reis per living slave. The seller's profits thus came to 95,000 reis, or 13,571 reis per slave. This was the gross profit, from which deduction must also be made for the cost of purchasing the slaves in Angola.

This cost was generally expressed in terms of goods bartered, and we do not know what it was in this case. It has been asserted that the Portuguese bought their captives at very low prices.

Our second example comes from the second half of the eighteenth century. It involves seven captives sent to Rio de Janeiro in 1762 by Captain João Proença e Sylva. Here is the tally for the sale:

Receipts (in reis)

2 young females, dead at sea	—
1 adult Negro sold to Ignacio Martins on 30 May	90,000
1 *molecão* (young man) sold to Manoel Francisco dos Santos on 4 June	64,000
1 molecão sold to Francisco Lobo on 14 June	70,000
1 *moleque* (child) died after debarkation on 14 June.	—
1 moleque sold to Manoel Machado Borges on 30 June	51,600
Total Receipts	275,600

Expenditures (in reis)

Sea transport and costs paid to captain	100,295
Services of a priest who baptized five captives	7,500
Medicine and fees for the treatment of a sick captive after debarkation	2,120
Food for slaves for 76 days at 60 reis per day	4,560
Commission for sale at 6 percent	16,536
Total Expenditures	131,011
Gross profit	144,589

What is striking in this account is first of all the high mortality rate in this lot: three out of seven died before any profit could be made. It is also surprising that it took a month to sell these four slaves, who went separately to different buyers. The cost of baptizing five captives is exorbitant, whereas the cost of food and the medical fees seem reasonable.

Let us compare the 1762 example with the 1612 example:

The account for 1762 makes no mention of import duties. Were these included under the head of "sea transport and costs paid to captain"? In that case, the transport costs from Angola to Brazil—14,326 per captive in 1762 compared with 9,600 in 1612—would be a composite of import duties and costs of the voyage.

The time elapsed between arrival and sale increased considerably. It took five days to sell the seven slaves in the 1612 lot. For the captives of 1762 it took at least one month (30 May to 30 June), and perhaps as much as 76 days, since there is a reference to 76 days of food after debarkation. Admittedly, 1762 was a year in which the demand for slaves was relatively low. It was a bad moment: mining was in decline and there was a crisis in the sugar market. Furthermore, the document does not state whether the slaves were sold at auction or privately.

The 1762 sale, moreover, was made by an agent who received a commission of 6 percent of the total receipts. In the 1612 sale no agent seems to have been involved.

Finally, we have no idea in either case how much was paid for the captives in Angola.

Our third case dates from the eighteenth century. We know about it from a tally sheet presented by Manoel Ferreira concerning fourteen captives sent to Bahia by Captain Manoel José da Rocha, a resident of Angola. These fourteen captives were brought to Salvador in 1795 by the galley *São Marcos*, commanded by Captain José de Matos da Costa and fitted out by Félis Francisco Ferreira:

Expenditures (in reis)

Duties on aforementioned 14 slaves at 8,700	121,800
Freightage for same	87,010
Paid in medical expenses at sea	7,000
Expenses connected with the death of 1 slave	800
Food for all until 12 August	12,680
Expenses (text is illegible)	58,500
Total	287,790
For monies belonging to above-named party	640,000
For monies to be given to Captain Manoel Roiz Barreto	48,000
Total Expenditures	976,000

Receipts

1 Negro molecão (young man) sold	110,000
1 Negro molecão sold	90,000
1 Negro molecão sold	93,000

1 Negress *molecona* (young woman) sold	70,000
1 Negress molecona sold	70,000
1 Negro molecão sold	90,000
1 Negress molecona sold	80,000
1 Negro conferado sold	70,000
1 Negress sold	64,000
1 Negress sold	69,000
1 Negress sold	56,000
1 Negress sold	70,000
1 Negro with two fistulae on the face and a wound on the leg	40,000
1 Negro who died on 12 July	—
Total Receipts	976,000

This account is quite different in form from the other two. It tells us about the duties paid on captives imported into Brazil, duties that more than doubled during two centuries (from 4,000 reis in 1612 to 8,700 reis in 1795). The freightage of 6,215 reis per head reflects a sharp drop in the cost of transporation compared with the 9,600 reis per head of 1612, especially considering the depreciation in the value of the real, which contained 0.007 grams of 22-carat gold in 1612 but only 0.002 grams at the beginning of the nineteenth century. What was the reason for this drop? Was the trade better organized? Was there increased competition among a larger number of ships? On the other hand, the selling price of a slave in 1795 was roughly equal to the 1762 price, with the slight rise, from 68,900 to 75,076 on the average, no doubt due to increased demand for labor: this was a period of prosperity for the sugar engenhos. Compared with 1612, the average price per slave had almost tripled.

The 1795 document makes no mention of a commission or agent, unless the sixty item under expenses, which is illegible, is in fact the total commission on the sale, which would come to 4,875 reis per captive or 5.79 percent of the total sale, a figure close to the 6 percent paid in 1762. On the other hand, we do not know the significance of the 48,000 reis paid to Captain Manoel Roiz Barreto. As for the 640,000 real figure, this was probably the gross profit earned by Manoel José da Rocha, the Angolan merchant who consigned to the vessel his cargo of fourteen captives, who no doubt traveled in the company of a good many other anonymous and precious "Negroes" and "Negresses."

Here are three examples, then: Unfortunately, we have absolutely no idea whether or not they were representative nor can we say with confidence that between 1612 and 1795 the price of imported slaves tripled and import duties more than doubled while the cost of transport declined.

Auction sales were not limited to Africans newly arrived in the ports of entry. Slaves were sold at auction after default on a mortgage, something that happened fairly often to sugar planters who were frequently forced to borrow from important merchants. These merchants, residents of the port cities engaged in the import-export business, made shrewd loans to senhores de engenho, offering advances against future harvests evaluated at well below the market price. These "advances" were generally in the form of commodities indispensable to the running of the plantation: tools, consumption items, and even slaves. If the sugar planter later found himself unable to pay back the loan, his slaves would be seized immediately and sold at public auction. This explains why the Portuguese government, convinced by the just arguments of the sugar growers, introduced as early as the second half of the seventeenth century a number of measures intended to prevent the ruin of growers stripped of needed manpower. The whole situation was a vicious circle that seems to have been hard to break, as the repetition of similar measures throughout the colonial period shows. Regulations alone could not do the job. The practice of seizing the slaves of debtors and selling them at auction continued in the nineteenth century, as we see from the following notice published in the *Jornal da Bahia* in 1854:

Notice—Dr. José Joaquim Simões, municipal judge of the third civil chamber of this city of Bahia and its territory . . .

Know that on 14 March inst., after session of this tribunal in its chambers on Direita do Palacio Street at ten o'clock in the morning, there will be sale by public auction of this tribunal, to whoever offers the most and makes the highest bid, of the following property:

Francisco, Nago, palanquin bearer and field hand, in good health, evaluated at 600,000 reis.

David, Nago, same description, in good health, evaluated at 600,000 reis.

Bruno, Nago, same description, evaluated at 600,000 reis.

Julio, Ussa (Hausa), field hand, with hernia, evaluated at 400,000 reis.

An ass with a serious flaw in its left hoof and undernourished, estimated at 200,000 reis.

As in all auctions, the price of the slave was set by the highest bidder. But we do not know whether imported slaves were always sold to the highest bidder: a public sale is not necessarily a sale to the highest bidder. But all signs suggest that whenever a seller had a particularly robust or skilled lot of slaves on his hands, or whenever demand exceeded supply, slave sales were true auctions.

Private sales were based on a prior understanding between buyer and seller, and the selling price was set in advance. We do not know when such a system was first established. Obviously it allowed for a certain flexibility in transactions. Private sales do not seem to have been practiced in Brazil until the slave trade was fairly well organized and the country enjoyed a relatively plentiful supply of labor. In my view the recourse to private sale was probably linked to urban development, which began in the late seventeenth century, for initially we find it being practiced almost exclusively in the cities, where large numbers of buyers required only a few slaves, either for domestic work or for jobs in construction and transportation. If a buyer acquired a skilled slave—a mason, carpenter, painter, cooper, carter, or fruit and vegetable seller—he might hire out that slave's services. The master would then live off the slave's earnings. This practice was widespread in large cities and in developed secondary and tertiary sectors of the economy. It gave urban life in Brazil a particular cast. In the nineteenth century, especially after slave trading became illegal, private sales tended to replace public sales. The massive transfer of slave labor out of the northern and northeastern sections of the country after 1850 seems to have been accomplished through private sales. This does not rule out the possibility that there were also auction sales in periods of high demand. That auctions did not disappear completely after 1850 is shown by newspaper advertisements such as the following: "B. Ariani will hold an auction on the 11th inst. at noon in Nova do Comercio Street to sell several slaves, several horses, and an ass" (*Jornal da Bahia*, 9 May 1855).

Ten years later, the newspaper *Diario da Bahia* published the following advertisement: "Sale at auction of furniture, slaves, fabrics. At the Estrella house, largo da Alfandega. Saturday 14 October [1865] at 11 o'clock, João Vigilio, tourinho, will sell at auction in his warehouse various items of furniture, china, glasses, fabrics, dry goods, watches, and a good slave, a light-skinned mulatto, age 21, excellent appearance, for valet or coachman."

Why were private sales held? A slave owner who found himself in financial difficulties might be obliged to sell off his capital in order to pay his debts or to obtain cash to meet his everyday needs. Others might wish to sell aging and relatively unproductive slaves, or else they might yield to a particularly attractive offer for a talented slave. After the middle of the nineteenth century, moreover, there was another reason for the increase in the number of private sales: the growth of banking institutions had made available new opportunities to those with capital to invest. This was especially true in Bahia, where a slump in the sugar-cane industry was compounded by the growth of a large body of free laborers, whose ranks were swelled by increasing numbers of freed slaves. Many of the traditional markets for slave labor therefore disappeared, both in the cities and in the surrounding countryside. The growth of banking made available other outlets for capital that would once have been used to buy slaves to hire out as laborers. The banks tempted Bahians with the prospect of less risky investments. By 1870 this led to a sharp decrease in the number of slaves owned by residents of the city and to a rise in the amount of capital invested in urban real estate, bank stocks, and government bonds.

This shift, hitherto little known, calls for a more detailed analysis. I shall discuss three decades: 1801–1810, 1851–1860, and 1871–1880. Sixty-five inventories of property of the deceased, chosen at random, have been used to obtain these results for Bahia.

1801–1810: Of the sixty-five decedents examined, only six possessed no slaves, or 10 percent of the total. Fourteen of the sixty-five were engaged in agriculture: four large planters (masters of sugar mills or *fazendeiros*) and ten small farmers of subsistence crops. In addition, there were eleven merchants, two soldiers, and two landowners. The other occupations represented in the sample included an alcohol distiller, a cobbler, a cooper, a goldsmith, a carpenter, a tailor, and a baker (one each). The remainder of the sample consisted of twenty-eight individuals with no apparent occupation: fifteen lived essentially on money earned by their slaves, for the rest of their property accounted for no more than 10–25 percent of the total estate. The fifty-nine slave owners together owned 540 slaves, or an average of 9.15 each. Four men and two women in the sample owned no slaves: their wealth ranged from 120,500 (a dilapidated house evaluated at 120,000 reis and furniture evaluated at 500 reis—a very precarious economic situation) to 5,895,303 reis, which was an average fortune for the time.

1851–1860: By this time we see a slight increase in the number of decedents who owned no slaves: there are ten in our sample. The fifty-five others owned 253 slaves, or an average of 4.6 each. Each slave owner owned from one to twenty-five slaves, and slaves accounted for at most 50 percent of the total estate. On the other hand, bank stock and government bonds begin to be fairly common. The occupations of the decedents are quite similar to those for the period 1801–1810: seven farmers, only one of them a large-scale planter, eleven merchants, three soldiers, two landowners, three curates, two barber-musicians, one lawyer, one cobbler, one cooper, and one boiler maker. Of the thirty-three persons for whom no occupation is indicated, thirteen lived by hiring out their slaves. Ten died without slaves, including five men and two women without occupation together with a merchant, a peasant woman, and a retired teacher. The smallest estate was that of a merchant who sold musical instruments and sheet music (663,155 reis) and the largest that of Rosa Maria do Amparo, a native of the city of Cachoeira in the Reconcavo, an unwed mother of five children (three boys and two girls), to whom she left 33,540,930 reis, all invested in bank stock.

1871–1880: a marked change has occurred. Forty-three percent of the deceased persons in the sample owned no slaves (28 out of 65). The average number of slaves per slaveowner was 3.29, compared with 9.15 and 4.6 for the previous periods. Of the thirty individuals for whom no occupation was indicated, only two lived on income earned by hiring out their slaves, and each of them owned only one slave worker, compared with 4–30 workers per owner in the period 1801–1810 and 2–21 workers per owner in the period 1851–1860. This dramatic change was certainly a consequence of economic changes linked to the abolition of the slave trade, which was a prelude to the abolition of slavery itself.

In the sample there are nine merchants, three teachers, two physicians, five small farmers, and six landowners, one large planter, one soldier, one alcohol distiller, one carpenter, one tailor, one baker, one fisherman, one artisan, one sugar refiner, and one public official. Of the twenty-eight individuals who owned no slaves, twelve men and five women were listed as having no occupation. About 55 percent of the estates consisted of property in real estate, 15 percent of liquid cash, and 30 percent of stocks and bonds. Six estates owed debts: three women (one itinerant fabric merchant, two without occupation) and three men (one fisherman, one teacher, one without occupation). The fisherman's assets consisted of a net, worth 50,000 reis, and a bed, worth 80,000 reis, and his debts amounted to 242,000 reis. As for the teacher, his only property was a piece of land evaluated at 250,000 reis, but he owed many small debts totaling 538,833 reis! The other teacher owned nothing at all, no real estate: the inventory proceedings were begun only to certify that the government owed him his salary for the month prior to his death. These were elementary school teachers, in Bahia a group recruited exclusively among the "colored," that is, emancipated slaves, so these figures give us some idea how such men were integrated into society. But for the moment our purpose is to understand what portion slaves represented of the wealth of a typical Bahian. In this final period, the smallest fortune was 312,000 (a man without occupation) and the largest, 31,273,317 reis, that of a food supplier.

Thus estates for all three periods were comparable in size, but the portion represented by slaves declined sharply. Both the number and the value of slaves owned decreased, owing, as we have seen, to economic changes that encouraged the immediate sale of idle slaves. In order to understand this late development, this veritable transformation of wealth in Bahia, we must first investigate the factors that influenced slave prices. It turns out to have mattered little whether slaves were sold publicly or privately. Price was of course of concern to both buyer and seller; it remains to be seen whether it also mattered to the blacks being sold.

DETERMINATION OF THE PRICE OF A SLAVE

The price of a slave was determined by many variables, some having nothing to do with the slave himself, others intimately connected with his person. The price depended on competition, distance from point of departure to point of sale, speculation, and economic conditions, as well as on the age, sex, health, and skills of the slave. Competition among the great powers played an important role in determining the price of slaves at the source. Slave traders in all periods attempted to be the first on the scene and sought to win the good graces of the native king or chieftain and to obtain permanent preferential status. This was true even for the Portuguese, who colonized a vast territory. Battles between European countries for control of these slave markets disrupted the flow of slaves and caused prices to rise. Countries also attempted to undercut the competition by offering their African suppliers more desirable merchandise at better prices. Tobacco, for example, played an important role from the seventeenth century on, and tobacco was a Brazilian product. Finally, the countries of Europe also competed for sales to end users of slaves. Here the assiento must have played a major role. Competition also led to smuggling, about which, unfortunately, we have very little information. We do know that after 1650 direct traffic begween Angola and Rio de la Plata became extremely important. This was an obvious triumph for the Portuguese, who managed to circumvent Spanish restrictions: slaves were exchanged for silver, and the profits were large enough that slaves who had already reached the coast of Brazil were rerouted to Rio de la Plata. Smuggled slaves also went to Spanish and English colonies, for the slave trader cared little where his profits came from. As early as the sixteenth century the English engaged in resgate in Portuguese territory and sometimes seized Portuguese slavers en route to Brazil. Another form of smuggling involved direct contacts between the Portuguese and the English, as in Bahia, where merchants did not hesitate to sell their first-quality tobacco to English merchants who traded it for slaves on the Mina Coast. The account books of Fort William in Ouidah record numerous transactions between Bahia and the Royal African Company. English ships entered Brazilian ports: for example, the *Broughton*, which was seized at Bahia in 1718.

The trade with the Mina Coast was doubly profitable for the Portuguese, because it enabled them to export contraband gold and then to reimport it without paying the duty known as the *quinto* to which Brazilian gold was subject. "Considering the hazards of the voyage and the immobilization of the gold for the considerable duration of the round trip to the Mina Coast and back, all to avoid the quinto of 20 percent to which gold employed 'at risk' in legal navigation was subject, it seems likely," says Pierre Verger, "that it could earn quadruple the amount advanced in exchange for slaves."

In the nineteenth century we find many ships flying foreign flags delivering slaves to Brazilian ports, but given the present state of the sources it is impossible to say whether they were financed by foreign merchants or by Brazilians attempting to circumvent the post–1830 ban on slave trade.

Another important factor in determining the price of a slave was the distance between the port of departure and the port of entry: shorter distances meant lower expenses and lower risks. In addition, a ship could make more round trips over shorter routes. In the mid-eighteenth century ships in the unregulated slave trade made an average of four round trips annually, compared with only 1.9 for the ships of the monopolies in the best of conditions. Thus it is easy to understand why some East African ports were abandoned in favor of West African ones. It is also clear why Mozambique was used as a source of slaves only in exceptional circumstances: during the Dutch occupation of Angola in the seventeenth century, for example, or during the nineteenth century when the ban on slave trade coincided with an increased demand for labor. The trip from Angola to Rio de Janeiro could be made in just over a month, whereas it took twice as long to sail from Mozambique, and the longer the voyage, the greater the cost in human life. The distance factor also played a role in the internal slave trade, and prices at the ports of entry were quite different from prices in the interior.

A third factor had to do with monopoly and speculation. In the sixteenth century, the price of slaves under the assiento system was different from the price in unregulated trade. The assiento granted a monopoly that required the use of intermediaries: it tended to raise prices, especially since payments were frequently deferred and carried high rates of interest. Direct private trade proved more advantageous to buyers, who formed partnerships to send ships to Africa in search of slaves.

After 1690, however, by which time the role of the assiento in supplying slaves for Brazilian sugar plantations was increasingly marginal, the emergence of a new class of merchants, independent of the sugar growers, resulted in the replacement of the assiento agents by a new group of intermediaries as greedy as their predecessors. By creating a true monopoly of supply, these merchants were able to charge usurious rates of interest on slaves sold on credit. It was these merchants who drew the greatest profits from the slave trade during the eighteenth and nineteenth centuries. Most of them were of Portuguese origin, and the firms established in the Brazilian ports were branches of parent firms in Lisbon or Porto. Following independence in 1822, these Portuguese merchants were replaced in part by a class of Brazilian and foreign merchants. But even then the supply of slaves remained a monopoly. Direct private trade worked to the advantage of slave buyers and users only during the late sixteenth century, when they were able to import slaves freely.

Monopoly means speculation: anyone holding a monopoly of supply can dictate his price to the market. But we must also take account of internal demand, which was affected by such disasters as famine and smallpox, which killed off many slaves. In 1616 and 1617, for example, smallpox decimated the slave population on the Bahian sugar plantations. The planters had to endure a terrible famine, and their situation became desperate. The war with Holland prevented them from replenishing their food and labor supplies. Yellow fever struck in 1686, again with disastrous consequences. Then, after a respite of a century and a half, a cholera epidemic in 1855 and 1856 killed some 30,000 slaves on the plantations of the Bahian Reconcavo alone. Famine was common in the northeast, where drought alternated with torrential rains. People often went hungry on the famous *massapé* lands, which contemporaries described as rich and opulent but which in reality soaked up too little water during rainy years and were quickly depleted (besides which they were less plentiful than planters of the time believed). On the cane plantations hunger was linked to the growing of products for export: high demand for such products meant less land for subsistence crops. Planters preferred to grow sugar or tobacco rather than manioc or legumes and started to supply what was needed for immediate consumption by importing food from long distances. In the late eighteenth century, for instance, Bahia received manioc flour from the port of Antonina, on the coast of Parana in remote southern Brazil.

The demand for slaves also depended on production. In periods of depression, when the price of sugar fell, slave purchases were reduced to guard against rapid or prolonged market fluctuations, especially since many planters bought slaves on credit, hence on onerous terms. By contrast, in times of prosperity, the demand for slave labor increased, which also increased the opportunity for speculation on the price of slaves. This was particularly true in the early eighteenth century, when the discovery of gold required that much additional manpower be found. The price of slaves rose rapidly until supply and demand were brought back into equilibrium. Later we shall see how prices dropped after 1730.

Thus demand stimulated supply. The profits of the slave trade were considerable. Even during the nineteenth century, when the trade was illegal, it was the basis of the fortune of such highly respected Bahian merchants as Antonio Pedroso de Albuquerque and José Pereira Marinho. Demand also stimulated an internal trade in slaves, which made possible the eighteenth- and nineteenth-century shifts in the slave population discussed earlier.

The final factor in determining the price of a slave was the method of payment. Sale on credit of course required repayment of the principal with interest. We lack the account records that would enable us to know the exact terms of such transactions. Our sources are mainly qualitative in nature, recounting the complaints of the sugar producers to the government in Portugal: planters complained of merchants who took advantage of the situation, because debts were pegged to sales of future production, which opened the door to all sorts of extortion. But circumstances also played a part: throughout the colonial period (1500–1822) Brazil had no official banking institutions. For all this time, and even during the first few years of independence, merchants quite naturally made themselves virtually indispensable as purveyors of capital needed by the productive classes. Now, to advance capital was to immobilize it, at great risk to the lender, since production was always subject to the unpredictable weather (drought, excessive rain) and to price fluctuations on the European market. The system of mercantilist capitalism tended in any case to deprive the productive classes of capital, because profits were exported to the home country: hard currency and productive wealth were transferred to Portugal, thus reducing the circulation of currency in Brazil. "Money hunger" in turn encouraged sales on credit. Thus circumstances conspired to the advantage of the merchants, who had to turn a profit in order to live. But at what level was the system profitable? The question remains to be answered, and with it the notion of "abuse" needs to be analyzed. Was what seemed abusive to the producer also abusive in the eyes of the merchant?

Abuse would have existed if the merchant class had followed a policy deliberately aimed at the destruction of the producer class, and hence of production itself, which would have been an absurd thing for the merchants to have done. Why would they have wished to sign the producers' death warrant, thereby destroying their own source of income? Profits that seemed abusive to producers because they reduced their own margins were doubtless seen by merchants as a just reward for the risks they ran. During the period 1690–1730, when the Bahian commercial class set itself up to supply the mining centers with slaves and merchandise, it did not forget its common interests with the sugar producers, even if cane growing and sugar refining declined to a position of secondary importance. Sugar continued to be exported, and the merchants continued to finance its production.

The same thing occurred in the middle of the nineteenth century, when Bahian merchants did everything they could to prop up the hopelessly crippled sugar industry, which the banks for the most part refused to finance. Thus the purchase of slaves on credit by sugar and coffee planters and gold-mine operators must be seen in the context of a sometimes shaky economy; indeed, only large-scale operators could buy on credit, for large amounts of property were required as collateral. In the cities, only those who owned land or other real estate could purchase slaves on credit.

Slaves were generally sold for cash to individuals who wanted them for domestic use or to hire out as laborers. This type of sale was associated mainly with the cities. The buyer purchased the slave either for his own use or on behalf of a third party. Sellers sold slaves by ones, twos, and threes, occasionally in larger lots. Cash sales increased with the growth of the cities and were most prevalent in the nineteenth century, after the slave trade was made illegal. Slaves sold at auction for execution of debts or after the death of their owner and the division of his property were also sold for cash.

One obvious question is whether there was a difference in price between slaves sold for cash and slaves sold for credit. Once again, quantitative data are lacking, but it seems likely that buying on credit cost the buyer more. This hypothesis warrants further research, for it touches on various hard-to-gauge factors that influenced the price of a slave: if the price of the slave dropped on the internal market but at the same time the price of export products rose, for example, the losses sustained by the two types of buyers offset each other. Even in this case, we must assume that the credit purchaser was free to sell his product to a vendor other than the one who sold him his slaves, an assumption that on the whole appears to be unwarranted.

Thus what one might call "external" variables were numerous and not easy to classify, though they surely had an important influence on the price of slaves. The "internal" variables, those attaching to the slave's own person, were equally numerous and just as difficult to comprehend. Among them were sex, age, state of health, and occupational skill.

It has been maintained that in the early seventeenth century sex played only a very limited role in establishing the price of a slave. Indeed, study of a few cases does show little difference in price between males and females: a "bearded" Negro between 25 and 35 years of age, 18,000 reis; a molecona, 17–19,000 reis; a molecão, 18,000 reis; and a moleque (male or female), 12–16,000 reis. But the economic conjuncture was rather special, since this was a period of very high demand and scarce supply, so that slaves of both sexes sold at high prices. In the agricultural Brazil of the seventeenth century, the work could be done equally well by men or women, since African women were used to working the soil. As soon as the slave supply stabilized, however, we find a very marked preference for male captives, as is shown by the composition of cargoes arriving from Africa in which the ratio of men to women was two to one. This proportion remained more or less constant over three centuries of slavery, which explains why Brazilian slaves reproduced less than North American slaves. The preference for male slaves actually increased with the discovery of gold. Although the work of extracting gold from the alluvial deposits in which it was mainly found did not require great strength, it was slow and difficult and required standing in water for long periods of time. It was assigned mainly to men. We lack data that would show the difference in price between men and women in the eighteenth century, but the average prices listed in manumission papers granted to adult slaves in Salvador between 1684 and 1746 show significant differences: men had to pay more for their papers than women, because the price of a male slave was higher than that of a female slave. These price statistics do not reflect the actual market situation, however, which was not influenced by such intangibles as human feelings and intimacy between slave and owner. It seems reasonable to assume that female slaves were on more affectionate terms with their masters and could purchase their freedom on better terms than their male comrades. In any case, in the slave system women were always considered less productive, more fragile physically, and quicker to age than men.

Nineteenth-century evidence confirms the findings shown in Figure 1. When wills were opened, for example, the estate was inventoried and any slaves to be sold were appraised. From auction statistics we have been able to glean the following information: for the years 1805–1806 and 1810–1811, prices ranged from 50,000 to 200,000 reis, but the average price of a male slave was 150,000 reis, compared to 100,000 reis for a female, or a difference of 50 percent. Certain very high prices are also significant: hearly all the slaves who sold for more than 150,000 reis were males. In 1805–1806, for example, of 149 men sold, 30 went for 200,000 *reis* apiece, or 20.1 percent of all males sold. Of 76 women sold, only 3 went for the maximum price of 200,000 reis, or 3.09 percent of all women sold. Similarly, in 1810–1811, of 80 men sold, 8 went for 200,000 reis, compared with only 2 women out of 42. In 1820 the average price of an adult female slave was 150,000 reis, that of a male adult, 200,000 reis. Thirty years later it was 390,000 for a female and 600,000 for a male.

All other things being equal, then, black men sold for more than black women, and sex was an important factor in determining the price of a slave.

Age was also important, perhaps even more important than sex, but

FIGURE 1

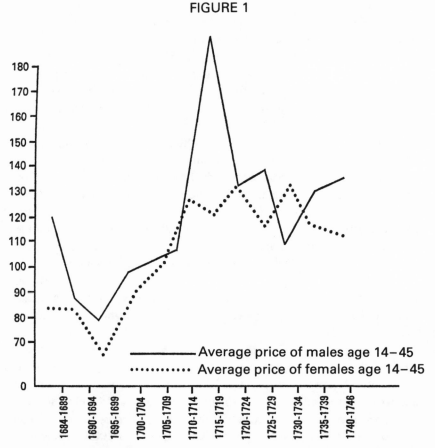

Source: Stuart B. Schwartz, "The Manumission of Slaves in Colonial Brazil: Bahia, 1684–1745," *Hispanic American Historical Review*, 54 (1974), 635.

again we have little information to go on. The documents speak of an old man (*velho*), an old woman (*velha*), a male or female child (*molequinho, molequinha*), adolescent (molecão, molecona), and of an adult Negro or Negress (*negro, negra*). The following list roughly describes the use of these terms:

child, age 0–7: molequinho, molequinha
child, age 8–14: moleque, moleca
adolescent, age 15–18: molecão, molecona
adult, age 19–35: negro, negra
adult over 35: velho, velha

Caution is in order, however, because confusion about the use of these terms was rampant during the slave era. I have come across several instances of the use of the term molecão (adolescent) accompanied by figures giving the age as nine or ten, and of the term moleque (young child) with the age given as eighteen or even twenty! What is more, many other terms are used in the documents, such as *rapaz* (young man), and *moço* or *moça*, rather vague terms for man and woman, respectively. This vagueness is quite understandable, moreover, given the difficulty of determining the precise age of an imported captive. Our informants were sometimes fully aware that they could not determine a slave's age with any precision: we find the mention of one "François, creole, age 40 more or less," for example, and this was a slave born in Brazil, whose age one might think would have been easier to ascertain thah that of an African slave. Or again: "Bernardina, mulatto child, who could be around three years of age, more or less." Only after abolition of the slave trade did age indications become more common and more precise, particularly for adults.

It remains true, however, that such age information as we have, however imprecise, enables us to determine the importance of age (real or imagined) as a factor in determining the price of a slave. The very young and the very old went for the lowest prices. During the years 1805–1806 and 1810–1811 their price ranged from 10,000 to 50,000 reis, or one-third to one-tenth of the price of a slave in the prime of life. Oddly enough, gender-related differences vanish, which suggests that the price of a female slave varied less over her lifetime than did that of a male slave. Estate inventories usually contained a fair number of older slaves who continued to be worth a good deal because they were in good health and were skilled in a profitable trade: women skilled as pastry cooks, lace makers, or embroideresses, and men trained as carpenters, locksmiths, or cobblers were valued highly until they had reached an advanced age. Yet in general the slave at the end of his active life was again worth only as much as he had been worth as a small child!

Obviously, sex and age did not constitute a complete physical description of human merchandise. The more robust a slave was, and the fewer physical "defects" he had, the more he was worth. As for a slave who was sick or decrepit, it was best to wait until the moment was ripe before putting him up for sale. Frequently the price had to be lowered to find a buyer: "José Joaquim da Silva, in his capacity as guardian of the orphans of the late Dona Florencia Joaquina da Conceição, declares the following: in the estate inventory in the possession of the undersigned is a female slave by the name of Rita, who, though appraised at 100,000 reis because she is old, found no buyer at this price when marketed along with other slaves; and also another female slave by the name of Rosa, appraised at 60,000 reis,,who was too small and too useless to sell for such a price, it being so high; and because of the expenses necessary to their upkeep, and their life being prejudicial to our wards, a situation which could be corrected by their sale, we hereby lower their assessments in the hope of attracting a prospective buyer." In our estate inventories for the years 1805–1806 and 1810–1811 (using the same statistical base as before by way of example), about 15 percent of the "skilled slaves" were sick or crippled. Their selling price ranged from 10,000 to 50,000 reis, the same as for children and old people. The price was so low because owners wished to get rid of relatively unproductive workers who only added to the cost of maintaining the slave labor force.

Finally, the fourth factor in determining the price of a slave had to do with the type of work of which the slave was judged capable. Does it make sense in speaking of a slave to talk about a trade or occupational skill? To be sure, of the slaves born in Brazil, some were actually put out to apprenticeship. One will (printed as an appendix to this volume) recounts the surely quite commonplace story of slaves whom their masters had trained for several years as barbers and musicians. Still, in a slave labor economy there is no rigid division of labor. In my study of emancipation, sale, and estate records I have found many slaves like the barber-musicians, capable of working in more than one trade: a man might be a painter and a mason or a field hand and a carter—ready to fill in wherever he was needed. Rather than speak of a slave's trade, therefore, I shall speak more abstractly of his "skill" or "qualification," words that better capture, I think, the realities of the time.

In our sample of estate inventories for 1805–1806 and 1810–1811, the proportion of skilled slaves (75.7 percent and 66.5 percent respectively) was higher than that of unskilled. The highest prices were paid for slaves in good health (here age counted for little) capable of working as tailors, masons, coopers, locksmiths, bakers, carpenters, and boiler makers (for men) and as seamstresses, lace makers, embroideresses, laundresses, and pastry makers (for women).

What about a slave's origins and color? Did these have an influence on the price of sale? Apparently not, even though some masters seem to have preferred slaves from certain tribes for certain kinds of jobs. Minas were reputed to make good servants, and Bantus were supposed to be good farm hands, as well as being gentle and docile. Color played no role in determining a slave's value.

THE EVOLUTION OF SLAVE PRICES: FROM SIXTEENTH TO NINETEENTH CENTURY

So many factors influenced the price of slaves that it is hardly surprising that over the course of three centuries of slavery slave prices varied considerably. Let us turn now to the long-term trend.

What happened will be clearer if we compare the evolution of slave prices with the evolution of sugar prices and, from 1810 on, of coffee prices as well. Average prices are given in the tables, with no distinction between males and females (because statistics are lacking). We are concerned here with the price of adult slaves in good health. Up to 1750 the price figures for sugar are an average of prices for white sugar and *moscouade* sugar. After that date, the figures are for white sugar only. Four broad periods have been selected: 1572 to 1650–1652; 1650–1652 to 1703; 1703 to 1750; and 1750 to 1888. The latter period is itself broken down into three shorter periods: 1750 to 1817–1821; 1817–1821 to 1850, and 1850 to 1888.

During the period 1572 to 1650–1652 Brazil increased its sugar production and exports to a rapidly expanding European market. Sugar was then a monopoly of the Portuguese. When Governor Mem de Sa, owner of the large sugar mill at Sergipe do Conde in the Bahian Reconcavo, died in 1572, the inventory of his estate showed African slaves valued at between 13,000 and 40,000 reis, with an average value of 21,800 reis. In the same period, an inventory of the Sant'Ana sugar mill, located in southern Bahia, showed slaves valued at between 13,000 and 25,000 reis, with an average value of 17,300 reis. It seems reasonable, therefore, to assume that the average price of a slave in this period was approximately 20,000 reis. By 1651–1652 this price had doubled. The increase reflected both the increased price of sugar and the increased demand for slave labor. During the late sixteenth century the number of sugar mills in Brazil increased, at a time when Dutch attacks on Brazil and on African slave ports were causing serious problems in maintaining a supply of slaves.

Between 1572–1574 and 1622–1623 the price of slaves rose more rapidly than the price of sugar (45 percent as against 11.6 percent). The low sugar prices in the period 1622–1627 might also be due to a short-lived depression. Even when the years 1622–1623, when sugar prices were

TABLE 3.
Slave and Sugar Prices
(1572–1652)

	Slaves				Sugar		
		Index				Average Indices	
Year	Annual average	1572–1574 = 100	1622–1623 = 100	Year	Average white sugar/ moscouade	1573 = 100	1622–1623 = 100
1572/1574	20	100.0		1572	(443)		
				1573	405	100.0	
				1574	405	100.0	
				1576(?)	570	140.7	
				1578(?)	765	188.9	
				1579	634	156.5	
1622–1623	29	145.0	100.0	1622–1623	452	111.6	100.0
1623–1624	35	175.0	120.7	1623–1624	421	104.0	93.1
1625–1626	31	155.0	106.0	1625–1626	516	127.4	114.2
1625–1629	30	150.0	103.4	1626–1627	477	117.8	105.5
1629–1630	30	150.0	103.4	1627–1628	688	169.9	152.2
1632–1633	30	150.0	103.4	1628–1629	684	168.9	151.3
1633–1634	34	170.0	117.2	1629–1630	544	134.3	120.4
1634–1635	42	210.0	144.8	1630–1631	460	113.6	101.8
1635–1636	39	195.0	134.5	1631–1632	505	124.7	111.7
1636–1637	50	250.0	172.4	1632–1633	583	144.0	129.0
1643–1644	41	205.0	141.4	1633–1634	686	169.4	151.8
1644–1645	41	205.0	141.4	1634–1635	658	162.5	145.6

1645–1646	42	210.0	144.8	1635–1636	838	206.9	185.4
1646–1647	52	260.0	179.3	1636–1637	1,082	267.2	239.4
1650–1651	49	245.0	169.0	1637–1638	1,160	286.4	256.6
1651–1652	55	275.0	189.7	1643–1644	855	211.1	189.2
				1644–1645	824	203.5	182.3
				1645–1646	843	208.1	186.5
				1646–1647	938	231.6	207.5
				1650–1651	828	204.4	183.2
				1651–1652	962	237.5	212.8

Source: Mircea Buescu, *300 anos de inflação* (Rio de Janeiro: APEC, 1973), pp. 42–44.
Note: Prices are given in Thousands of reis per slave and reis per arrobe of sugar—1 arrobe = 14.745 kilograms.

depressed, are taken as a base, the slave price index is sometimes higher than the sugar price index. Bear in mind, however, that the data are incomplete, riddled with gaps, and provide no information at all about the price of non-African labor. It appears that sugar planters in this period used much more native Indian labor than had been thought until recently. We know virtually nothing about the value ascribed to Indian labor, comparable in many respects to black slave labor.

For the period that runs from the restoration of the Portuguese monarchy in 1640 to the beginning of the eighteenth century, during which the search for gold became Brazil's leading economic activity, we have almost no statistics on the price of sugar or slaves. The years 1652–1703 were broadly speaking years of difficulty for sugar, especially after 1670. The value of the real declined steadily until 1668, when it reached a level that would be maintained for nearly a century with the aid of Brazilian gold. We have enough information to establish Tables 3 and 4.

Again, slave prices rose more rapidly than sugar prices, which makes sense given the demand for slaves in the mining regions and the depression in the sugar market. To get a better idea of the change in slave prices, let us try to compare prices in gold-mining and sugar-growing regions. Though the trends are parallel, there are considerable differences in the price levels. It is difficult to give a very sophisticated analysis with such sporadic data as we have, but Table 5 gives some idea of the orders of magnitude involved.

The rush to the mines thus drove up prices, especially during the first two decades after the discovery of gold. After that the pace of inflation became less hectic. Prior to the discovery of gold, the mining regions were empty. Slave prices in 1703 were nine times higher than in 1690, while the price of sugar increased enormously. Inflation also affected other commodities: a chicken that sold for 80 reis in 1690 cost 5,250 reis in 1730, and the price of an *arrobe* of beef went from 160 reis to 48,000 reis over the same period. Thus the increase in slave prices was relatively modest. Whereas in the previous period slave prices had climbed much more rapidly than sugar prices, now slave price increases trailed behind price increases for other commodities. The reason was probably that demand for slaves was higher then in the sugar-growing regions, where the supply was less elastic. In the mining regions, the slave market was not so tight as the market for foodstuffs. Because slave prices were so high in the mining regions, all available slave labor tended to flow there from the agricultural regions, thus maintaining some semblance of equilibrium between supply and demand, whereas foodstuffs were hard to transport and it took some

TABLE 4.
Slave and Sugar Prices

	1650–1652	1703	Index (base (1650–52 = 100)
Slave (unit)	52,000	100,000	192.3
Sugar (arrobe)	895	1,300	145.5

Source: Mircea Buescu, *300 anos de inflação*, p. 74.
Note: Prices are from 1690 to 1936 (in reis).

TABLE 5.
Slave and Sugar Prices in The Mining Region

	1690	1703	Index base 1690 = 100	1730	Index base 1690 = 100
Slave (unit)	50,000	450,000	900	417,000	834
Sugar (arrobe)	1,280	48,000	375	—	—

Source: Mircea Buescu, *300 anos de inflação*, p. 81.
Note: Prices are from 1690 to 1736 (in reis).

time to establish a local infrastructure for food production. Thus slaves were relatively less expensive than food in the mining areas.

How did slave and sugar prices evolve in the sugar-growing regions? Table 6 gives figures for Bahia:

The picture that emerges from these figures is fairly clear: a sharp rise in the price of slaves did great damage to the sugar economy. At the peak of the famous gold cycle, the price of a slave had risen much more rapidly than the price of sugar; expressed in terms of change in the purchasing power of a unit weight of sugar, the figures are − 52.9 percent for 1705, − 58.8 percent for 1740, and − 19.1 percent for 1750. The figures explain

TABLE 6.
Slave and Sugar Prices at Bahia (in reis)

Year	Slaves		Sugar (arrobe)	
	Price	Index	Price	Index
1690	50,000	100	850	100
1705	200,000	400	1,600	182.2
1740	200,000	400	1,400	164.7
1750	120,000	240	1,650	194.1

Source: Mircea Buescu, *300 anos de inflação*, p. 86.

why the sugar industry suffered decapitalization and why planters sought to get rid of laborers who had become a burden to support. They also explain why the resumption of activity in the sugar industry occurred only when slave prices fell (1750) and sugar prices began to rise toward levels not seen since the beginning of the century. With this background, what can we say about the evolution of slave prices after the great inflation of the gold cycle 1690–1750)? Once again we lack statistical data for Brazil as a whole. We do, however, have some figures for the province of Bahia: statistics on sugar prices to consumers and on the price of slaves. These are the figures on which the following analysis is based. I shall divide the period 1750–1888 into three shorter periods:

1750 to 1817–1821: This second era of prosperity for sugar growers had a peak between 1787 and 1817–1821. This was also the time when the slave trade was most unregulated. No insurmountable difficulties were encountered in bringing slaves to market, and demand was growing at a healthy pace. Domestic inflation seemed to be under control.

1821 to 1850: This next period lasted almost thirty years, until the slave trade was abolished in 1850. This was a period of depression in the sugar economy. From 1830 on trading in slaves was illegal, though slaves continued, despite all the prohibitions, to arrive from Africa at an increasing pace as 1850 approached. These slaves were for the msot part swallowed up in a vast internal slave trade; demand came mainly from south-central Brazil, where coffee had supplanted sugar. Price disequilibria in this period were not due to either inflation or deflation.

1850–1888: This period saw runaway inflation from 1850 to 1869 (when the war with Paraguay ended), followed by decreasing inflation up to 1880, after which prices stabilized during the final years of the empire. During this period, sugar and slave prices moved in a fairly coherent manner: slave prices peaked in the 1860s and 1870s, then dropped again in the 1880s. The fall in prices was due to the replacement of slave labor by free labor of European origin, as immigrants came to work in the coffee fields from the 1860s on. The substitution of free labor for slave labor took some time, however, so that its effects were not really felt until around 1890. At the same time the sugar industry fell into a depression—this time a terminal depression, at least for the state of Bahia—which resulted in a shift of manpower from sugar to coffee, a movement that reached its peak between 1860 and 1874. The price of sugar declined as soon as the inflationary period (1850–1870) was over. Inflation or not, the Brazilian real declined steadily in relation to the pound sterling throughout the

TABLE 7.
Slave, Sugar, and Coffee Prices at Bahia (in reis)

	Slaves		Sugar		Coffee	
Year	Price (average)	Index	Price (arrobe)	Index	Price (arrobe)	Index
1750	—	—	1,295	103.6	—	—
1760	—	—	1,515	121.6	—	—
1770	—	—	1,290	103.6	—	—
1780	75,000	42.8	1,890	151.8	—	—
1790	125,000	71.4	2,190	175.9	—	—
1800	150,000	85.7	2,595	208.4	—	—
1810	175,000	100.0	1,245	100.0	1,245	100.0
1820	200,000	114.2	1,815	145.8	3,540	208.4
1830	250,000	142.8	2,160	173.4	3,465	207.8
1840	450,000	257.1	—	—	—	—
1850	500,000	285.7	2,685	215.6	3,975	319.2
1860	650,000	357.1	6,675	536.1	6,735	341.4
1870	650,000	357.1	6,510	522.9	6,030	484.3
1880	450,000	257.1	5,835	468.6	7,220	579.9
1888	400,000	228.5	4,195	336.9	9,600	771.0

Source: (1) for slave prices, data from estate inventories, AEB, judicial section, 1740–1890; (2) for sugar and coffee prices, data from accounts of the hospital of the Santa Casa de Misericordia, Bahia, 1750–1890.

nineteenth century. Finally, coffee prices rose steadily from 1810 to 1888, except for the one year of 1870 (this is the period for which continuous statistics are available).

This long period saw a sharp increase in the price of primary export products (sugar and coffee) relative to the price of slave labor, creating especially favorable conditions for the preservation of the slave labor system in Brazil. The sugar industry, though caught in crisis, experienced a marked rise in prices, which explains in part why cane growers in the northeast continued to battle to maintain production until 1880, only to renounce all claims and demands for compensation as abolition became imminent (1885). On the one hand, the crisis in sugar hit cane growers hard, forcing them to sell their laborers to coffee plantations in the south; on the other hand, those cane growers who did survive became increasingly powerful and dominated the industry. In the 1880s they began to impose or propose new solutions to the problems of the sugar industry, using more rational and profitable methods based on the concentration of fields and the use of modern sugar-processing plants to replace old mills dating back to the colonial era. The transition from the family-owned

TABLE 8.

Minimum and Maximum Prices of Slave in Bahia (in reis)

Years	Minimum price		Maximum price		Average	
	Women	Men	Women	Men	Women	Men
1820	10,000	15,000	550,000	700,000	270,000	347,500
1830	30,000	20,000	500,000	600,000	235,000	290,000
1840	20,000	10,000	880,000	1,200,000	430,000	595,000
1850	33,000	30,000	900,000	1,100,000	438,500	585,000
1860	40,000	50,000	2,000,000	2,500,000	980,000	1,225,000
1870	50,000	40,000	2,000,000	2,500,000	975,000	1,230,000
1880	50,000	100,000	1,100,000	1,800,000	545,000	850,000
1888	50,000	200,000	600,000	900,000	275,000	350,000

Source: Katia M. de Queirós Mattoso, *A carta de alforria como fonte complementar*, in *Moderna História Econômica* (Rio de Janeiro: APEC, 1976), pp. 149–163.

sugar mill to the plant owned by a joint-stock company occurred just as the abolition of slavery was being debated. Thus abolition became an issue when a slave-based system of production no longer made sense; slavery became a relic of the past and an impediment to progress, one that had to be eradicated as quickly as possible. Thus the reorganization of the sugar industry, coupled with the arrival of European immigrants at the coffee plantations, led ineluctably to a decline in the price of slave labor that foreshadowed the impending end of the slave system. The trend is clearly visible in the spectacular drop of slave prices after 1880 (see Table 8). The price statistics given in the tables should be regarded only as indicators of orders of magnitude and not as actual measures. This is particularly true of slave prices: average price figures obscure variations due to sex, age, and state of health.

A comparison of Tables 7 and 8 clearly shows the progression of prices, and in particular the whiplash administered to inflation by the definitive abolition of the slave trade. In the period 1870–1888, however, the minimum price of a female slave stood steady at 50,000 reis, whereas that of a male slave quadrupled during the same period.

Such an unadorned statistical finding leaves us hungry to know more. Up to now I have attempted to view the slave trade in historical and economic context. We have seen captives arrive by the shipload, generally in the dark about what was happening to them and reduced to silence by the diversity of their languages and customs. They were sold as merchandise, transported, warehoused, treated, displayed, appraised, and set to work. Whether controlled by monopolistic trading companies or private shippers and their agents, the slave trade, domestic and trans-Atlantic, was always linked to the development of Brazil. It was made possible by the desire for wealth, the greed, of certain Africans. Heavily populated black Africa drained itself to populate the Americas. The relatively stable institutions and cultures of black Africa broke down in the face of the insatiable demand for slaves. And so millions and millions of African captives became Brazilian slaves over a period of three long centuries. In the slaves' collective memory the Africa of their ancestors survived, but the slaves themselves had become "different."

Our next task is to describe the lives of slaves who seem anonymous only until one takes a closer look. To be a slave in Brazil was an unenviable fate to be sure, but a fate quite different from that which awaited the African captive delivered to a Virginia cotton planter or to a cane grower in the Antilles. What were the slaves' hopes? What games did they play? How did they labor and toil? What were their dreams? The purpose of the next section is to rescue these men and women from the anonymity in which they have been kept for so long by the combined effects of the old slave system and the new statistics.

PART 2

Being a Slave

F O U R

The African Adapts to Brazil and the Brazilians

SLAVERY: AN OLD CONDITION IN A NEW WORLD

Because certain forms of slavery had existed for centuries on the continent of Africa, Brazilian historians used to say that blacks imported from across the Atlantic were docile and ready to accept their new status as slaves. This assertion is based on the unwarranted assumption that what was true of a limited area of Africa was typical of the continent as a whole. In fact, slave hunting became widespread in Africa only as a result of the slave trade—as that trade grew, and for its benefit. It was the business of capturing slaves for sale to European colonies that reinforced the power of those African kingdoms whose warriors supplied the slavers. In any case, there were major differences between slavery as practiced in Africa and slavery as practiced in Brazil. In Africa slaves were not necessarily assigned to productive tasks. Some were personal slaves of powerful lords, in some cases of their own tribe, in all cases of their own color. Africa's slaves never left their native region and so remained in familiar surroundings physically and psychologically. Living in a known culture, they easily adapted to an almost familiar way of life. The slave system was a venerable part of a stratified society, and slaves were protected by a range of well-defined traditional institutions. Subequatorial Africa—the region that furnished most of Brazil's slaves—was the part of the continent in which true slavery—slavery for productive ends—was least practiced prior to the advent of the colonial slave trade. In the warrior states that hunted and sold slaves to the slavers exploitation of slaves as practiced on the other side of the Atlantic was unknown. In Brazil slaves were used first to produce export crops and to extract precious metals and stones; in urban centers they worked as artisans and provided social services. Thus relations of exploitation in Brazil were closer to certain forms of slavery in the ancient world than to the patriarchal slavery of Africa. What is more, this resurgence of an ancient mode of production occurred in the heart of an expanding capitalist economy, in which the coexistence of new and old forms of slavery created a novel system. Indeed, it is doubtful whether it is correct to speak, in an undifferentiated way, of "relations of production and exploitation" in connection with such social services as transport of freight, navigation, and domestic chores. Was the slave who hired himself out on the labor market both exploited and exploiter? Was the slave who himself owned slaves at once slave and master? Was there more than one kind of slave? How can we characterize social relations between different groups of slaves, and between slaves and other social classes? We cannot begin to answer these questions until we know more about the endless variety of material and emotional circumstances in which Brazilian slaves found themselves over the course of the three centuries during which slavery was practiced in Brazil. It is pointless to try to impose an a priori model. A much better approach is to look first at the variety of situations in which Brazilian slaves lived.

To speak of "material and emotional circumstances" is already to take a step in the right direction and to view the slave as a member of a larger society. How was the transition made from captive to slave? To answer this question we must take up the story of our captive where we left off: after his sale to his new master but before he has begun to work in the job from which his new identity will derive.

FROM THE CARGO OF CAPTIVES TO THE SLAVE "HEAD": DID THE SLAVE REGAIN HIS IDENTITY?

For endless hours the African captive waited in anguish for the slave ship that would carry him to Brazil. We do not know how much time elapsed between his capture and his arrival in America, since the documents record only the time of crossing. Nor do we know how much time elapsed between his arrival and eventual sale. During this distressing time of captivity, slaves must have formed friendships, however hesitantly, with their companions in misfortune. If, by chance, a comrade from the slave depot or the crossing happened to turn up working in the same mine or town or on the same plantation, firm bonds of friendship were likely to develop. Such friendships, called *malembo*, were the beginning of socialization. They created real solidarity among captives, who felt a powerful obligation to help one another. In 1836, for example, a freed slave started an organization whose purpose was to repatriate some two hundred other freed Bahian slaves. He chartered a British ship for five million reis (the equivalent, at the time, of 875 pounds sterling) to carry them back to the port from which they had sailed: Onim, present-day Lagos. This man had been part of a shipment of slaves brought to Bahia in 1821 by the ship *Emilia*: "Having acquired a certain reputation among his fellow emancipees, he used it to induce them to return to their native land. To finance the operation he sold various slaves from his own personal property and granted freedom to six others who were to accompany him." Of the two hundred who sailed for Africa, sixty had belonged to the *Emilia's* cargo. Then there was the celebrated African king known to the Brazilians as Chico-Rei. Captured along with several members of his family and community and sold in Minas Gerais, he managed to gain his freedom and, one by one, bought the liberty of every member of his tribe.

Striking as these examples are, similar stories are not rare. Slaves who enjoyed such bonds of friendship with their fellows were better off than the majority of captives, who were sold singly and delivered alone to their buyers. Often they found themselves isolated, since most masters mixed slaves from different tribes for reasons of security. Initially the black African was a "captive" wrested from his native society, and he remained a captive until he became a member of slave society. The transition was more difficult for those who had been taken by surprise and suddenly lost all the family, tribal, and communal ties that had given them a place in society. Desocialization led inevitably to loss of personhood. The slave became a thing, an object, an item of cargo. He entered a state that nullified not only his possessions but his being: whatever he may have been in his own society, now he was a captive whose fate lay in the hands of others. The buyer wanted him to be malleable, economically and socially, so that he could be assigned work that would bind him to his master. Accordingly, the slave was denied any legal or civic status. It was his function, his job, that determined his situation. The conditions of slavery were as varied as the jobs that slaves performed, but in all cases the slave remained entirely subject to the whims of his master. Thus slavery is not fully characterized by the relations of production. To speak only of relations of production is to neglect an understanding of the situation of individuals who did not necessarily participate in any definite mode of production, who were assigned jobs and functions on which the very existence of the ruling class depended—the usual relationship between exploiters and exploited was stood on its head. Nevertheless, the relation of the slave to society as a whole was always defined, implicitly or explicitly, in terms of his lord and master. The master set the norms and laid down the rules that governed this relationship. That said, does it make any sense to ask whether the slave could, under such conditions, regain his personhood? The question is surely complex, and by breaking it down into simpler questions perhaps we can formulate an answer.

First, we may look at the laws that governed social relations in slave societies: The slave was legally "inferior" to his master; he was private property, a "thing" with no legal status; and he was not in control of his fate. Looking at the question in this way, it is difficult to see how the slave could have acquired legal personhood, even if he had a place in society and in social relations of domination.

But from a psychological standpoint the black man's very survival unquestionably depended on his "repersonalization," on a certain acceptance of his position in social life. The question now takes on an entirely new meaning and assumes a fundamental importance. To maintain that human beings could have survived without adapting in some degree to their situation is of course absurd. Now, adaptation surely depended on the slave's relationship to his new environment, and the qualities of the master, his family members, and his lieutenants were surely just as important as the qualities of the individual slave and of the group of slaves among whom he lived. Ultimately, the slave's new social personality would be created by his insertion, along with other black men whose minds were still formed by African models, into a society shaped by a white model. This difficult process of social integration created constant tensions. Such was the lot of the slave forced to adapt to the slave system; he was forced to work hard, to humble himself, to obey and show loyalty to infallible masters. Humility, obedience, loyalty: these were the cornerstones of the slave's new life. For slaves were merchandise of a very special kind, and their buyers and owners always discovered in the end that slaves were also human beings, with whom it was possible to enter into close relationships, provided of course that the blacks showed themselves to be loyal, obedient, and humble. The slave's social being, his acceptance by free men in a society based on slave labor, depended almost entirely on whether or not he proved to be loyal, obedient and humble. These three essential qualities were the key to the personality of the "good slave": the slave who possessed them could acquire the competence, the know-how that brought power sufficient to regain some sense of identity. With the power that came with skill the slave could feel less fearful; some of the wounds born of capture and loss of homeland could heal; and the slave could then acquire a new language, a new home, a new and unique identity born of a tacit but solid social contract.

The means used to train slaves to show apparent loyalty, obedience, and humility could be either violent or gentle. Masters generally preferred persuasion to coercion. Sugar planters in the northeast dropped violence and threats in favor of patriarchal and paternalistic forms of manipulation. They sought to make the slave a servant, a member of the extended family, to involve him in a modus vivendi that saved owners the expense of surveillance and diminished the risk of attacks on his person or property. The slave, for his part, acquired a certain social identity. He was assigned specific social roles and even gained some social influence, some importance in the eyes of free men, thanks to his master's backing and protection. Some slaves became overseers, stewards, or group leaders and thus seemed to circumvent authority. But this new social identity was really the result of identification with the master's family. In fact, the master struck a bargain with the slave: "Give me your loyalty and I shall give you protection and my family's identity." Slaves went from "living with" their masters to identification, at least in part, with the master class, which in turn tried to accommodate them. The result was a very unusual situation, of a sort likely to confound social analysts, many of whom have drawn the conclusion that this type of relationship represented a perfect adaptation of the slave to his new environment. In spite of these intimacies, however, the world of the masters and that of the slaves remained culturally and socially distinct and antagonistic: confrontation between them was inevitable. The apparent mildness of relations between masters and slaves and the seeming adaptation of an obedient and humble slave work force were in fact effective and subtle manifestations of black resistance to a society whose goal was to strip blacks of their moral and cultural heritage. We shall see how the slaves were able to make use of the social constraints imposed on them by their masters; ultimately they were able to restore some equilibrium to the system, making it possible for them to live amicably and in some ways to cooperate with their owners. But this equilibrium was fragile and could be upset by a trifle, leading to suicides, escapes, and individual or collective rebellion. Then the master was forced to resort to violence and repression. In fact, in the northeastern part of Brazil, a section reputed to be so attractive to slaves and so easy for them to adapt to, escapes and rebellions were most numerous and conflicts between masters and slaves most violent. Paternalistic as they were, masters lived in constant fear that blacks would react in unanticipated ways. For that reason they created instrumentalities to ensure their social and economic survival in case of trouble—even in areas where slave violence was not a reality but only a possibility. "Preventive" violence, for example, was intended to reduce the slave to humility and obedience. Since disciplinary violence had to take account of religion and the law, it was generally rather moderate. But excesses did occur, and repression sometimes provoked resistance and led to the death of a slave. About such problems there is no dearth of evidence—on the contrary.

In this dialectic of adaptation and inadaptation, resocialization and resistance, an important role was played by "senior" slaves. New arrivals had to be integrated not only into the culture and society of the ruling class but also into the group of fellow slaves, to whom the newcomers were linked by economic, emotional, and religious bonds. Adaptation to the society of the masters, adaptation to the community of slave brothers: both processes were important to the slave's conquest of a new identity. It was as difficult for the new slave to adapt to his fellow slaves as to the society of the master. But the problems encountered were different in the two cases. The newcomer was embraced by a group of men of his own color, themselves slaves engaged in the same kind of economic activity. But the masters were careful to mix slaves from different tribes and communities in the hope that a less homogeneous group would be less inclined to rebellion. Some masters went so far as to stir up tribal rivalries by systematically assigning members of one tribe to supervisory roles and members of other tribes to hard labor. In the cities, different religious confraternities accepted members of only one tribe up to the beginning of the nineteenth century. Black Africa was endlessly diverse. Sudanese blacks, for example, had experienced a level of political and social development far in advance of anything known to the Bantus, whose civilization was still at the level of rudimentary community organization. These political and social differences were compounded by religious differences, and the role of religion in African societies was a very important one. The Bantu religions were quite different from the Yoruba religions, and the Muslim black had little in common with his "pagan" comrades. The latter eventually created a new religion, a Brazil-based survival of old African religions. Later on I shall discuss the religious question more fully, and we shall see how Islam, which had already undergone a transformation in Africa at the hands of Islamized blacks, would be further transformed on Brazilian soil. Here, the newly arrived slave encountered other slaves whose customs were diverse and whose families were dispersed. Customs and families were the linchpins of African society. Even if the blacks of Brazil were able to create a new social organization, distinct from that of the whites, that new community was as strange to the newcomer as was the society of the white man. How was he going to adapt? One might imagine, for instance, that if new and old slaves managed to establish family ties, newcomers might find themselves on familiar ground as soon as they were able to take their bearings within the new family. But the number of men was always larger than the number of women, and master rarely looked favorably upon marriages between slaves. Thus the African could not hope to find his social identity through the family in the narrow sense of the word. Marriage was not the linchpin of the new slave communities; rather, we must look to relationships between neighbors, coworkers, and participants in leisure activities and other associations of many kinds.

For such relationships to develop, the group had to accept the newcomer and the newcomer had to wish to join the group. And wishing was not enough, for the new arrival immediately encountered problems of language and religion. The religious difficulties were less serious than the linguisitic ones. But learning Portuguese, which became the vernacular of slaves who could not understand one another's native tongues, took time, and there was a real language barrier between new arrivals and the rest of the slave community. As for religions, the slaves of Brazil quickly evolved a syncretic religion acceptable to almost all Africans, which incorporated elements of the Bantu, Yoruban, Fon, and Catholic religions. Only Islam, which in any case was really a significant factor only in the cities in the first half of the nineteenth century among a "black elite" that was often hated and feared by other blacks, was left out of this synthesis that embraced the bulk of the slave population. The African's chief need was to be accepted by his group. It was the group, ultimately, that determined the quality of daily life, for white society was even more "alien" to the newcomer than the society of his fellow slaves.

Slaves born in Brazil, and who therefore spoke Portuguese, were called creoles. Generally they were raised in the master's family and bore a strong imprint of white society. Their problems of adaptation were quite serious, for they were soon seized by the desire to be as fully assimilated as possible. There was some social mobility in slave society: a slave could go from laborer to artisan or domestic servant, for example. There was also the hope of manumission for those who accepted western values and renounced their African heritage. In reality, freed men were always rejected by white society and thrown back onto the black community. The black community, which was constantly receiving new members from Africa, was not necessarily ready to reject the cultural heritage of its African ancestors in favor of the white man's heritage. Thus slave society was constantly riven by tensions between the creoles and the Africans. The creole was the victim of the irreducible contradictions between black and white. He was the slave who had the greatest difficulty in forging his own identity; powerful whites expected much more from the creole than from the African, and forgave him nothing. Hence for the creole the requirements of obedience, loyalty, and humility took on a whole new dimension. Masters considered him a human being responsible for his attitudes, whereas the African *bossale* (the one who is born far away), who barely spoke the white man's tongue, was usually regarded as an ignorant child to be educated and trained. What a creole was supposed to learn as a child the bossale was allowed to learn over a lifetime of labor. The master usually took notice of the African cultural heritage and often viewed the African slave as a "savage" in need of education in all areas. Thanks to this mind set, it was actually easier for an African slave to win emancipation than for a creole slave. To whites, Africans were less dangerous competitors than creoles and granting an African his freedom represented, in many cases at least, a smaller loss. What is more, solidarity among Africans was much stronger than among creoles. The bonds among new arrivals from Africa made a better cement than the creoles' desire for assimilation. This solidarity among Africans proved useful in obtaining letters of manumission, which restored to some slaves the liberty they had lost. Finally, it is again the Africans to whom we are indebted for the survivals of African tradition in Brazil. They felt the need to forge a new culture, a culture that would be their original and vital response to the difficulties of adapting to the new environment in which they found themselves obliged to live.

The black man arriving from Africa faced a simple dilemma: either he did not adapt or refused to try—in which case his only alternatives were struggle to the death, suicide, flight, or revolt—or else he did manage to integrate himself sooner or later and to one degree or another into the new society, in which case he took on a new identity. This new identity was the product of a twofold adaptation: a tactical adaptation to the white model, to the masters' demands for obedience and loyalty, together with a sincere adaptation to a mode of life and a mode of thought created by a heterogeneous group of slaves. Along with this adaptation went tension, caused by attempting to imitate the white model on the one hand while maintaining African tradition on the other. In fact, most slaves eventually learned to obey, to pray, and to work in order to win their masters' approval. At the same time they succeeded in the delicate task of adapting to the new culture created by previously arrived slaves and creoles. This dual apprenticeship was indispensible to the new slave's survival and the key to his new identity.

To Obey?

For the slave, the necessity was to obey; for the masters, to win obedience. Obedience could take many forms. It depended on partners, on the work required, and on the conditions in which that work was performed.

To begin our analysis we may distinguish between societies according to whether they are more or less hierarchical and more or less rigid. In Brazil urban slaves were not organized in the same way as rural slaves. Obedience took different forms in the fields, in the cities, and in the mines. The obligations of a slave who worked as a shepherd were different from those of a domestic, an artisan, or a peasant.

Brazil's first need was for farm hands. The fortunes of northeastern and east-central Brazil were based on the large-scale production of primary export products, primarily sugar cane, especially along the coast. The plantations made use of a highly stuctured system of exploitation, which led to the development of a rigid social hierarchy. Sugar was originally grown on vast tracts of land granted by the Portuguese crown to *sesmarias*, or planters who had shown they could produce a good yield. The concessionaire was obliged to do everything possible to develop an efficient system of production. It was not enough merely to sow and to reap; the harvest had to be transformed into a consumer product: sugar. This need gave rise to an agro-industrial complex, the so-called engenho, which demanded a fairly high degree of rationalization. Jobs in agriculture and industry awaited slaves to fill them. The engenho was a major enterprise, and without division of labor it could not have succeeded economically. Slaves found themselves taken in to a highly structured system, in which command and control methods were adapted to the needs of sugar production. Even after Brazilian agriculture had shifted from sugar to coffee, cotton, and subsistence products, its organization retained the indelible mark of these early days. At first sight the system would seem to have been one of two distinct classes: masters and slaves, rulers and ruled, whites and blacks. In this patriarchal system absolute control of production seemed to be the prerogative of those who owned the land and even more the means of production, the slaves and the machines of the sugar mills. An engenho's land was not worth much in colonial Brazil if that land was virgin or if the manpower required for the coming harvest was lacking. In this agrarian society the slave was therefore an indispensable instrument of production, but his job was fixed and there was little prospect of social mobility. Innumerable writers have described this traditional agrarian society, with a few masters at the summit and a mass of indistinct, industrious, and obedient slaves at the base. This picture is really oversimplified, as we shall see; it is in fact incorrect to draw too stark a contrast between this agrarian type of society and the societies that developed in the mining and livestock-raising regions of the country. On the whole, however, it apparently was easier for some degree of familiarity and cameraderie to develop between slaves and free men in the mines or in the vast sertão than in the engenho. In mining areas, all the master asked was that the slave produce a satisfactory quantity of gold or diamonds. In general the master held only temporary title to the land on which he set his slaves to work. When his fortune was made or the earth's resources were exhausted, he would sell his slaves or sell them their freedom. Or if he moved on in search of new riches, he would have to rely on the slaves to uncover a new seam or to pan for gold in the streams. Little by little the slave might become a partner in the venture. This trend was in fact facilitated by the central government. The crown granted sugar planters almost full powers to govern their lands, where they reigned as absolute masters. By contrast, in the mining regions the central government hastened to establish a strong military and police presence, for it was essential to achieve an abundant and steady output by whatever means proved necessary. The industrious or clever slave, the slave blessed by the gods who discovered the extra nugget or the precious diamond, might well succeed in earning himself a personal nest egg. The master was entitled to require a certain minimum output, the amount for which he was responsible to the government under the terms of his contract. Beyond that, the slave was in control and even enjoyed the government's protection. Slaves in the mining regions could therefore rise in the social hierarchy and become free men, because the society in which they worked was more open than the society in the agricultural regions of the country.

In the vast livestock-raising regions of the interior, social boundaries were even more fluid. The territory was relatively unpopulated and the climate harsh. No one owned the land, and people of different nations fought over it for many years, especially Spaniards and Portuguese. The master who owned the cattle led the same nomadic life as the slaves who helped him with the herd. Society in the Brazilian sertões was primitive and not especially hierarchical, because the number of slaves required was small and because masters themselves lived a primitive life. In addition there were poor whites involved in the activity, the so-called *peoes* and adventurers of every stripe. In this relatively free land of nomads, slaves were subject only to the same constraints as everyone else who had to cope with the austere environment. In the nineteenth century, when large salt houses were established in Rio Grande do Sul for the production of dried beef, some of this cowboy population settled in the area. The new society that developed in the cattle centers quickly became stratified, taking for its model the patriarchal society of the agrarian regions. The number of slaves increased while the chance of rising in the social hierarchy decreased and controls were tightened. Thus field hands, mine hands, and slaves of the sertões experienced very different fates, and their relations with the society that employed them were also quite different.

What about urban slaves? What was the slave's place in the city? Could he hope to find himself in a social environment flexible enough to allow for adaptation and advancement? Brazil was not a particularly urbanized country in the period 1600–1900. By 1820 approximately 7 percent of the population resided in cities, almost all of which looked to the sea and the mother country for their livelihood: Pernambuco, Bahia, and Rio were nothing less than economic fortresses. They arrogantly lorded it over a vast hinterland, whose small towns, hamlets, and villages were only way stations on inland routes. Only the mining province of Minas Gerais, whose towns were inhabited by agents of the royal government and large numbers of merchants, was urbanized to any significant degree.

The Atlantic ports and the mining cities of the interior played an important role in Brazilian life, as centers of commerical activity, social services, and government. In a system in which slave labor predominated, inevitably much of this would be entrusted to slaves. Slaves were assigned jobs that the European population viewed as base; even poor Europeans avoided lowering themselves by doing certain kinds of work. Besides, all emigrants came to the colonies hoping to enjoy a higher status than they could claim in Europe. Travelers' accounts depict slaves engaged in the most varied tasks as far back as the early seventeenth century. Free labor was rare in any case. Slave workers were indispensable, and in every city of Brazil we see the figure of the slave owner eager to hire out his slaves.

Urban society seems to have been less divided and less structured than rural society. In the cities lived numbers of people who were neither slaves nor high officials nor important landowners nor great merchants. This growing intermediate stratum consisted of professional men, lower level clergy, minor civilian and military officials, artisans of every stripe, small and medium merchants, and sailors. Does the existence of a middle class suggest greater social mobility for slaves? Undoubtedly it does, and it would be useful to know what proportion of this group consisted of freed men. Be that as it may, urban slaves surely were often more independent of their masters than were rural slaves. The slave artisan might live at some distance from the residence of his master, to whom he was obliged only to pay a lump sum out of what he earned from his work. The master who hired out his slave as a stevedore, painter, or sailor kept an eye on him to be sure, but he was also obliged to allow the slave a certain autonomy. Urban slaves were free to walk the streets and to form friendships with the humble free men with whom they worked; they certainly felt themselves to be less prisoners of their condition than did rural slaves. Some degree of social mobility was possible because of this relative independence, which lessened the traditional antagonism between master and slave, ruler and ruled.

The privileges enjoyed by urban slaves seem to have been shared by domestic slaves. It has often been said that masters chose as personal servants slaves made in the image of the white man: born in Brazil, often into the owner's family, and raised, educated, and *criados*—literally, "created"—in the big house. When it became necessary to sell some of these slaves, their masters waxed eloquent in praise of their qualities, and the newspapers described them as valuable and capable individuals. Domestic slaves could easily make themselves indispensable to their masters, to whom they gave their daily devotion and perhaps also the money earned by work done in addition to normal household chores. Many domestic slaves went through the streets with plates of candies or lace which they carried on their heads and sold to earn not inconsiderable profits for their owners. But life was by no means idyllic for these slaves, always under the eye of the master, always watched and monitored. In order to have any hope of rising in the social hierarchy and ultimately of gaining his freedom, the household slave had to exhibit, even more than the ordinary slave, the cardinal virtues of obedience, humility, and loyalty imposed by the master.

For the slave, then, obedience was not simply a necessity. Obedience of course made the master happy, but the slave had longer-range goals in mind. The field hand's horizons were more limited than the horizons of the slave in the mines or towns. But in all cases obedience was the only available strategy, for the black man could not rise in the social hierarchy and achieve some life of his own unless he made use of the values of the white society in which he lived. Using obedience as a protective shield, he could recreate his fragmented world, or rather create a new world colored by the Brazilian surroundings and yet all his own. But once obedience was accepted as a tactic necessary for survival and progress, the slave had to learn how to make this tactic pay dividends in everyday life. Before he could benefit from his apparent docility, the slave had to undergo a three-fold apprenticeship: to learn the language of his masters, to learn to pray to the Christian God, and to learn a useful skill.

To Understand, To Pray, and To Work

Adaptation through language, prayer, and work had two faces, for as we have seen the slave had to live with two communities: the slave community and the community of free men. Thus it was a double lesson that awaited him as he learned to speak Portuguese, to pray to the God of the Christians, and to do his job on the coffee or sugar plantation, in the gold or diamond mine, or in the city.

The language problem was not an issue for the creole slave, who had imbibed the language of his masters since childhood. As for the African slave, it was rare for him to encounter at his workplace another slave who spoke his own language. To the master or, more often, to his overseer—generally a mulatto, black, creole, or occasionally an African who had been in Brazil for a long time—fell the responsibility of teaching the new arrival the rudiments of Portuguese. Learning continued through contacts with fellow workers or with the chaplain. Priests were actually seldom found on the plantations, and by the eighteenth century one no longer saw Jesuit missionaries versed in certain African languages who were assigned to travel about the countryside seeking to convert "black pagans." The masters were in any case not very demanding instructors: if the slave could understand simple orders, that was enough. This was especially true of small agricultural communities, which had little contact with the outside world. By contrast, in the nineteenth century, we find growing up around the coffee plantations inns in which black slaves and poor whites could meet over a glass of whiskey and where the Africans could pick up a few well-chosen curses and enough of a vocabulary to permit elementary conversation. Only slaves in constant contact with their masters, especially the domestics, became truly bilingual, and their children, raised alongside the master's children, learned an African vocabulary as impoverished as the Portuguese vocabulary of their African relatives.

Schooling of slaves was strictly prohibited in Brazil, and even emancipees were not allowed to attend classes. This restriction remained in force throughout the slave era, even in the second half of the nineteenth century when the slave system was already in decline. The few masters and priests who decided to teach slaves to read and write were violating the established rules. For this reason Brazilian slaves have left no written archives. There are no "Slave Souvenirs" of the sort that are so common for the southern United States to tell us about the emotional lives, the actual experience, of these subjugated men and women. There is much to be learned from the white man's account of the black, of course, but the slave was unable to tell his own story. We therefore have no choice but to try to understand him through his behavior.

Masters were content if their slaves could speak rudimentary Portuguese. Consider, for example, the following newspaper advertisement that appeared in 1855, describing the African "Antonio, known by the name 'Antonio Vapor,' of the Nago nation, tall, more than 50 years of age, and who speaks in a rather confused but quite understandable manner." Or another advertisement, which says of an African slave from Mina who disappeared in 1858 that he is "tall and fat, with big lips and very white teeth and speaks very well." The language problem was quickly solved for the master who was content merely to make himself understood. Ultimately the awkwardness of the slaves in speaking Portuguese distorted the language spoken by Brazilians of all social categories. Even today in northeastern Brazil it is possible to recognize in the pronunciation and vocabulary of descendants of great cane-planting families linguistic anomalies directly inherited from plantation blacks. To say *fio* for *filho* (son) or *faze* for *fazer* (to make) is the mark of a person educated with Africans or the descendants of Africans. Furthermore, the Africans introduced a variety of new words into the Portuguese vocabulary which rapidly became part of the language of Brazil: *molambo* (rags), *moleque* (adolescent), *mucama* (nurse), *tanga* (loincloth), *mandinga* (witch doctor), *cacula* (second eldest son), and many more. It is difficult to know whether the African or *bossale* chose deliberately to remain in a world where the means of communication were limited, where he could keep his distance from his oppressor and yet exert an influence on him. The game was quite subtle, and every slave had the opportunity to use his own skill to connect up his past with a present that bore his own personal stamp. These were humble victories, to be sure. For the ladino or creole slave, who of course spoke Portuguese, the problem was different: whether or not to preserve the African vocabulary of his ancestors.

The master who needed to make himself understood so that he could give orders and organize his slave's working day also attempted to instruct the slave in the rudiments of the Catholic religion and to teach him how to pray. Slave society counted on the support of the Church to teach workers the virtues of patience and humility, resignation and obedience to the established order. Brazilian Catholicism was a religion of formalistic obligations, an authoritarian religion in which the patriarchal family head assumed the role of religious leader. On plantations where there was a chaplain in residence, he was totally subordinate to the owner and entirely cut off from his bishop. He was responsible for educating the master's children and for saying mass, hearing confessions, and celebrating baptisms, marriages, and funerals. He was in no way prepared to practice or preach a religion of liberation. On the contrary, the religion he preached was one of penitence and fear. For the clergy, the cornerstones of morality were paternalistic charity for the masters and conformity and asceticism for the slaves: "There is no labor," said Father Vieira in a sermon delivered to the slaves of an engenho in the Reconcavo of Bahio at the festival of St. John the Baptist in 1633

no way of life, more similar to Christ's cross and Passion than yours. . . . Profit by this to sanctify your labor in conformity with, and imitation of, such an exalted and divine exemplar! In an engenho you are the imitators of Christ crucified because your suffering is very like the Lord's suffering on the cross. . . . Here, too, cane it not lacking, cane like that mentioned twice in the Passion. The Passion of Christ occurred partly in the night though he did not sleep, and partly in the day though he did not rest, and such are your nights and your days. Christ was naked and you, too, are naked. Christ was mistreated in every way, and so are you. Of irons, prisons, lashings, wounds, and ignominious names your imitation is made, which along with patience will win for you the rewards of the martyr. . . . When you serve your masters, do not serve them as one who serves men but as one who serves God. Because then you will serve not as captives but as free men, and you will obey not as slaves but as sons.

Similar exhortations may be found in the sermons preached by the regular and secular clergy. For the slave heaven awaited, but only after a life of privation and punishment. This was the Church's way of justifying the shipment of slaves from Africa to Brazil. In the cities parish priests also practiced a highly formalized religion, in which sacraments were distributed in procession-spectacles, leaving to the lay confraternities and tertiary orders the real work of spreading the gospel. Slaves in fact had little personal contact with priests and chaplains. Most agricultural communities were visited by priests only on the feast day of the patron saint of the locality, at which time marriages, baptisms, and confessions were heard one after another in joyful chaos. The job of instructing new arrivals in religion was generally left to other slaves, whose mission was limited to explaining the outward signs rather than the inward content of religious practice. Such outward signs included the sign of the cross, the Credo, and the litanies of saints. The first prayer taught to the new slave was: "By the sign of the Holy Cross, deliver us, my God, Our Lord, from our enemies." This was accompanied by three signs of the cross. In great houses slaves were assembled every Sunday and holiday for prayers at the hour of vespers and sometimes also in the morning and evening. It is easy to imagine what became of these Christian prayers when recited by slaves who knew little Portuguese and even less Latin. Some ejaculatory prayers were distorted into incomprehensible and meaningless formulas: for example, Resurrexit sicut dixit became "*Reco, Reco Chico disse,*" "*Kist, Kist, Kist*" was all that remained of Benedict XIII's prayer, "Praised be our Lord Jesus Christ." Most slaves were born, lived, and died amid the external appearances of religion but without any real contact with Christian doctrine. It was up to them to maintain or create a proper inner life, or even to practice ancestral religious rites under the benevolent eye of the master, who looked upon it all as play. For the master the real sign of Christianization was humility and obedience at work, or the slave's use of a religious vocabulary to greet him with "Your blessing, my master," to which the master invariably responded, "God bless you, amen." These formulas are still widely used in traditional areas of northeastern Brazil.

To obey was therefore to learn the rudiments of Portuguese and the rudiments of Christian practice. Most important of all, however, was to learn to work well. This meant submitting to group discipline. On the plantations, for example, just as the chaplain represented the master in role as educator and religious leader, the *feitor* or overseer represented him in his role as organizer of work and disciplinarian. The master could thus remain aloof and thereby preserve his image as a severe but just father, a kind ruler, and a mediator. In the coffee or cane fields, the slave worked in a team of 12–15 men or women. If deemed to have a talent for a more skilled job, he would be put to work under a more senior slave. The sugar mill and its machinery required all kinds of specialized workers. In the cities as well as on the farms masons, carpenters, cabinetmakers, and barbers had to be trained. More specialized jobs were often reserved for creole slaves or for blacks trained in Africa by their clan or tribe (for artisans were quite common in African villages). Children destined for a trade were placed in apprenticeship with an adult when they reached the age of eight, under the watchful eye of the master or overseer, who determined whether or not the young slave was capable of acquiring the necessary skill. In the cities masters found it profitable to hire out the services of well-trained slaves; it was common to place young slaves with older workers, often freed slaves, who became the temporary masters and educators of their young apprentices. Domestic slaves were of course exempt from the surveillance of the overseer and master, but they were closely watched by the mistress of the house. At the slightest sign of insubordination a slave could be sent to work in the fields, since the lot of the field hand was considered harder than that of the household slave. Masters who were not landowners could sell their troublesome slaves to coffee planters or to mine concessionaires in remote provinces.

Corporal punishment also served to maintain discipline by example. But recourse to such measures was not ordinary. No one would deny that some masters and mistresses were sadists. Generally speaking, however, neither the master nor the overseer went about whip in hand, ready to punish every minor infraction. Much more subtle methods were used to obtain obedience at work and humility toward the master. Masters preferred to work on the emotions of their slaves. They sought first to inspire respect, and a job well done could lead to mutual respect between master and slave. Whip and whipping post, chains, brass masks, irons, and pillories were last resorts for masters unable to obtain discipline by other means. They were used only when a slave refused to accept his position. When the black man did not manage to carve out the area of freedom he needed, when he found neither family nor group nor associates nor amusements of his own, then but only then did he refuse to accept the discipline of work and enter into the terrible realm of refusal, punishment, and rebellion.

Work discipline was not the same on a large sugar or coffee plantation as on a family farm where tobacco and manioc were grown and where the slave lived at close quarters with the master's family, whose joy and suffering he shared. But the master was always the all-powerful ruler and commander, to whom the slave owed labor, humility, and loyalty. From the master's point of view, the well-adapted slave was the complacent slave. But if the master saw complacency as a virtue, how did the slave see it? The slave's goal was to transform obedience into pride and dignity. He sought to be a man of many loyalties, which is to say, his own man: not merely a conscientious and efficient instrument of "white" power but a man sharing in responsibility for the African community. Before attempting to describe the structure of black society and the nature of solidarity among blacks, I want to examine the slave's true value in white society. By value I mean not price but influence and esteem. This matter, of course, is highly subjective.

WHO KNOWS WHAT I AM WORTH?

Legally, the slave was an item of movable property. His master deemed him worth the purchase price plus the cost of caring for him so that he could work. In the historiography of Brazil there are two powerful schools: one holds that slaves were very badly treated, the other that they were much better treated than most of the Brazilian population of today.

The slave's obligations were to work in obedience and "Christian humility." The master's obligation was to protect his worker, who was after all a precious capital investment capable of providing a good return if properly cared for. Was the care the master took of a slave precisely proportional to the value he ascribed to that slave? That is hard to say, because some slave owners were responsible and others negligent. We have seen, moreover, that slave traffickers provided a constant flow of new manpower. Masters may have found it more expedient to replenish their "stock" with new workers. In the seventeenth and eighteenth centuries the life expectancy of many plantation slaves has been calculated to be no more than seven years, which proves that seven years of labor provided a sufficient return on the capital invested in the slave's purchase and upkeep to make the investment worthwhile. Sometimes the master found it more advantageous to increase his sugar or coffee harvest than to plant maize and manioc, only to find himself short of cash to purchase what he needed to feed his workers. To judge from contemporary literature and government regulations, slaves could not always eat their fill, were not always decently clothed, and died for lack of essential medical care. The blackest descriptions come to us from such Jesuits as Georges Benci, Antonio Vieira, or Antonil. But the regular clergy in this period surely sought in every way possible to attentuate the unbearable aspects of slavery as an institution. The clergy believed that the slave, too, had a soul in need of protection. And the church was concerned not only with saving slaves but also with saving their privileged owners. For the latter, salvation depended on charity. Hence good priests castigated wicked masters. The government, too, had an interest in protecting the labor force, since it wished to increase its own revenues by increasing production. The better a slave was cared for, the more productive he became.

The slave owner moreover was a veritable entrepreneur, who surely would not have deliberately allowed the capital needed for his enterprise to deteriorate. We know that the slave diet was far richer in calories, proteins, and carbohydrates than the diet of a poor Brazilian in the twentieth century. Slaves ordinarily ate manioc flour, corn, dried meat, game, local fruits such as bananas, oranges, lemons, and papaya, and molasses. Slaves residing near rivers or seacoasts ate fish and shellfish. In the cities slaves entitled to earn a little money of their own could go to the market and buy tasty and inexpensive dishes prepared by other slaves. In the countryside the "custom of Brazil" (as West Indians called it) was for the slave to have the use of a small plot on which he planted manioc and vegetables. Frequently he sold excess crops to his master or in the market of a nearby town. There were Homeric disputes between slave owners and church officials, because the master wanted his slaves to farm their own plots on Sundays, whereas a regulation adopted in 1700 required masters to give slaves one day off each week and to respect the Sabbath rest.

It is also widely believed that the slave died young because he worked too much. How much work is too much is a highly relative notion in fact. There is no doubt that slaves did work a great deal. Masters required all slaves to work in various jobs for fifteen to seventeen hours a day, and by tradition they were inflexible on this point. The great Brazilian sociologist Gilberto Freyre, whose renowned *Masters and Slaves*, the second edition of which was published in Rio de Janeiro in 1936, painted an almost idyllic portrait of Brazilian slavery, asserts that masters nearly always attached higher priority to productivity than to the slave's health or life. Some historians have described slaves in the mines as working to the point of exhaustion or even death. With more ample documentation and the use of travelers' reports, however, it has become possible to say that things were not as simple as they might seem. Terrifying accounts of slave labor do have some basis in reality, but broadly speaking the burden of work was unbearable only for short periods. In the countryside there were slack and busy times, following the cycle of harvests and seasons. In the mines heavy rains interrupted all activity. Night work was impossible everywhere, except in the sugar mills during the time when molasses was being cooked. The working day was marked by numerous pauses. Children and old people brought huge pots of water and soup to workers in the fields. There were also many nonworking holidays in the Brazilian calendar: Mauricio Goulart has calculated that there were no more than 250 working days per year.

Thus the high mortality rate among slaves cannot be explained as the result of excessive labor. It was a consequence, rather, of working conditions. The slave worked in very harsh climates. In the northeast it was hot and humid, sometimes very humid, throughout the year, and sudden changes in temperature were common. In the space of an hour the temperature could drop from 24 degrees centigrade to 18 degrees. In this part of the world slaves always wore light cotton clothers. Covers and coats were rare, and slight chills, left untreated, turned into chronic ailments that reduced resistance to bronchitis, diphtheria, and pneumonia. In central, western, and southern Brazil winters were harsh, temperatures often went down to freezing, and there was no heat in either the master's quarters or the slaves'. Slaves often did not have enough covers and woolens to protect themselves against the cold. Treatment for illness was crude at best. Few trained physicians traveled to the plantations to treat patients. The story is told of a group of French pharmacists who had signed on as crew members of French vessels, only to desert those vessels to travel about rural Brazil offering their services and especially their drugs to cure slaves on the coffee plantations. They made a fortune. This episode took place in the nineteenth century, but the two previous centuries also had their share of quacks and patent medicine salesmen. Even trained physicians, often unable to make the right diagnoses, found themselves as helpless in the face of illness as those whose only schooling was derived from common sense, greed, or the empirical teachings of witch doctors. Medicine in this period was based on medicinal plants. When the master of a sugar mill or coffee fazenda paid a doctor to make regular visits to the plantation, the same doctor treated both the master's family and the slaves. In the nineteenth century certain large coffee operations employed their own doctor and maintained a separate building as a hospital. A slave served as nurse.

Numerous diseases became endemic in Brazil: tuberculosis, syphilis, lice, scurvy, malaria, and often fatal dysentery and typhus. These diseases affected the entire population. Slaves often had less resistance than whites owing to poor hygienic conditions in the slave quarters. The mortality rate in Brazil was quite high in both the free and slave populations, but there were many elderly slaves, both men and women. In 1885 a law known as the "sexagenerian law" liberated nearly 120,000 slaves over age sixty, which was considered a ripe old age for that era. In addition, the black mortality rate was higher than the mortality rate for whites and those of mixed race, because whites had been subject to a process of selection lasting several centuries. Whites and mulattoes were inured to the hardships and showed themselves more resistant than blacks to certain infections. Blacks died at a greater rate because they could not adjust physically to the new conditions in which they were forced to live.

Thus the slave had to work to adjust not only to a new way of life and new forms of work but also to a new biological environment. His master asked him to accept white values and to seek his owner's approval here below and in the Christian heaven hereafter. Did slaves accept the white man's world? And if so, how did they relate to it? For slaves knew better than their masters their origins, their shortcomings, and their worth. Very quickly, too, they understood how indispensable they were to the white masters whom they served.

FIVE

Solidarities

The rules of the social game in Brazil obviously were set by the masters, who controlled the slave-based economy. But the slave could either accept those rules or reject them. To be sure, it was very difficult to reject all the rules, for to do so meant attempting escape or risking death. But there were a thousand ways to accept and yet bend the rules. Though there were a few violent uprisings, which will be described in due course, for the most part social peace was ensured by subtle ruses, stratagems, and adjustments coupled with covert resistance. For this system to work, the slave needed a certain period of time to adjust to his new way of life. And masters and slaves had to live together long enough to allow slaves to create refuges and to learn the limits of tolerable behavior. Because the Church was well aware of this need for time, it was not very exigent in matters of slave religion. It knew that Christians were not made in a few hours and that real conversion took months if not years. Masters also knew that the education of workers took time and that by themselves they could not do the whole job. They looked to the Church for help, as well as to the slave community. Thus the world of the slaves and the world of free men were sharply divided and yet closely dependent on each other. To be a slave in Brazil was to seek to overcome the contradictions between these two worlds while at the same time overcoming tensions within the slave community itself. The slave had to give up old ways of life, but if he succeeded in making a new life for himself he received compensation in the form of new and liberating resources—liberating in the sense that they created new modes of thought and new emotional bonds. The masters were aware of this: to them, the newly landed black seemed primitive, timid, and hostile—quite a depressing figure. They knew that some blacks would remain that way until they died. But they also knew that most would in the space of a few years become skilled, experienced workers, learn their catechism, and adopt a fairly sober way of life. Such slaves were said to have "adjusted to the country"—in other words, they had become completely assimilated and adapted to their new way of life. Most creoles were "adjusted" in this sense, and slave owners had a saying that "one creole is worth four *bossales.*" Mulatto creoles were the most prized, though they had the reputation of being haughty and violent. Brazil was said to be "Hell for Negroes, Purgatory for Whites, and Paradise for Mulattoes." Whatever he was— black or mixed white or Indian, creole or bossale—the slave remained a slave in the eyes of the law. Africans were almost always in the majority in the slave community, where social adaptation occurred. Each slave had to resolve his own personal problems; some were more successful, some less, in confronting issues stemming on the one hand from the clash of master and slave and on the other hand from the antagonism and suspicion between Africans and creoles, blacks and half-breeds.

Social relations in Brazil in the seventeenth, eighteenth, and nineteenth centuries were thus complex, more complex than is suggested by the usual simplistic image of a two-class society, divided between a ruling class of free men and a subjugated class of slaves. Social hierarchies within the "subjugated" class were just as keenly felt as hierarchies within the "ruling" class. Relations were sometimes better between master and slave than between two slaves or between a slave and a freed man. Nevertheless, slaves were eager for solidarity with other slaves. They achieved this solidarity through an extremely complex set of social practices about which little is yet known. These practices touched on every aspect of social life: the family, the group, religion, rebel and outlaw communities. They are the signs that reveal the success or failure of adaptation. And finally, problems and tensions existed within the slave community as well as between slaves and their masters.

A FAMILY FOR THE SLAVE?

The nuclear family (father, mother, and children) does not appear until quite late in Brazilian society, long dominated by the patriarchal model, in which the paterfamilias gathered together, under his authority and his roof, uncles and aunts, nephews, unmarried sisters and brothers, distant cousins, bastards, and godchildren, to say nothing of *agregados.* Agregados were free men or manumitted slaves, poor whites, mulattoes, or blacks —wards of the family who were considered full members of the family

108 / Being a Slave

community. Slaves, too, were part of the family—all slaves, not just domestics. Thus it was not unusual for an urban family of modest means to number twenty or so individuals. To live in such a strange community one had to submit to its rules and be ready to follow orders. In the countryside agregados worked lands belonging to the family head, from whom they received food and protection. They were like a private police force, which the masters needed to maintain because the authorities were so far away. The agregados served the master personally. In the cities they worked at jobs and turned their earnings over to the family. Whether emancipated or free they lived in the shadow of the family that offered them protection in exchange for service. For powerful lords, wealthy sugar planters, mine concessionaires, or coffee growers, it was a matter of prestige to maintain a large number of relatives and agregados under one's roof. To refuse such protection when it was requested was to lose caste. In these extended families, whether rich or poor, the slave occupied a humble position. Even the poorest families owned at least one slave. The master of the household was the father of all, and slaves, like other family members, had to persuade themselves that they were "sons" of the house—less privileged than other sons, but sons all the same. The family was intended to be the place where the slave learned to live his life as a perpetual child. It was the Brazilian family that taught the slave how he should behave toward other slaves, emancipees, and free men.

Was the Brazilian family based upon a couple whose union was blessed by the marriage sacrament of the Roman Catholic Church? In remote areas, where priests seldom visited, husband and wife did live together without the blessing of the Church. A wedding might be held if the opportunity arose, as during a missionary visit, for example. Only the ruling classes considered Catholic marriage a social necessity. The middle and lower classes did not marry. Blacks and whites established "natural" families, which the Brazilian Church was perfectly willing to accept. Common-law marriage or concubinage was the lot of almost the entire white and black population, and these unions produced many illegitimate children: in Bahia as late as the nineteenth century, one-fifth of the population listed in the census was born outside of religiously sanctioned wedlock; in São Paulo and Minas Gerais a quarter of all infants baptized were illegitimate. Common-law marriage may have discouraged childbearing, however, for many couples were childless. It was not reluctance to sanction miscegenation that stood in the way of legal marriages—far from it. In Paraty, for example, a small city in southern Rio de Janeiro state, religious marriages in which white men married mulatto women accounted for more than 14 percent of all marriages, simply because there were more white men in Brazil than there were white women. Racial endogamy in Brazil was limited to areas where all social categories were represented. The general tendency was for upward social mobility to be coupled with a "purification of the blood," so that wealthy blacks aspired to marry women whiter but poorer than themselves.

Obviously there was a world of difference between the Brazilian family and the black African family whose members all came from the same community or ethnic group. In Africa, the words "brother" and "cousin" did not necessarily imply consanguinity. Members of the same ethnic group generally regarded one another as brothers. "Cousin" really meant "friend." Distant cousins, uncles, and aunts were considered members of the family, which was never limited to parents and children alone. What defined the African family was common ancestry. When progeny became too numerous, a branch would break off and start a new line. African societies were thus based on lineage.

What about the black slave family that developed in Brazil? Cut off from his lineage, could the slave establish a family of his own within the broad family of his master? If so, what kind of family? Did Brazilian masters, like their North American counterparts, exhort their slaves to marry and have children? Indeed, in the United States, the slave family played an important economic role as the institution through which food, clothing, and lodging were distributed. As the family created new emotional ties and responsibilities and came to possess a house and a small plot of land, the slave tended to feel more attached to his master, more willing to accept discipline and follow orders, and this situation prevented the development of class consciousness. Moreover, when the slave trade was abolished in the early nineteenth century, the prolific black family became the master's only source of slave labor. Legislation in most slave states prohibited slave marriages, but plantation regulations took no notice of these laws. For the slave owner, the nuclear family, the couple with many children, was an economic necessity and not a moral or religious imperative.

In Brazil, if contemporary accounts and tradition are to be believed, things seem to have been quite different. Cut off from his roots and from his natural environment, the Brazilian slave lost his essential points of reference. His family ties were destroyed. Despite the exhortations of the Church, masters were little inclined to allow their slaves to marry. In contrast to what happened in the United States, in Brazil the slave supply did not dry up until 1850. Buying adult blacks was cheaper than raising slave children: the child mortality rate was quite high, and masters had to wait ten or fifteen years for a child to become really productive. What is more, male slaves outnumbered females by two or three to one. This ratio decreased after the slave traffic was halted in 1850, but in rural areas up to 56 percent of the slave population continued to be male.

The shortage of women encouraged temporary liaisons. The first official census of Brazil, in 1872, shows that only 10 percent of Brazilian slaves were married or widowed. In rural areas few slaves married, but in the cities slave marriages were as common as marriages in the free population. As mentioned earlier, concubinage was common in the middle and lower classes. Certain confraternities required new members to regularize their situation, however, and the Church did all it could to persuade masters to arrange marriages for their concubines. Civil law in fact provided no privilege for couples sanctioned by the sacrament of marriage, and masters were allowed to put asunder couples united by the Church: father, mother, and children could be sold to different buyers or given away to different takers. It is not difficult to understand why slaves saw no advantage to getting married and why masters preferred not to encourage bonds that might raise problems of conscience if it proved necessary to sell one member of a family.

A law governing slave marriages did not appear until quite late: in 1869 the government prohibited the separate sale of married slaves. The law of the "free womb" of 1871 declared that all children of slaves were born free and prohibited the separation of parents and children under twelve. Finally, the regulations of the manumission fund set up in 1872 to pay for the liberation of slaves gave priority first to married slaves, next to slaves with free-born children (children born after 1871), next to slaves with children under eight, and next to couples whose children had been emancipated but had yet to reach age twenty-one. Then came slave couples whose minor children were still slaves, then mothers of minor children, and finally couples without children. This legislation is unfortunately the only information we have about manumissions authorized by the Brazilian government, and it tells us little about the problem of slave marriages. Yet this problem preoccupied public debate in the final years before abolition, during which there was much discussion of the issue in the newspapers. It can be stated as a general rule that slaves did not marry.

Were slave unions solid and lasting? Often the master chose a mate for a slave whom he wished to "marry," and there is no doubt that the sexual lives of slaves were not as free as they would have wished. That is why Brazilian slaves had so few children. Many sought abortion rather than bear a child into slavery, and men, it seems, practiced coitus interruptus. Sexuality for slaves was a response to physical needs, not a means of procreation. On the plantations the men's dormitories were separate from the women's, and even legally married couples had to resort to furtive nighttime encounters. The masters' policy was to make sexual liaisons difficult but not impossible. Thus African polygamy gave way in Brazil to a succession of brief encounters.

When, in spite of all these obstacles, children were born, the family was generally without a father: *"Pater incertus, mater certa."* It was the slave community as a whole that served as family to the child born of an ephemeral union. This was true of children whose parents were both slaves as well as of children of unions between master and slave. The social life of the group was more important than family life as such, which was practically nonexistent. For the slave child, the formative experiences were with neighbors, work, recreation, and mutual aid through religious associations. Public life took precedence over private life. Communal feasts and other community events were the high points of the slave's life; limited home life and severe poverty were the other side of the coin. Solidarity among slaves existed outside the nuclear family, and fatherless children turned to their mothers and to other slaves in the group for needed support. The wills left by freed slaves often tell us of fathers who, though they became wealthy, did not think of buying their child's freedom until they were on their deathbeds. They did not find the situation scandalous. Mothers, on the other hand, always sought to have their children freed, even when they themselves had to remain slaves after paying for the child's manumission.

Thus the education of the slave child usually consisted of two somewhat incompatible components. On the one hand masters and free men tried to win the slave's affection while training him to be obedient, humble, and loyal. On the other hand the slave community sought to win the child's exclusive allegiance. The white children with whom the slave child often spent his early years were themselves raised by slaves, African *mucamas*. White and black children heard the same lullabyes and stories carried over from Africa and firmly entrenched in Brazilian folklore today. On a large estate such as a sugar engenho or coffee plantation black children moved freely, participating in games with white children and receiving caresses from all the women of the house. One traveler speaks of "ebony Cupids" tumbling about with the dogs before the admiring eyes of their masters, including the chaplain. We have no idea how many slave mothers died in childbirth, or how many lacked time to take care of their children. The young slave, whether he became a *cria da casa*, or protegée of the master in whose home he was raised, or a butt of teasing by white boys and girls, was much closer to the white community than to the black. In the master's house he found stability and tenderness, which influenced his emotional life. For him the master would always be the father he never had. This was true to a lesser degree in the cities, where limited living space meant that black children were relegated to the slave quarters of the house or even to another dwelling. Rural slave children generally went to the slave quarters only at night. Mothers, exhausted by their day's labor, often entrusted the education of their children in large part to rather strange characters who played the same role of father and family head in the black community as did the master in the white community. The slave community came to life at night; it had its own rituals, its own morality, and often its own language and social practices. Thus the slave child had to face the same difficulty as the adult newly arrived from Africa: he had to learn to live in two worlds, between which he was eventually obliged to choose.

At what age did the child make this choice? At what age did someone decide that the time for games was over and the time of apprenticeship had begun? By age seven or eight the slave child had to make himself useful. At that age he became aware that his status was lower than that of free children: the first major shock. The master's orders became specific and unchallengeable. A child selected to work in the household had to undergo as difficult an apprenticeship as one sent to work in the fields or as an artisan. In fact, the child had to obey not only his white "father," now the "master," and his white "mother," now the "mistress," but also the master's domestic servants or the artisan in charge of his training. Black masters were sometimes very harsh, for they knew that they occupied a privileged position in the slave hierarchy and in many ways treated other slaves with disdain. The child had to develop his own defenses and in any case suffered emotional damage. His childhood world crumbled. The lesson he learned may be summed up thus: succeed at the trade for which you have been chosen by special privilege and hope thereby to rise in the slave hierarchy and perhaps one day to buy your freedom, or else fail and be relegated to the mass of unskilled manual laborers, for whom life is especially difficult. Children sent at age seven or eight to work in the fields suffered a blow that was hard, to be sure, but perhaps salutary, in that the ambiguity characteristic of the early years of the child's emotional life was abruptly dispelled. The child soon learned that the abyss between master and slave was unbridgeable, even if he continued to feel unavowed affection for his mistress. He formed ties to his new companions, which might prove useful if he decided to seek manumission later on. The black community took charge of him, all the more readily because the age of apprenticeship corresponded to the age at which young blacks were initiated into African society. The masters, who had no notion of the religious nature of these initiation rites, were willing to tolerate them insofar as they facilitated the child's integration into the work community. Cut off from his natural father (whose identity was often unknown), and cut off, too, from his surrogate father, the now remote master, the slave child found his bearings in the larger family or black workers and worked to regain his lost emotional stability. In the black community, whose ancestral roots had been severed, new allegiances were formed with adoptive parents, and new religious bonds developed. When this black community succeeded in organizing itself, it was a force for the master to reckon with, and the community did not always look kindly on slaves who enjoyed, or had enjoyed, the master's special favors. In exchange for the illusory privilege of living on intimate terms with his master, as a domestic servant, for example, the slave had to be at the owner's beck and call day and night. He could not share in black communal life. Better fed, better clothed, and better housed than other slaves, and less burdened by work, was the domestic slave or privileged artisan a turncoat, a "white"? Some behaved in insolent and authoritarian ways and never learned to navigate skillfully between the two different worlds to which they belonged. Young slaves sometimes resorted to deception in order to remain in the good graces of their masters, and yet they were unable to win acceptance by their fellow slaves.

In town the master's presence was less oppressive and more remote, because slaves and their owners did not generally live under the same roof (unless the slave was an especially valued domestic servant). It was also easy to meet other members of the same ethnic group. The urban child was less divided in his loyalties between black and white than was the rural child. It was easier for him to stay with his mother, or rather to run after her. The city streets swarmed with so many black children that municipal councils threatened to impose sanctions on masters who let "the children [of their slaves] grow up in the streets." Open-air merchants kept one eye on their children and the other eye out for clients, and at bridges, where women gathered to do the washing, one often heard the laughter of children at play.

Sought-after Associations: Godparents

Only young slave children knew the joy of being, in a relative sense, free. For any slave beyond age eight, life was filled with mistrust. Slaves did judge and criticize their masters, but woe unto him who allowed the master to catch him at it. The master, for his part, was never so imprudent as to trust fully in any slave, for he knew too many examples of old slaves who, after years of apparent loyalty and affectionate devotion, vanished as soon as they had their freedom, as well as young slaves who suddenly became insolent and lazy on the day they obtained, in compensation for loyal service, a written promise of manumission. Slaves were cunning and masters suspicious. It is by no means clear that the battle between them was always one-sided. For even though the master had law and force on his side and could kill a stubborn slave if he wished, the slave, too, wielded some potent weapons: he could undermine the master's authority, and even more he could disrupt production by sabotage, evasion, rebellion, or suicide. The slave system required constant compromise if two apparently irreconcilable camps were to live in peaceful coexistence. It is hard to imagine any sincere complicity between masters and slaves as groups. Yet friendships occurred more often than one might suspect between individual masters and slaves. Slaves also formed friendships with freed men and other slaves. These were matters of individual choice, of elective affinity, of personal sympathy between man and man. Such personal sympathies were institutionalized in the god parents.

The godfather (*compadre* in Portuguese) and godmother (*comadre*) bore responsibilities similar to those of a parent. At baptism each slave was assigned a godfather. For adult Africans who were baptized en masse, the godfather was an unknown individual imposed on the slave much as baptism itself was imposed. But for the creole the godfather was chosen by the slave and had to agree to take on the role. To be a master's godson was a privilege that afforded special protection within the slave group. Sometimes the godchild was actually the child of a master unwilling to admit publicly that the newborn was his own. The godfather was obliged to help his godchild, not only spiritually but also materially, and in Brazil he rarely failed to take this obligation seriously. Relations with godparents served as the model for all other interpersonal relations. The godparent relationship was perfectly adapted to the rules of Brazilian society, based as it was on the broad, extended, patriarchal family. Furthermore, the godparent relationship extended beyond just the godparents and godchild to embrace the families of the godparents and the newborn; the newborn's family received an important social boost. The slave mother of a child taken to baptism by its mistress became the comadre of the mistress and was allowed to greet her by saying, "How is my godmother today?" Subtle forms of affection could spring up in this way between masters and slaves.

Not all masters were white or free, moreover. Miscegenation and manumission—both aspects of social mobility—began early in Brazil and continued to be common throughout the seventeenth, eighteenth, and nineteenth centuries. It was common, moreover, for a slave without legal status to own one or more slaves. Actual practice was, in this respect at least, totally in contradiction with the law. Thus masters were found in every class of society. There were white masters, masters of mixed race, and black masters. Their behavior did not depend on their color or social position but on their quality as individuals. But for the slave the master —whether rich or poor, white or black—was always a "white" master, because to be "white" in Brazilian society meant to adopt certain superior attitudes, to wield a certain power.

The term godparent also had a broader meaning. A slave might choose a godfather to represent him, for example, to plead his case before his master. A fugitive slave wishing to return home but afraid of his master's wrath might appear accompanied by a third party. Or a slave who had amassed enough funds to purchase his freedom but found his master unwilling to set him free might call upon a godfather to argue in his behalf. Or again, a slave unjustly convicted of a crime might might seek out an adviser, often a law graduate, to appeal his sentence. For a freed slave the former master often played the role of *patrono* and continued to feel responsible for the man or woman who had been his slave and remained bound to him through a whole range of ritual forms. Is it therefore correct to say that "godparents" were usually protectors belonging to a higher social class? No. Parish records actually show that godfathers and godmothers often belonged to the same social class as their godchildren. Slaves, for example, were chosen as godparents of other slaves because they enjoyed the esteem of the entire community. "Senior" slaves were willing to serve as godparents to many children, and it is quite possible that relationships of this sort, which were accepted by the established Church, actually concealed attempts to reconstitute the African family. Though it is difficult to demonstrate this for slaves, we can see it much more clearly among freed men. Quantitative analysis of wills and estate inventories of manumitted slaves reveals a constant concern to assist godchildren, especially those still living "in captivity," who might be helped through a monetary bequest to buy their freedom. Black masters set free favored godchildren ahead of other slaves. Bonds between slaves were much stronger than bonds between a master-godfather and his godchild. Indeed, masters were masters of their own generosity, and if something displeased them they could easily take back what they had given. Thus solidarity based on individual esteem was uncertain and often illusory. To be sure, the widow whose single slave was her only source of income, the invalid whose slave became an attentive and tireless nurse, and the adult who continued to feel genuine affection for the woman who had nursed him as a child were common enough figures in Brazil. But as a general rule, in spite of individual sympathy, godparenting, and other special relationships, and in spite of the fluidity of the constantly evolving "white" community, it remains true that personal bonds between master and slave had less effect on the slave's emotional equilibrium and social advancement than bonds formed with other members of the slave community.

CIRCUMSTANTIAL ASSOCIATIONS: WORK

Of fundamental importance was the solidarity that stemmed from the slave's working life. Normally, 80–100 slaves, mostly adult men, worked together on an engenho. All lived together in the *senzala*, a large, rectangular, one-story building along which ran a covered gallery. Each dormitory had a single window that opened onto the gallery; often this window was incorporated into the door, the upper part of which could be left open. The master's house, or "big house," dominated the senzala. The owner could observe everything that went on from his room. A rare privilege for a slave on a sugar plantation was to be allowed to live in a small cob hut with one window and one door, located at the forest's edge. The slaves' only furniture consisted of crude cots with filthy straw mattresses covered with scraps of cloth, together with a few stools and chests. A small amount of clothing was handed out: two shirts and two pairs of pants or two skirts per year. Only generous masters provided jackets. Artisans and domestics were better housed and clothed.

The working day, interrupted by meals taken in common, varied considerably in length over the course of the year: in the northeast during the summer it ran from twelve to fourteen hours, and twelve hours or slightly less in the winter. A gong or bell signaled the waking hour, which was followed by a brief period for washing up. Then the slaves marched over to the master's house to receive their orders. In Brazil, unlike the Antilles where masters were chronically absent from their plantations, the owner or one of his children usually lived on the engenho, and no owner would think of staying away at harvest time, even if his overseer was a good manager. Before the day's jobs were assigned there was a brief prayer. The work consisted of planting, weeding, harvesting, transporting, repairing boats, roads, and buildings, tending animals, gathering wood for fuel and crates, fishing, and sometimes raising food for local consumption. Sugar mills need highly skilled workers such as purifiers and sugar boilers. During the first two centuries of colonization these jobs were filled by free men, but gradually they were replaced by slaves. Like the domestics, these skilled slaves were treated fairly well. Sometimes they were paid in cash. But everyone, from overseer down to cane cutter, worked all day long. Sugar cane is a demanding crop, which requires considerable tending at planting time, constant weeding with the hoe, and a large crew at harvest. Goats, cattle, and horses had to be kept from trampling the young shoots. Each slave was assigned a job, to plant a certain area, say. At harvest time he had to cut 350 bundles a day, with twelve canes in each bundle, and each woman had to tie as many bundles. Slaves actually preferred this method of organizing the work, which left some free time once the assigned task had been accomplished. During weeding time, however, he was allowed no respite. The sugar mills were veritable beehives of activity. Songs could be heard during the hours of heavy labor, punctuated by the cries of the overseer and team captains. At ten in the morning and three in the afternoon a small meal was served and the slaves were allowed a moment of rest; these were the only breaks in a day of hard labor under constant surveillance.

The milling of the cane was a very dangerous operation: the cane had to be placed between the mill wheels, and it was easy to lose a hand or an arm. This job was assigned to a team of seven or eight women: three carried cane, one placed it in the mill, another passed the cane trash through the mill a second time, another prepared lamps for lighting, and yet another threw the cane trash into the river or into a storehouse for use as fuel. The furnaces, cauldrons, purifiers, drying racks, pottery shops, and packing stations employed still other men and women.

The life was rude, monotonous, and disciplined. The work seemed endless. Leisure time was entirely at the discretion of captains and masters, unless bad weather drowned the cane and spoiled the harvest. We know very little about how the daily life of slaves on a sugar plantation was affected by the master's moods, by market fluctuations, or by the weather. According to *Pilgrim in the Americas*, one master made his slaves work on Sundays to keep them from visiting nearby plantations where the slaves, "given to sorcery and all belligerent," spent their Sundays drinking rather than attending mass. But when night fell and sounds of African drums and dancing started up, this same master went to bed pleased and reassured: silence would have been far more mysterious and troubling than the noise of these slave "amusements." For the slave's night was his own. Tired though he may have been from the day's labor, he returned at night to the great family of slaves, in whose refuge he could finally feel himself. Unfortunately, little is known about the feasts and rituals of these people of the night, with their lively songs and obscure gestures. This was a nation without archives, at whose humble communal joys we can only guess.

Yet there could be no communal life without a sufficient number of slaves. On smaller farms (growing cotton, tobacco, or subsistence crops) that employed only five or six slaves, or in the sertão where slaves were rare, communal activities were much more difficult to sustain. Isolated slaves could not fortify themselves with, or draw pleasure from, the knowledge of belonging to an active, fraternal community. No doubt such slaves were more likely to imitate whites and thus to lose fairly quickly African communal traditions and notions of the sacred. Gold and diamond mines employed somewhat larger numbers of slaves, usually fifteen to thirty per mine. Even more than the slave in the sugar fields, the slave miner was assigned a job to complete and enjoyed some free time when it was done; with this freedom he could sometimes amass a small nest egg. But the great age of mining ended around 1760, and as the mines were exhausted their slaves were either sold to other concessionaires or retrained as agricultural workers and thus condemned to the same fate as their brothers on the engenhos or fazendas of other regions.

The slave miner lived with his master in a crude straw or cob hut in which everything was makeshift. Covered with mud, these huts might be used to store gold or diamonds, but they were still wretched dwellings. No one gave a thought to making the place comfortable, since the concessionaire's only thought was to get rich quick and return to Europe. Courageous and crude, these adventurers were not particularly strict with their slaves, because panning for gold was hard work that had to be done in a painful physical position, the slave standing with his back bent over the stream and often with his feet in the water. Slaves had their growth stunted or became bowlegged, and many young adolescents acquired life-long deformities. Men wore jackets and pants, smoked tobacco that was distributed four or five times a day, and stopped at least a half-hour for lunch and two hours in the afternoon. Seeking quick fortunes, many concessionaires sought to deceive the royal tax collectors. Slaves sometimes became involved in machinations from which it was difficult to escape: the master might propose a partnership that was risky for both parties. Indeed, if a slave discovered a very large diamond or denounced his master for smuggling, he could be set free by the government. Thus it was in the master's interest to maintain good relations with his slaves. But the slave's cards in this game were more apparent than real, for he worked alone and often did not know how to take advantage of his strengths. He got no support from other slaves—on the contrary. Violence and competition prevailed among slaves as well as masters in the wild rush to acquire gold and diamonds. The slave miner's first concern was to protect himself—from the master, driven by greed and ready for anything, even murder, as well as from other slaves, desperate to amass enough money to buy their freedom. Many did manage to win their freedom, and then, but only then, did they begin to feel solidarity with those who continued to wear the yoke of slavery: religious confraternities were particularly numerous in the province of Minas Gerais. Life in the mines was therefore as harsh for the slave as life in the fields. Physically it was even more precarious. Sexuality was more repressed, owing to the small number of women employed in the extraction of gold and diamonds. But the slave was better off because of the prospect that he might gain his freedom, and he dreamed of liberty as he toiled at hard labor from sunup to sundown.

Coffee plantations did not really begin to develop until the second decade of the nineteenth century. Coffee growing expanded most rapidly after 1850, when the slave trade was officially abolished in Brazil. Plantation owners were forced not to waste black workers, who had become very expensive, and even to use whites hired locally among the smallholders displaced by the new plantations. White workers, many of whom were forced to do the hardest jobs such as land clearing and woodcutting, were always demanding higher wages. To the slaves they were a living example of the free life slaves wanted for themselves. Nevertheless, despite the presence of this large free population, the coffee planters introduced a patriarchal system modeled on that of the cane and cotton plantations in the northeast. It is widely maintained that coffee planters were more enlight-ened entrepreneurs and more efficient farmers than cane planters: the pa-triarchal economy is supposed to have given way to an industrial economy in which the slave was no longer a member of the family but an anony-mous worker, indeed a money-making "machine." In reality, however, daily life on the coffee plantations was quite similar to daily life on the engenhos of the northeast. After a breakfast of coffee, molasses, and boiled corn, slaves again recited their morning prayer while lined up in front of the master's house, waiting to be divided into work teams. Generally there were some fifty men and women, all wearing the broad hat characteristic of coffee workers, which they would raise to greet their master, at the same time uttering the words: "Praised be Our Lord Jesus Christ." To which the master would respond: "Praised be he for ever and ever." The oldest slaves worked the lands nearest the house, while younger men and women went off in separate groups, carried by carts known as *maxambula* to more remote fields. In the distance one could hear the *quimzumba*, songs in African tongues led by the *mestre cantor*. Each group was watched by two "leaders," almost always slaves. The ten o'clock meal was served in wooden or tin plates: corn porridge, black beans, and pieces of lard covered with a thick layer of manioc flour. The kettles on the cart were also filled with sweet potatoes, cabbage, and turnips, and everything was highly seasoned with pepper and parsley. At one o'clock there was another break for coffee together with a kind of corn muffin. In winter workers might warm them-selves with whiskey. Dinner was served at four o'clock. Then work re-sumed until nightfall, when the cry was heard to "Stop work!" ("*Vamos largar o servico!*"). Yet it was not uncommon on coffee plantations for work to continue even after nightfall. Night work, known as *serão*, could con-tinue until ten or eleven. In winter the coffee beans had to be dried. And it was always necessary to prepare the next day's meals, to cut wood, and to tend the animals. Before going to bed slaves were served a ration of corn, a piece of dried meat, and some manioc meal.

Outwardly, then, there was little apparent difference between the life of a slave on a coffee plantation and that of a slave on an engenho, except per-haps that the working day was slightly longer for the coffee worker. Yet master-slave relations seem to have been more cordial in the northeast than in the center-west. This happened no doubt because slaves working on the coffee plantations came into contact with many free white workers. Free workers were often better prepared than slaves, better at working the land, so that comparison favored the white worker. This preference for whites drove a wedge between master and slave and encouraged radical protests within the slave community. As slave living conditions improved, rebellions increased. Ideas popularized by the abolitionist movements helped to raise slave consciousness. To prevent slaves from meeting, many masters eliminated the Sunday rest and instead gave selected groups of slaves afternoons off during the week. Some slaves were allowed to use their time off to plant coffee or vegetables, which they then sold to their master or to inns on the highways. The Swiss traveler Pradez recounts that on one fazenda in Rio province he came upon a tavern run by an old slave "aunt." She sold whiskey, tobacco, mirrors, hats, and cotton clothing of better quality than that supplied by the master. White men kept taverns on the major roads and often received goods stolen by slaves or even contraband coffee. Their relations with slaves, who were the best clients, were quite cordial. Other friends of the slaves included tailors and seamstresses, some free, some manumitted. For the masters they cut to order trousers, white shirts, and short jackets for men and skirts, blouses, and scarves for women, who generally chose what design they wanted. Every two years the slave received a wool coat, and every year he received a new blanket. Clothes were washed and mended only once a week. Housed, like their brothers in the northeast, in usually dirty senzalas, and sometimes forced to work in wet clothes, slave coffee workers also suffered from the same diseases and were at the mercy of the same healers and barbers with their herbal remedies and bloodletting, which constituted the only available therapy. Coffee planters often abandoned slaves ill with tuberculosis or leprosy, and wretched groups of vagabonds formed and finally sought refuge in the cities, to the dismay of city leaders, who railed against such unscrupulous owners. Coffee growers in any case considered a working life of fifteen years optimum for a slave. It was only after the slave trade was abolished in 1850 that masters began to take better care of their slaves and to employ physicians on the fazenda.

The life of the slave on a coffee plantation, therefore, was quite similar to that of a slave on a sugar plantation. But the lives of city slaves were quite different. In town workers fell into two distinct groups. One group consisted of whites—poor but free men who had come to Brazil to try their luck—and manumitted slaves, whose numbers increased steadily from the eighteenth century on. The other group consisted of slaves, who gradually replaced free workers of European origin in lower status jobs. This dichotomy was accentuated by the division between artisanal and manual labor. Manual labor lost all prestige and came to be regarded as slave work. Even artisanal work was of course considered slave work until the nineteenth century. Eventually labor became so abundant that free workers attempted to have municipal governments reserve certain jobs for them, such as stevedore and sailor. Since urban slaves were dispersed among many owners and assigned in many cases to work by themselves, was it possible for them to form groups that fostered solidarity? On the plantations slaves lived and worked together. The slave who panned for gold found it hard to make friends with other slaves, his competitiors in the race to accumulate enough money to buy freedom. But what about the slaves in the Atlantic ports and in the cities of the mining regions? Did they form friendships with other slaves in the same craft, or from the same tribe? Consider the case of the old capital, Bahia. I have systematically examined 6,593 letters of manumission granted in Bahia between 1779 and 1850. These "freedom charters" were recorded by a notary. The common life of the slave is recorded in precise, personal terms in these official documents, which allowed the master ample scope to explain why and how he came to manumit this particular slave, whose qualities and humble life story were often described in great detail.

One thing is certain: the urban slave was generally not as highly trained for his work as tradition would have it. Domestic slaves were easily turned into "breadwinners" who went out on behalf of their masters and sold their ingenuity, their wares, or their physical strength. The urban slave was a person of many talents. Some obviously had learned in Africa or in their master's employ a specific trade, such as cook, coachmen, embroideress, seamstress, caulker, mason, boilermaker, carpenter. They could sell their skills, provided there was a market for them. Other slaves sold their talent as salesmen. Everything was for sale in Salvador: tinware, fruits and vegetables, corn bread and muffins, dried meat and fish cooked African-style. The *ganho* (or slave for hire) sold his physical strength: he could work as a chair carrier or stevedore, essential jobs in a city of steep slopes. The British consul James Wetherell has left us a good description of these black porters and stevedores:

> When they work, they are as naked as can be: their clothing consists of a roughly made and inadequate pair of shorts. They carry smaller items on their heads, while larger objects, such as wine casks, are suspended from poles that they carry on their shoulders. I have seen large blocks of wood carried by thirty or more Negroes, and the

whole thing looked like an enormous centipede. As they carry these heavy loads through the streets, they chant a sort of chorus, a useful way of warning people to get out of the way, for it is hard to hear anything amid the surrounding tumult. The choruses generally begin with a chanted remark by one of the Negroes on something that he sees, often something faintly ridiculous. The others respond in chorus. Collectively the Negroes carry very heavy loads, but each of them individually could not carry as much as a European. They are very independent and would pass up a chance to earn some money rather than carry more than they think right. From their habit of carrying things on their heads, they hold their bodies quite erect. Women in particular are very skillful: an orange, a cup of tea, a bottle, a lighted candle are all placed on the head, leaving the hands free. They seem to carry objects with equal sureness on their bare heads or on the scarves they use as turbans.

Slaves normally specialized in trades for which there was a demand or which were chosen for them by their masters. The possibility of shifting large numbers of slaves from one occupation to another helped to stabilize a market in which demand varied with circumstances and competition. Slaves were often simply placed in a labor pool. It was possible to hire a slave by the day, the week, the month, the year, or longer. For short periods (a day or a week) a verbal contract generally sufficed, but for longer periods a document was drawn up and signed before a notary. It specified the duration of the work, the services to be performed, and the price. The employer was obliged to supply room, board, clothing, and medical care to the hired slave. Since the slave owed a specified number of days of work, if he fell ill the duration of employment would be extended to make up for the lost time. In the cities, slaves sometimes became regular workers and received a daily wage, all of which had to be turned over to the master, who might decide to give the slave a "bonus." But if the master did not contribute to the slave's upkeep, he owed him remuneration. The system was thus highly flexible: sometimes the master provided room, board, clothing, and medical treatment, sometimes he offered only room and medical treatment, and sometimes he left the slave entirely on his own. In the latter two cases, the slave had only to pay his master a fixed sum each day. This sum was obviously determined in such a way that it would have been difficult for the slave to save much of what he earned. Still, it is clear that urban slaves enjoyed much greater freedom of action than rural slaves.

Although they were not always under the surveillance of their master, they were vulnerable to market conditions and to competition with other slaves. Masters also suffered from competition. Slaves were sources of income, and in this respect the interest of the master coincided with the interest of the slave. For that reason masters did not interfere with certain slave organizations, whose goal was to help slaves win their daily struggle to earn a living.

Because slaves in the same trade competed with one another, these slave organizations tended to be based on ethnic origin. The black community was divided into more or less hostile factions. The government found it advantageous to encourage hostility between different "peoples," as well as between Africans and creoles, blacks and mulattoes, freed men and slaves, in order to prevent them from forming a common front against the ruling establishment. The risk was in fact high in a city like Salvador, where nearly half the population consisted of slaves, and whites were in the minority. Toward the middle of the nineteenth century, whites represented about 25 percent of the population of Bahia. Division by ethnic group was apparently sharper among men than among women, perhaps because in trades practiced mainly by men the effects of the law of supply and demand were especially harsh. Generally speaking, men of different "nations" gathered at different cantos, or streetcorners, to await their clients. Women had fewer cantos, and the ones they had were less exclusive than the men's. While waiting for customers they wove straw hats and baskets or made small iron chains and bird cages for parakeets, as well as pearl bracelets and leather objects decorated with seashells. They also mended the precious umbrellas that were carried in accordance with African custom, by those who had been "nobles" in their homelands: made of yellow nankeen, these umbrellas added a gay note to the many colors in the street. The freed men who gathered at a particular canto obeyed the orders of a so-called canto captain. While waiting they sat on three-legged stools. Itinerant barbers came and shaved them, and black women sold corn and tapioca pudding that the *ganhadores* ate with bread or African-style rice prepared with dried meat and a peppery sauce or else with yams and grilled whale meat. At the cantos freed men were often joined by slaves practicing the same trade, and the friendships that grew up between members of the same ethnic group who did the same kind of work proved solid and durable. They were responsible for the foundation of many manumission societies and religious confraternities, which helped to encourage solidarity and mutual aid among urban slaves.

Refuges and Refusals

It was through work that blacks achieved the basic security indispensable for survival. If they did their work well, masters eased up on surveillance and left them alone. Slaves helped one another on the job, so that each man enjoyed the esteem and support of the entire group. But all people need some autonomy, and slaves could not get all they needed from the working group whether in town or in the countryside. Other refuges were essential. Slave owners were aware of this and tried to meet the need through religious associations or confraternities. But slaves found other refuges from their condition—some mysterious, some violent—and when these seemed to pose a danger to the slave system, the government and slave owners did not hesitate to combat them with every means at their disposal. In a sense, every slave association, whether authorized or prohibited, represented a refusal of, a protest against, an oppressive system. For slaves, to unite was to protest, even if that protest took the form of behavior sanctioned by the masters.

REFUGES ACCEPTED BY THE MASTERS

Slaves had little in common apart from their work. And even then there was much diversity: what did field hands have in common with shepherds and cowboys, or those who worked in the forests with those who worked in the savannah, or ancestor- or totem-worshippers with the followers of Islam? But Slavery in fact, even as it destroyed the underpinnings of African society and indiscriminately mingled members of different ethnic groups, preserved the essential religious values of African society. Slave society was a melting pot out of which came a novel religion of which slave owners had no inkling. We are still largely in the dark about the nature of this religion, and the interpretations that I am giving are tentative and should be treated with caution.

The slave was confronted with two forms of religious practice. First there was was the Catholic religion, which, though difficult to assimilate, enjoyed the prestige of being the masters' religion. It was based on a trinitarian God, more feared than loved, a God who was vengeful in this world but held out the promise of paradise in the next. Then there was African religion or, rather, there were African religions, as varied as were the peoples and communities of Africa itself. Gradually, however, these African religions tended to coalesce, to evolve toward a form acceptable to all, to broaden to the point where they could serve as a coherent cultural reference for the entire black community. Little by little there developed new forms of religion not based on the European or on any single African model. The slave saw his religious life as proceeding on two different levels; neither could be reduced to the other, and the two were compatible only because they did not intersect. The term "syncretism," which is often used to describe the religious practices of black Brazilians, is in my opinion a misnomer, for there were in fact two parallel religious modes based on two entirely different sets of values. It was quite possible to be both a good Christian and a good "pagan," for both religious systems were complete unto themselves. To be sure, from the early days of slavery until as late, perhaps, as the eighteenth century, there was a chaotic profusion of unorganized cults in Brazilian African communities, cults that are often referred to in the sources as "games" or "amusements." But three "solutions" to the religious problem quickly came to the fore: the Bantu solution, the Fon-Yoruba solution, and, in the cities only, the Islamic solution.

Bantu religions were based on ancestor worship, which slavery destroyed by breaking the family tie. Bantu spirits were natural spirits, associated with certain African rivers, forests, and mountains. Again slavery broke the link, this time with nature. As a result, Bantu religions in Brazil were very susceptible to outside influences, and Bantu slaves adapted the Catholic and Indian cults of the dead to their own traditions. In the religious meeting places spirits—African *orishas* and Indian *cabocles*—were invoked separately, each in their own language, in a ceremony involving a trance that brought together members of two oppressed communities: Africans and native Indians. Or, to take another example, Bantus reinterpreted Catholicism in such a way that saints Benedict and Iphigenia became black saints who were worshipped as familial and national ancestors. It is common to contrast these Bantu cults with the Yoruban cult, which remained closer to African models: for example, the candomblés of Bahia, the *chango* of Pernambuco and Alagoas, and the *batuques* of Porto Alegre were Yoruban religious ceremonies. Nago slaves from Guinea and Dahomey, who began to arrive in Brazil in large numbers during the eighteenth century, had a powerful influence on the less highly structured cults of the Bantus. Among the Yoruba of Africa, the orisha, or spirit, was the leader of the family, and each orisha had his own "confraternity" to chant for him. In Brazil, the ancestor worship disappeared but the confraternities remained. Priests grouped the worshipers of all orishas in a single organization. Each spirit was invoked in turn, in a specified order known as the *shiru*. In Africa, as soon as a worshiper was possessed by his orisha the ritual came to an end. In Brazil, divine possessions proliferated. The Yoruban cults, quite common in both urban and rural areas, were highly organized, centered on a *terreiro,* or cloistered religious community, in some cases equipped with its own buildings and places of worship and always with its own hierarchy. The slave found security in these cults, and the community enjoyed having its own sacerdotal hierarchy, a source of social prestige for those who rose from the ranks of ordinary worshipers. The religious leaders became the leader of the entire community, an extended family like the patriarchal family but free of all interference from whites. The slave had a period of time set aside for the Christian religion and another for an African religion. We do not know what psychological stress this situation may have caused. The need for solidarity and for a spiritual life must generally have encouraged the newcomer to accept the cult established by the most influential community leaders. But try to imagine what it must have been like for a Muslim to find himself in a group of slaves practicing an animistic religion, or for a Bantu to join a community where Yoruban influence dominated, or, even more complicated, for a creole slave to confront black religions whose meaning he no longer understood. All these individuals must have been forced to find some compromise, to grope toward a modus vivendi in which unresolved contradictions must have produced constant tension.

Masters authorized dances and celebrations in keeping with African customs, provided there was no conflict with morality or religion. They encouraged surviving African "folklore" but never allowed the open practice of genuine religious cults, which seemed to them incompatible with Christianity. Since the masters' aim was to hasten the adaptation of black arrivals, such officially sanctioned folklore in many cases quickly lost its spontaneity and became an artificial exercise, particularly when it was sponsored by the civil and religious authorities and organized within the framework of a Christian confraternity placed under the patronage of Our Lady of the Rosary. These confraternities, based on Portuguese models, had earlier been introduced into the Congo by Portuguese missionaries, who had some success in converting subjects of the Congolese kingdom. Congolese slaves were therefore allowed, with the master's approval, to continue to worship in their own way, and a papal bull of 1681 gave instructions for organizing the celebration of the feast of Our Lady of the Rosary, set for the first Sunday in October. This included the election of a "king" and "queen" and of male and female judges, as well as African songs and dances, all under the watchful eye of whites, who even gave the elected leaders of the black community cash gifts to pay for the festivities.

How free were the slaves to choose their own leaders? Did the white-approved hierarchy coincide with the actual hierarchy of the black community? The responses to these two questions depend on the organization of the black community and on the charismatic qualities of its leaders. It was in the countryside that the master's influence weighed most heavily. In the cities, white supervision was much less rigid, and blacks, owing to their large numbers, could gather by "nation." We must be careful, however, not to underestimate the negative aspect of these ethnic solidarities, which destroyed the unity of the slave community and exacerbated inter-African rivalries.

The urban slave who sought to join a black community also faced another obstacle. In town, African culture was the culture of an ill-defined social class, which included both freed men and slaves. How many generations did it take before the children of a freed slave became socially assimilated, without any ties to the African culture of their ancestors? In some port cities, moreover, there was a constant influx of new arrivals from Africa, whereas the number of new arrivals from Europe was small, so that white society itself was heavily influenced by African culture.

As in the countryside, the first urban black associations were religious. They were modeled after religious confraternities, some imported from Portugal, some developed in Brazil itself, whose purpose was to involve laymen in the mission of spreading the faith. The earliest confraternities in the colonial cities had a white membership, and only after the towns began to grow in the late seventeenth century and the number of slaves and freed men increased did we see the first "colored" confraternities emerge. Free men, freed slaves, and slaves were grouped according to ethnic background: for example, Our Lady of Baixa-dos-Sapateiros of Bahia admitted only Angolan blacks, whereas Our Lord of the Redemption was composed exclusively of Gégés. Other confraternities accepted only mulattoes, and hence creoles. By the eighteenth century, however, less exclusive confraternities were formed, and in the following century, when civic associations increasingly supplanted religious organizations, ethnic distinctions lost almost all significance. These urban confraternities had a very simple hierarchy—the same for both black and white confraternities. The directorate, which served for one year, consisted of male and female judges, a procurator charged with investigating the private lives of members, a treasurer, and a secretary. The directorate chose the years's "king" and "queen." Wealthy confraternities had their own church, while others occupied an altar in a convent or a parish church, where black and white confraternities sometimes came together.

As both a religious organization and a mutual aid society, the confraternity was supposed to cultivate the faith of its members and, through dues collected, to aid those in need, including invalid slaves cast out by their masters and young women without dowries; money was also collected to pay for manumissions. For reasons of social prestige masters often made large gifts to selected confraternities. Collections were organized both inside and outside the church. Some confraternity members left bequests to the community when they died. As a result, certain confraternities became economically powerful and invested in real estate or spent large sums to decorate their chapels; they also made loans at interest and played an important social role. The confraternity was a corporatist institution that fostered social cohesion and helped to regulate social relations between groups separated by skin color, economic power, and cultural heritage. What proportion of the slaves and freed population belonged to confraternities? Were they reserved for a privileged few? Organizations claiming the patronage of Jesus or his mother or some favored saint were so numerous that it seems reasonable to assume that nearly every black could have found at least one community ready to meet his or her material and spiritual needs. It was easy to belong to more than one confraternity if piety demanded, since these were primarily religious organizations and not mutual aid groups. Confraternities organized celebrations, masses and processions, confessions and communions; they taught religion and kept a watch on the spiritual life of the faithful. Unbaptized members were not admitted. Neither were unmarried couples, at least in theory. Confraternal constitutions were approved by the authorities. The wills of freed slaves preserved in notarial archives are most edifying: among the members of confraternities one finds a constant concern to enjoy a "good death." In the churches we can still admire all sorts of paintings and sculptures on the themes of Christ on the Cross, Christ in the Tomb, and the Mater Dolorosa. Death, burial, and indeed all rites of passage—from confession to communion to extreme unction to prayers for the dead—fell within the purview of the confraternities. Close as the Brazilian black may have remained to his African culture, and to whatever degree he participated in traditional forms of worship of which we know very little because he was obliged to hide them, he was intensely preoccupied by the desire to die a good death. He counted on the protection of his creator, the Virgin Mary, his patron saint, his guardian angel, and all the saints in heaven. And he took a passionate interest in the funeral rites, be they splendid or simple, and prayers for the repose of his soul that his confraternity would observe after he was gone.

We cannot state with any assurance that these confraternities, Catholic in form, also provided the institutional setting for the practice of African religious cults. In Salvador, however, we do find some support for this hypothesis: the Nago-Yoruba of the Ketu nation met, we are told, in the church of the Barroquinha and formed the Confraternity of Our Lady of the Good Death, which staged a procession every August 15. But oral tradition of the Nago-Yoruba, who still practice their religions in Bahia today, holds that it was not until 1830 that a true African religion was organized when a "saint's father" (*Babalorixa*) and a fortune-teller and priest of Ifé, the god of divination (or *Babalao*), were brought from Africa. The two priests are supposed to have come to Brazil as slaves of two freed women who returned to Africa to find them and bring them back. In any case, African cults never practiced their rites in the same places used for Catholic rites. The African or his children might practice two religions simultaneously, but each had its own rules, its own setting, its own physical space. It is therefore hard to see how Catholic churches could have been used by African cults.

No doubt blacks did, however, take advantage of the freedom of association they enjoyed in the confraternities to make contacts that may well have led to meetings for other purposes. In Salvador, at any rate, African cults remained clandestine until the middle of the nineteenth century. They were severely persecuted by the police. Consider, for example, the following excerpts from the press for 1855, eloquent in their dryness:

Arrested and placed at the disposition of the police were Christovam Francisco Tavares, emancipated African, Maria Salomé, Joanna Francisco, Leopoldina Maria de Conceição, Escolastica-Maria de Conceição, free creoles, slaves Rodolpho Araujo Sa Barretto, mulatto, Melanio, creole, and African women Maria Thereza, Benedicta, Silvana with nursling, and Maria, also with son, who were at the place known as Engenho Velho in a meeting to which they referred as a *candomblé*. [*Jornal da Bahia*, 5 May 1855]

On the night of the twelfth, a house in Victoria parish known as a *candomblé* and used for various purposes as a meeting place, was encircled. Most of the group consisted of gullible people who gave offerings to have their fortunes told. The thirty-two people arrested were transferred during the morning of the day before yesterday to the prison of the Aljube. [*Jornal da Bahia*, 15 April 1855]

African cults probably always existed in colonial Brazil, meeting clandestinely and sporadically in the hope of escaping persecution. The dominant class did not concern itself with these cults unless they somehow threatened law and order.

Toward the end of the eighteenth century a new type of association between freed men and slaves in the cities began to emerge: the so-called manumission societies, a sort of loan fund managed by Africans. Each member had a small square stick on which an official of the society marked his deposits with cuts. Another African was given responsibility for collections. The money collected, generally in small copper coins, could be loaned out at interest, especially for the purpose of purchasing manumission. At the end of the year, dividends were distributed. It is not known whether the membership of these associations was restricted to people of certain ethnic groups, but we do know that at about the same time various lay organizations for mutual worker aid were formed, such as the Society of Artisans or the Poor Man's Protective Society. Only blacks could belong to these groups, whose statutes make no reference to any ethnic restrictions.

As the nineteenth century progressed, ethnic antagonisms, which had been so important in earlier periods, gradually faded. The evidence of wills shows clearly that emotional bonds no longer have anything to do with belonging to the same African nation. A change of attitude? A desire to establish a true African community by glossing over controversial issues? It is hard to know for sure. In any case, it seems that lay associations of this type did not exist in the cities of the interior, and especially in Minas Gerais. There the confraternities must have supplanted for the propagation of the faith the religious orders banned by the government, whereas in the Atlantic ports the Jesuits, Franciscans, Carmelites, and Benedictines played a major role in catechizing Africans. In the interior, the secular clergy, all of Portuguese origin, were the sole representatives of religious authority, and as society in the mining regions was regimented and closely watched, the Catholic priest must have seemed more like an army chaplain than a pastor. The confraternities were therefore an essential part of the government's efforts to attenuate the system's authoritarian aspects. They helped to bring blacks into the fold of official Catholicism. The prescriptions of Christian morality were here taken more seriously than in the northeast, and slaves were married to prevent concubinage. Many black confraternities in the Minas accepted whites as members, no doubt owing to fraternization on the job between free men and slaves. Manumission was never a leading concern of confraternities in the mining regions, because slaves could always hope to strike it rich and overnight become wealthy enough to buy their freedom.

The confraternities were real melting pots for Africans: everyone enjoyed the same social condition, without distinction as to ethnic background or color. But antagonisms did sometimes develop between creoles and Africans, freed men and slaves, mulattoes and blacks. For example, in the diamond region of the Minas, the confraternity of Our Lady of Tijuco split into two groups when a creole faction left to found the confraternity of Our Lady of Mercy, the confraternity of the "natural creoles of Brazil." Among the freed slaves of the Minas there was a large mixed-race population, and relatively well educated half-breeds were able to wield substantial influence in the face of white society. It was no longer color that divided the economic forces, but social status, since some blacks as well as mulattoes were able to become artisans, professionals, and even landowners and farmers. This trend developed around 1760, as mine output declined, leading to a decrease in new slave arrivals. The slave stock was not replenished. Hence it was easier to assimilate, at least in appearance, those already there. The opposite happened in the coffee-growing regions, where one found few blacks or half-breeds working as artisans owing to competition from large numbers of white European immigrants. In these areas solidarity was usually the result of violence and confrontation.

INDIVIDUAL REBELLION

The following notice appeared in the *Journal da Bahia* for 14 November 1857:

Fled on 31 January while on his way to buy bread at Bonfim, the Mina slave David, average height, stout, three lines on either side of his face, always smiling, he has been spotted between Calçada and Bonfim. It is believed that he has been taken into a home, and a complaint has been lodged already for work days lost and for objects that he took with him. Whoever captures and returns him to his master at Hospice no. 44 shall receive a reward of 20,000 reis.

Or consider this notice, published in the *Diàrio de Rio* in 1826: "Disappeared from the home of Antonio José Moreira Pinto, a nameless bossale black."

Along with suicide and murder, flight was a way for the maladjusted slave to give outward expression to inward rebelliousness. The runaway slave fled not only his master and his work but the insuperable problems of daily life. He also fled his station in life, his lack of roots in either the slave or the white community. David, sent to buy bread in the Bonfim district of Bahia, was certainly no newcomer to Brazil, whereas the runaway in Rio had landed quite recently, so recently, in fact, that he had not yet received a new name. Not speaking Portuguese, he took a great risk in trying to escape. But both men refused the lot of the slave, always to give and never to receive, and both chose to run away in search of support, assistance, and affection. Creoles and ladinos, men and women, young and old, people of all walks of life and many different backgrounds filled the "runaway slaves" columns of the Brazilian newspapers. Slaves left city jobs as well as plantations: "Fled from the Timbo plantation belonging to Ignaçio Borges de Barros, a slave named Maria, Nago nation, short and fat, face highly marked, missing upper portion of the right ear, because of which she always wears a turban on her head. Anyone returning her to her owner or providing accurate information as to her whereabouts shall be well rewarded for his trouble" (*Jornal da Bahia*, 23 January 1855). Slaves fled in the worst of circumstances, unaware that distinctive signs, as in this case Maria's ear, would lead to easy detection. The country was strange, immense, hostile. Only a few slaves living along the borders could hope to reach a neighboring land. Some stowed away on ships sailing for Africa, only to be discovered at the first inspection. Some hoped to find a better master and only went from Charybdis to Scylla. Any escapee who did not find refuge with a group was doomed to be captured. Communities of rebel slaves were repeatedly established throughout the long history of Brazilian slavery. Some runaways were lucky enough to be accepted by Indian tribes. If a slave succeeded in marrying an Indian man or woman, the law declared both the slave and the children of the marriage free, for the government, solicitous of the Indians' welfare from the early eighteenth century on, hoped in this way to prevent unscrupulous masters from reducing the Indians to slavery by encouraging intermarriage with slaves. Sometimes a slave would try repeatedly to return to the plantation after being sold in town. Another might flee the country for the city. Some even had counterfeit manumission papers drawn up. Some runaways got what they wanted: the person with whom they sought refuge purchased them from their former master, giving the slave the right to work for a master of his own choosing. It was practically impossible to live by oneself in a country as vast as Brazil, but even when couples fled together they were in for a very dangerous adventure. Consider this story, for example, told by Hercule Florence, who, during a voyage to Amazonia in 1841 found on an island near the Itupuerama Cataract a black woman who had been living alone for three months. She and her husband, both slaves at Camapuà, had run away, traveled down the river Pardo and back up the Parana and the Tiete, finally taking refuge on a little island where they built a cabin. They had six happy months together, hunting and fishing, until one day the husband drowned while trying to swim across the river. An hour after being discovered, the woman was returned to her master.

We have no idea how many slaves ran away. It must have been more difficult to flee a plantation than a job in the city. Escapes were probably easier during wartime. Running away probably became quite tempting in the 1870s, by which time a fair proportion of the free population subscribed to abolitionist ideas and was willing to aid fugitives. What about slaves who saved enough money to buy their freedom but whose masters refused to manumit them? Did they then attempt to gain their freedom by running away? If so, they did not often succeed. One slave, for example, had made a fortune while working on his own, away from his master, and owned six slaves of his own. In exchange for his freedom he offered four of those slaves to his owner, when he was recognized and arrested by the police. The master flatly refused to free the man and, to add insult to injury, took possession of his six slaves.

Fugitive slaves were almost always captured. Informers were attracted by offers of reward. Those who might help were deterred by fear of punishment. The Brazilian church offered no right of asylum. Captured fugitives often refused to give the name of their master. They rotted in prison, and some slave owners were hardly eager to have them back, for it was often more expedient to "forget" about a fugitive than to pay the costs of his capture and upkeep. In 1876 the Aljube prison in Bahia held 403 unclaimed fugitives. Throughout Brazil prisons were crowded with abandoned runaways.

The slave who fled an unbearable situation had nothing to lose and hoped to improve his luck. But, for others there seemed to be no exit, and in their despair they resorted to suicide. Suicides were more common in the cities than in the countryside, even though the urban slave enjoyed greater autonomy than his brother in the fields. Police reports, in their cruelly crisp style, tell us some things that drove slaves to suicide: the impossibility of complaining to the authorities about unjust treatment, inability to pay the master the sum due under the terms of a contract for a slave de ganho, false accusations, fear of being sold and forced to move long distances, a failed escape attempt, a discovered theft. It was always fear that led to suicide, for which many means were found: asphyxia from swallowing one's own tongue, hanging, strangulation, eating dirt. It was common to punish slaves caught eating dirt by forcing them to wear zinc masks. But what could be done about the slave who let himself die of consumption? Slaves who decided that they wanted to die stopped eating, lost weight, and faded away: this was the so-called *banzo,* or slow suicide, a kind of terminal nostalgia. Slaves committed suicide far more often than free men: in 1865, for example, four out of five suicides in Sergipe involved slaves. In Rio in 1866, it was sixteen out of twenty-three. And in Bahia in 1848, it was twenty-eight out of thirty-three, including two creole slaves. These figures may be misleading: if an angry master killed a slave, he might try to disguise the death as a suicide, whereas conversely, suicides by free men or women might have been declared to be natural deaths so as to obtain a church burial.

Sometimes slaves reacted to their plight not by running away or committing suicide but by resorting to violence. With the same shovel, hoe, spade, or knife he used on the job a slave could kill the master or the overseer who was always punishing him or his mother or his friend. Recalcitrant slaves, or those reputed to be recalcitrant, were sometimes subjected to terrible punishments. Repression led to rebellion, a vicious circle from which the slave could escape only by invoking the law of an eye for an eye, a tooth for a tooth. The least punishment that a master could inflict on a slave was to confine him, usually in chains. Every plantation had its iron collars and bracelets and masks and trunks (see Glossary) for holding slaves fixed by the neck or ankle or torso for days at a time. In the nineteenth century even free European colonists were subjected to the trunk on coffee plantations. Until 1824 it was legal to mutilate disobedient slaves—they could be branded with hot irons, their fingers could be crushed with thumbscrews, and their ears and toes could be cut off—and such punishments were not uncommon. But the whip remained the primary instrument of repression. Its use was not abolished until 1886. To be sure, in 1830 a regulation prohibited administering more than fifty lashes at a time. As a result, punishments of 300–400 lashes were spread out over several days, which lessened the danger of killing the slave, the likely result if the entire punishment had been meted out at one session. Reaction to such punishments sometimes took the form of collective violence, as was the case with eleven slaves from Campinas near São Paulo, who murdered the overseer Malaquias in 1868. This overseer detested the slave Raphael and used any pretext to whip him or tie him to the stake. One day the slaves begged the overseer to pardon Raphael. When he refused, they killed him with shovels. A case of unpremeditated murder? That is not clear: these slaves meted out their own justice, because the courts were closed to them. They could not take complaints to court directly but had to be represented either by their master or by a third party, which was not easy, particularly in the countryside.

Slaves who committed murder were always sentenced to death until 1876, when the death penalty was abolished for everyone in Brazil. Brazilian historiography and legal anthologies stress this problem. The masters never felt entirely secure. Even when the danger of overt violence was small, they still worried about being poisoned. Repeated small doses of certain poisons were known to cause death. So great was the fear of slow poisoning that when a master found out that one of his slaves was a "sorcerer" or "witch doctor" who knew something about herbs and magic, he often hastened to sell him. He also knew that the slave who hated his white masters had his own ways of taking revenge, such as voodoo magic that could make people sick or kill as surely as a poisoned arrow. Whites trembled before the dark forces that they believed Africans capable of unleashing. It is difficult to say whether crime was more common in the slave than in the free population: the few existing studies of the question are not very convincing. It appears, however, that the crime rate was lower among slaves, probably owing to tight surveillance and strict regimentation.

Subtle forms of opposition, not quite criminal, were extremely common, however. Forced to labor, buffeted back and forth between white and black leaders, between the masters and their friends, the slave— obedient, loyal, and humble as he was, and utterly devoid of power and authority—had his own means of protesting against his situation. He was capable of many kinds of sabotage. Some acts the master eventually discovered, such as thefts of food, clothing, money, and above all merchandise, which was constantly spirited away from coffee fazendas and diamond mines. Other forms of protest undermined the authority of leaders: slowdowns, repeated work stoppages, spoiled work, harassment of blacks and creoles who served the master. Protest began in the master's own house. A cook ordered to do a chambermaid's work by a tactless mistress would never do the job properly. The queen of the household was the old black nurse, one of the senior members of the black community, the "uncles" and "aunts" of whom the slaves were sometimes more wary than they were of their white masters. Deceiving the master was a game justified by the oppression of which the slaves were victims. Slaves sang the following song with anger in their voices:

> Branco diz o preto furta
> Preto furta com razão
> Sinho branco tamben furta
> Qunado faz a escravidão

> The white man says: the black man steals.
> The black man steals for good reason.
> Mister white man also steals
> When he makes us slave

One form of collective resistance was for a group of slaves to make off with a portion of the harvest and sell it to a dealer in stolen goods. In a system based on forced labor, rebellions—some organized, some not, some spontaneous, others planned—were inevitable. It may have seemed less risky to slaves to rebel as a group or to hide in so-called *quilombos* than it was for individuals to run away or disobey orders, and collective action was certainly less desperate than suicide.

COLLECTIVE RESISTANCE: QUILOMBOS AND INSURRECTIONS

A quilombo was a hideout where fugitive slaves gathered. To flee to such hiding places was not the same thing as to engage in organized insurrection against white power. The slaves hiding in the quilombo wanted no trouble and resorted to violence only if attacked by the police or army or if necessary for survival. Quilombos and *mocambos* (forest hideouts) were found all over Brazil from the sixteenth century on. Does this indicate a reaction against the slave system? a return to African ways of life far from the masters' rule? a protest against the conditions of slavery more than against slavery as such? a desire to practice African religions in freedom? The quilombos were all these things. They were a product of the instability of the slave system, of an unimaginative work regime, of harsh discipline, injustice, and mistreatment. They offered a resolution to the problems of slaves torn between the white and the black community. They appeared suddenly in large numbers in a society in which blacks were in the majority and the police were totally incapable of preventing the establishment of such marginal communities. The *quilombolas,* as the slaves gathered in the quilombos were called, found the support they needed to live on the fringes of society. Yet quilombos were never planned. They grew up spontaneously. A single hideout might shelter black Africans and creoles, slaves and even free men victimized by some discriminatory law. Among the free and freed men in the quilombos were often deserters, thieves, murderers, sometimes joined by men who had been forbidden to practice a certain trade. Thus the inhabitants were quite a varied lot. Most quilombos were hidden in hard-to-reach rural areas, far from the cities, the highways, and the plantations. This was the case, for example, with the celebrated quilombo dos Palmares, which was established in the seventeenth century in the interior of the present-day state of Alagoas, then attached to the captaincy of Pernambuco. It was also true of the very famous mocambo of Pará, established around 1820 northwest of Manaus in the forest along the Trombetas River. But some quilombos were established just outside of large cities. The army did not manage to destroy the Bahian quilombo of Cabula, hidden in the heavily wooded recesses of the woods around Salvador, until the early nineteenth century. A royal "provision" of 6 March 1741 laid it down that a quilombo was any clandestine group of more than five fugitive slaves. Nineteenth-century provincial laws reduced the number to two or three. But there were enormous differences between a quilombo inhabited by hundreds or even thousands of fugitives and a hut that offered refuge to a handful of slaves. The larger quilombos created whole new social organizations, with their own hierarchies and economic and political authorities, while the smaller ones were shifting, unstable alliances among fugitives who lived by pillage and behaved rather like guerrillas. It is said that when the quilombo of Palmares was destroyed in 1695, thirty thousand fugitive slaves resided there, and that when the mocambo of Trombetas was destroyed in 1823, it was home to some two thousand people! Most quilombos were inhabited by a few hundred men and women. Their population varied with time and circumstances. The only ones we know much about are those with which the forces of law and order came into contact. All signs suggest that hostility from the outside forced these communities to organize and become truly independent centers of production. To delve a little more deeply into life in the quilombos, I have chosen three that seem to me typical.

My first example is the quilombo dos Palmares, mentioned earlier: in 1630 Holland established a base in Pernambuco. The Portuguese recruited a black regiment led by the black hero Henrique Dias, who helped them fight the Batavian invaders. But other blacks, such as Calabar, organized to fight their former masters and collaborated with the enemy, while still others simply fled, thereby bringing down upon themselves the fury of both the Dutch and the Portuguese. Hiding in the lush, impenetrable forest of Palmares, where resources were abundant, these fugitives established a "republic," sixty square leagues in area and containing several towns: Zumbi, Arotirene, Tabocas, Dambrangaga, Subupira, Osenga, and Macaco, the capital, a fairly large town of some 1,500 dwellings. In 1643 the republic of Palmares had a population of six thousand. By 1670 it had climbed to twenty thousand. Subupira, the military training center, was a fortified village of eight hundred huts. The first elected leader of this republic was "King" Ganga-Zumba, who was murdered in 1678 because he had agreed to negotiate with the whites and to sign a peace treaty. His successor, the legendary Zumbi, embodied the idea of black resistance. Each king governed from his own village, which became the capital of the quilombo. They were assisted by a council of elders, chosen from among the heads of other villages. The king and village leaders had their own bodyguards. In Palmares one could find priests of all religions, Catholic and African. Any fugitive slave who sought refuge in the quilombo dos Palmares was considered a free man. On the other hand, a slave captured and brought to the quilombo remained a slave, though he was allowed to purchase his freedom. Only the leaders were well dressed. Ordinary people were not allowed to carry arms. Murder, adultery, and theft were severely punished. Palmares, like all quilombos, lacked women, and residents did not hesitate to embark on female-hunting expeditions to remote engenhos and towns. People lived by fishing and gathering as well as by raising corn, manioc, sweet potatoes, beans, and sugar cane. all of which were grown within the republic's borders. Hunting provided meat. Cattle and other livestock were not bred, but chickens moved around the huts. Masons, carpenters, tinsmiths, weavers, and potters all practiced their trades, and Palmares traded with the Dutch and even with the Portuguese. It took eighteen Dutch and Portuguese expeditions in all before Palmares was subdued, and historians still argue about whether the experiment should be seen as a novel but rational attempt to create an elective monarchy or as an expression of cultural resistance, of "tribal regression." Was this a "flight to Africa?" And if so, to what Africa, since Palmares was home to men from so many different backgrounds and social classes?

Innumerable expeditions were also required to subdue the quilombo of Trombetas in Para. In the Para region Indian workers were plentiful and there were relatively few Africans. The quilombo was established in 1821 when the *cafuzo* (mixed black and Indian) Atanasio, a slave of Major Martinho da Fonseca Seixas, took to the forest with forty companions. It took in survivors of two other well-known quilombos—Inferno and Cipotema, which were destroyed in 1812—along with other fugitives, who arrived in groups of twenty, thirty, or even a hundred. Atanasio was a despot who liked to sow fear everywhere. He had his subjects grow manioc and tobacco of good quality. His men gathered cacao and *salsaparilha* (sarsaparilla), a spice used in cooking and as a medication. These products were traded in large quantities in the port of Obidos, where the quilombolas of Trombetas did not hesitate to show themselves. There commercial contacts reached as far as Dutch Guyana and remote regions inhabited by scattered Indian tribes. The police managed to destroy Trombetas in 1823, but Atanasio, taken prisioner, escaped and established a second quilombo in the same region which endured until 1835. Survivors of that quilombo then moved farther upriver and founded the hamlet of Cidade Maravilha, the "marvelous city," a city so peaceful that its itinerant merchants could travel freely downriver to sell their wares. We know that in 1852 some of them came to have their children baptized in Catholic churches. If they happened to encounter their former masters, they asked for a blessing and were allowed to go unmolested.

Our final example is the quilombo known as Buraco do Tatu, near

Salvador, founded in the middle of the eighteenth century. It lived by theft, preying mainly on blacks who came to town from nearby plantations to sell food on the open market. This quilombo had confederates in the free as well as the slave population of Salvador, who provided it with food and weapons. To avoid possible reprisals, white planters preferred to collaborate with the fugitives of Buraco do Tatu, who, because they were not inclined to make total war on the whites to liberate their captive brethren, were not felt to be particularly dangerous. The village of Buraco do Tatu consisted of thirty-two rectangular houses arranged in six rows separated by a broad central street. Each house sheltered a monogamous couple, to judge from the lists drawn up when the quilombo was destroyed, which show sixty-five adults, including one creole black and two "sorcerers," one a *mandingue,* the other an old woman. The lists do not mention children, because children found in the quilombos generally became the property of members of the expeditionary force sent out to crush the fugitives. The village was quite similar to Bantu villages in northwest Africa, with its ramparts reinforced by a series of twenty-one traps, cleverly camouflaged with leaves and branches, a booby-trapped entrance, and a central house. Inside the village were a few fruit trees and herb gardens. Two leaders shared power: Captain Antonio de Souza, the military leader, and Teodoro, the administrative head of the community. Each leader had a wife who was given the title of "queen." In 1763 it took two hundred men, mostly Indians, to destroy this quilombo. During the attack four quilombolas were killed. None of the prisoners was sentenced to death. The leaders were sent to the galleys, the rest received corporal punishment. Thirty-one slaves were returned to their masters and branded with the letter F for fugitive, as set forth in the royal ordinance of 1741. The story of Buraco do Tatu is truly exemplary: like nearly all the quilombos of Brazil, it had fewer than one hundred residents and was established near a town in which it had many confederates. It was a community of rebels, welded together by the solidarity born of intransigence in the face of oppression.

These groups of hard-core intransigents naturally provoked a reaction by the forces of law and order. As early as the seventeenth century we find mention of an official known as the *capitão-do-mato* or *capitão-do-campo* (bush captain), generally a free man of color whose job was to capture fugitive slaves. He went from plantation to plantation inquiring whether any slaves had escaped. Accompanied by trained dogs and perhaps one or two men, the bush captain was adept at man hunting. If he captured a fugitive, he received an amount proportional to the distance covered. The law required the master to retrieve his slave from the prison of the nearest town, where he had to pay the costs of captivity plus the amount due to the bush captain. Quite a few of these bush captains neglected their duties. Some hired other people to do the job, while others put captured slaves to work for their own benefit. Often they were paid by the mother, concubine, or wife of a fugitive to look the other way. Since this system did not work very well, various quasi-military organizations were set up in the nineteenth century: "companies" of forest patrols, infantry, and militia. For major expeditions the army and Indians were brought in. Yet the number of quilombos continued to grow rapidly, even in the nineteenth century when the forces of order were well organized; this suggests that Brazilian society was unable to quell the rebellion in its midst, and indeed that many Brazilians served as its accomplices.

The problem was rather different when it came to dealing not with relatively peaceful quilombos but with open rebellion that posed a threat to the established order. Although the government could tolerate reasonably inoffensive marginal communities, it was terrified of organized insurrection. The law defined the enemy: "A gathering of twenty or more slaves intending to secure their freedom by means of force." Fear of mutiny was endemic in areas where there were large numbers of slaves or descendants of slaves. This was the case in the agricultural and mining regions and even in some parts of northern Brazil where natural crops were gathered. Actual insurrections were rare; most of the time it was just a matter of rumors that an insurrection was being planned. Conspirators were almost always arrested before they had time to act. If a spontaneous, unplanned uprising occurred, it was generally disorganized and easily put down.

The best-known (as well as the most studied) insurrections occurred in Bahia between 1807 and 1835, that is, at the end of the colonial period and in the early days of independence. Decolonization and the establishment of a nation state (1808–1840) created two kinds of tension in Bahia: tension within the slave class and tension within the class of free men, where there was conflict between the interests of the most powerful groups and those of the less fortunate. Each white mutiny and slave rebellion had its unique characteristics, shaped by specific but ever-changing economic and political circumstances. In the uprising of 1807, the plan was for the slaves from the engenhos of the Reconcavo to join the slaves of the city at the city gates. Together, these slaves, led by Hausas, were supposed to attack the whites, kill the masters, poison the public fountains, seize several ships anchored in the harbor, and sail for Africa. But the plot was betrayed and the rebellion nipped in the bud. Its leaders were sentenced to death. The secret was better kept in December 1808, when Nago and Hausa slaves organized a similar uprising: it took a pitched battle fifty kilometers outside of Salvador to put down the rebellion. Another plot was foiled by troops in 1810. Four years later, slaves attacked a fishery in the Itapōa region, killing the administrator, his family, and several whites who happened to be on the premises and setting fire to the buildings. Troops were sent up from nearby Salvador, and after a battle lasting several hours the rebellion was quelled. Of the fifty-six dead found on the field of battle, nearly all were, once again, Hausas. Witnesses reported that their battle cry had been, "Freedom, long live the Negroes and their King, death to whites and mulattoes." A court condemned four men to be hanged on the square of the Piédade and twenty-three others to be deported to Mozambique after a public flogging.

The wave of rebellions nevertheless continued in the towns as well as on the engenhos of the Bahian Reconcavo. Between 1816 and 1835, for example, there were five major uprisings. In 1830, twenty armed slaves *de ganho* attacked the slave depot belonging to the merchant Wenceslau Miguel de Almeida and freed one hundred newly arrived captives before they were taken by the police. But the last, most serious, and best organized of all the insurrections, which caused genuine panic in the white population of the city, took place on 25 January 1835. It came close to succeeding. The twenty-fifth of January was the date of the very popular festival of Our Lady of La Guia, which was celebrated in the church of Bonfim. The time set for the uprising to begin was the hour when slaves left their homes to fetch water from the public fountains. The plan, simple yet clever, was to distract the police by setting fires, which would also force the troops to leave their barracks. The insurgents, abetted by the ensuing confusion, would then disarm the soldiers and join the slaves from the Reconcavo. The plan had more chance of success than its predecessors, for previous rebellions had for the most part begun outside the city and the troops had been able to crush them fairly quickly. But once again, the plot was betrayed and the revolt cut short, despite a promising beginning: a small group of slaves did manage to intimate the guards of the provincial president's palace for several hours and to hold off an entire battalion of infantry.

The rebellion of 1835 was organized by slaves adhering to Islam. Was it a kind of "holy war" against the Christians? J.-J. Reis, in his study of insurrections among Bahian slaves, has shown that the role of the Muslim slaves was one of organization, of enforcing discipline and setting an example. The way Muslims helped one another inspired other Africans deprived of family, home, and community. Yet the 1835 uprising, like its predecessors, remained a "prepolitical" movement. It was political only to the extent that its goal was to seize power in order to redistribute it. Islam functioned as a common language, a catalyst. It welded together the slave community. The rebels' battle cry was, "Death to the whites, long live the Nago," and the fighting had no religious overtones. After 1835, moreover, the masters, seeing the situation as it was, declared war on Africans, and above all on freed Africans, large numbers of whom had been found among the rebels. Those who were arrested were deported to Africa. The government attempted to encourage Africans who wished to return to their native lands to do so. For the rebels looked upon whites, mulattoes, and creoles as so many enemies to overcome. Here we touch upon one of the reasons that all these attempts at rebellion failed: the slave community lacked cohesion and unity in its struggle against the authorities. It was unable to overcome its internal conflicts, its divisions between creoles and Africans, blacks and half-breeds, freed blacks and mulattoes.

Another reason for the failure of the rebellions was the effectiveness of repression: the army was strong and informers were plentiful. By attacking the entire free population—whites, creoles, and mulattoes—rebel Africans ultimately aroused a united "Brazilian front" against them. Solidarity born of intransigence came and went as slaves lived their daily lives. And the white authorities knew how to take advantages of every chink in the rebels' armor. Eventually the uprisings became the pretext for new proscriptions. Every rebellion led to more and more minute regulations. In 1807, for example, slaves were forbidden to move about freely after nine o'clock at night without written authorization from their masters. In 1814 *batuques*, songs and dances accompanied by a drum, hitherto considered innocuous, were banned. In 1832 a municipal ordinance provided for a fine of 8,000 reis or four days in prison for any slave owner who allowed a slave to loiter in town "for longer than required to make necessary purchases." Regulation after regulation was established, the combined effect of which was to limit slave movements so effectively that rebellion became impossible after 1840. Exploiting the panic created by the insurrections, the ruling classes terrorized the rest of the free population, cowed as it was by the black avalanche. The rulers exploited tensions between slaves and freed men of different ethnic stock and prevented the formation of a unified group bound together by common interests.

Thus those who rejected the slave system, from inhabitants of peaceful quilombos to members of secret associations of would-be rebels, never succeeded in rousing the entire slave population. The intransigents remained marginal and for the most part led precarious lives. To dissatisfied slaves they represented an almost mythical possibility of escape. But the dissatisfied were never able to unite and so to give force to their dream of freedom. For most slaves that dream eventually faded; the maladjusted managed to adjust and in many ways those who should have come together drew apart. This socialization created new men whose hopes were not incompatible with the organization of society as a whole. In the next section we shall discuss the new dreams of manumission and assimilation and try to understand how these affected the daily lives of humble men and women.

THE HOPE OF MANUMISSION

As we have seen, Brazilian society was able to afford its slaves limited but real areas of freedom—freedom essential for allowing slaves to forge new individual and social identities. The slave's life had two sides: a dual hierarchy, a dual morality, dual rules of behavior. To accept this dual life was really the only viable solution, since escape and rebellion nearly always ended in failure. Socialization eventually integrated the slave into this Janus-faced world, but his integration was ambiguous. The slave adapted by accommodating himself to his new surroundings. But insofar as he remained a slave without any possibility of individual advancement, he was imperfectly integrated into the larger society. Not until he became a free man, or at least envisaged the possibility of becoming free, did the slave complete the transition from wretched captive to hopeful citizen, cleverly and ambitiously seeking to improve his lot. Only then did the slave truly adapt to his environment, like the spider, the tortoise, or the chameleon; only then did he make use of cunning, that arm of the weak and oppressed, to make himself seem humble, loyal, and obedient to his masters and yet a worthy brother to his companions in servitude. The slave thus experienced his dual life as a temporary state of affairs, which would eventually lead to a better life, not the remote paradise promised by the priests but the life of freedom to be gained through manumission.

In reality, very few slaves were set free because in the first place manumission was a matter decided by the master and beyond the slave's control. Manumission could not be obtained unless the master wished to grant it.

A master might wish to free a slave who had worked for many years and brought sufficient return on the capital invested in him, or he might wish to realize his investment immediately. Manumission provided quick and easy cash and was less risky than selling the slave on the market, where the price depended on market forces and on the slave's condition. The master might also wish to reward a slave for services rendered by him or his parents. Finally, the master might wish to get rid of a troublesome slave who threatened to disrupt the tranquillity of his family or his plantation or to dispose of a sick or elderly slave or of a child too young to work. On the eve of abolition many masters granted freedom to dozens of slaves on condition that they agree to work for free for seven more years—a legal means of prolonging the time of slavery. Some masters attempted to replace black workers with Europeans: this happened in coffee-growing regions, where the slave system fell apart earlier than it did elsewhere.

All slaves wished to secure their freedom, but how many had the means to do so? How many harbored in their heart of hearts that fear of the unknown that prevented them from making any real effort to make their dreams come true? The masters, as we have seen, were often adept at offering their slaves an environment in which they could feel secure. What did freedom mean to an elderly slave with no special skills, a field hand, who found himself liberated but without land and free only to go, not to stay on the plantation that he had come to know, whose white and black communities had become his second home? How heavily did the desire for freedom weigh in the heart of a timid urban slave, unsure of himself and in need of his master's assistance to find work in a highly competitive labor market? What did freedom mean to a crippled, sick, or suffering slave? And what about the bitterness of freedom for the slave who was forced to part from the white child she had nursed, raised, and loved? The reward of freedom had its pitfalls and could end in despair when manumission was imposed, as it sometimes was, by an all-powerful master.

If a slave really wanted freedom, could he obtain it? In more than 90 percent of the cases, freedom was bought for a sum of money which was difficult to come by. Slaves in the mines and cities had a clear advantage over field hands on the plantations, yet the field hands constituted the bulk of the Brazilian slave population. Field workers rarely sold any of the crops they raised on their private plots, which went first to supplement their daily rations. They produced for a subsistence economy, not for a market economy. Their best hope was to obtain their freedom free of charge by serving their former master as an *agregado*, or plantation supervisor. But agricultural society seems to have been quite rigid. The slave who gained his freedom, who generally had no land of his own in the vicinity, became a marginal individual. Field hands were therefore less combative than city slaves, particularly in the traditional agricultural regions of the northeast, where sugar planters preferred to share their lands with free farmers rather than manumitted slaves. To tell the truth, our information about agricultural land ownership in eighteenth- and nineteenth-century Brazil is too fragmentary to enable us to state with any confidence what the differences were between the various regions of this immense country. Clearly, however, in an agricultural society based on the large-scale plantation, the "white model" could in no way be imitated by the freed slave. Between the humble farm he might one day be able to possess and the engenho or fazenda of the master, the gap was enormous. What is more, the freed slave could not become a farmer without his former owner's help. Near Salvador, for example, were abandoned fields worn out by sugar growing. These were often rented to freed slaves, who planted subsistence crops for sale in town markets. Other agricultural slaves—to be sure, a very small minority—were lucky enough to be assigned to sell the products grown on the plantation. Such slaves knew both the town and the countryside: they farmed the land but sold what was grown in town, something that whites looked upon as degrading but that enabled the slave to earn some money of his own. But it was mainly the urban slaves and the slaves in the mines who dreamt of emulating white models, of moving into a higher social class, of rising from servitude to freedom. Yet the figures suggest that freed slaves accounted for no more than 0.5 percent to 2 percent of the population of cities like Rio, Salvador, and Paraty (the only ones investigated thus far). The rate of manumission may have been higher in Minas Gerais, but that remains to be proven.

Thus only a small number of slaves saw their dreams of freedom come true. Although manumission did provide some means of social mobility, it was only individuals who improved their social position, never whole groups. What good, then, were associations formed in the workplace or through lay and religious organizations if they benefited only certain slaves and never the whole group? This is an important question, and we must look to the freed slaves themselves for an answer. The third part of this book will be devoted to this subject.

What kind of slave could hope for manumission? Without undue generalization we can answer this question in part by examining rules of behavior. Let us look at a few black African slaves, a few slaves of mixed race, some from the cities, some from the mines, with an eye to determining what strategies they adopted in the hope of crossing the threshold between slavery and freedom. The first thing an African had to do was learn Portuguese, a visible sign of his integration into Brazilian society. By exhibiting obedience, humility, and loyalty he could then win his master's affection. We must be careful not to think that the master's feelings for his slave ever grew warm. This would be to commit an anachronism: in the patriarchal Brazilian system the "father" never forgot himself so far as to compromise his authority. Affection in this context does not mean tenderness but esteem coupled with pride in owning a trustworthy slave. To please the master was to enter into a personal relationship with him. It was then up to the slave to cultivate the master's good opinion. By doing a good job, the slave pleased his owner, remunerated the capital invested in him, and sometimes earned enough of his own to purchase his freedom. In this respect, slaves in the mines and slaves de ganho in the towns were far better off than field hands. But domestic slaves could hope to obtain their freedom for nothing, though they had to wait longer for it. Patronage and godparenting could strengthen the bonds between a master and a slave who did his job well. The master's family and, more commonly, the slave community and confraternities sometimes afforded slaves protection. Here again, the slaves imitated their masters and turned for assistance to tertiary orders, convents, lay and religious organizations that played the role of banks (there were no state or private banks in Brazil until the nineteenth century, and Brazilian banking was so poorly organized at first that deposit banking did not arrive until the second half of the century, and even then banks did not inspire much confidence). The slave who needed money could thus usually find a group willing to lend it to him. Or, if not, he could turn to a friend, a slave or freed man, to hold his savings or to lend him the money needed to purchase manumission, assuming that his master seemed willing to give it to him. Obviously, a skilled slave in good economic times would be more likely to earn the money needed for manumission than a general laborer who had to face competition from many other people without work. In hard times it was better to belong to a wealthy owner or to have friends (slaves or freed men) who were well established in business. For the government protected free workers, and the best way for a slave to earn money to purchase his freedom, apart from working in the mines, was to run a small business or work as an artisan. The slave who was a good businessman could secure a faithful clientele. This particularly true of cities in which slavery was an old tradition and most of the free population had descended from manumitted slaves. It was not true of cities to which slavery had come more recently, or where large numbers of European immigrants competed for work as artisans and shopkeepers. This was the case with Rio de Janeiro, which, as the national capital, received a fairly large number of European immigrants, especially Portuguese. It was also the case with São Paulo, which became an important coffee-exporting center at a time when the abolition of the slave trade dried up the supply of new slaves and made masters extremely reluctant to grant manumission to slaves needed to work on the plantations.

The slave who really wanted freedom was not in a position to demand manumission. Certain factors were simply beyond his control. In short, the older the slave tradition, and the smaller the number of European immigrants, the more likely the humble, obedient, and loyal African was to secure his freedom, provided he had the necessary help to do so.

Creoles and slaves of mixed race had the great advantage of having been educated by their masters. They had learned a trade and enjoyed close relations with their masters from early childhood. Many were freed before they reached adult age, some as early as baptism. At a time when child mortality was high, all they had to do to grow up as free men was survive. Of course their mothers might remain slaves forever, but even they looked to their children to win their freedom some day. Creoles and half-breeds were not always lucky enough to be set free while still young. Those who were not had to be wary of the slave community, which always distrusted them. We shall see in the next chapter how difficult relations were between Africans and creoles. The slave born in Brazil tended to gravitate toward the masters; his life was more complicated than that of the Africans.

Whether black or half-breed, African or creole, the slave who came to Brazil was a new man. We have seen him living or surviving in the bosom of his family, his community, his job. And we have seen him dream of manumission. By looking more closely at this dream, we can gain a better idea of who the Brazilian slave really was.

PART 3

The End of Slavery?

To be a slave in Brazil, then, was not to be utterly without responsibility, humbly and faithfully obedient to omnipotent masters, and in a state of total dependence. This was one of the novel aspects of Brazilian slavery: to be a slave in Brazil was, I think, to accept the contradiction inherent in assuming the past and adapting to the present while hoping for a better future. Past, present, and future were all illuminated with the glow of freedom: slaves regained, in part at least, the unforgotten freedom of their lives in Africa by cleverly adjusting to their new lives in Brazil. For Brazilian society was neither more rigid nor more cruel than any other. The colonial land was virgin and open, and social mobility was not impossible as we have already seen.

In Portuguese there is an untranslatable word that sheds some light, I think, on how the black man more or less successfully adapted to his new estate, surroundings, and fate: *jeito,* which roughly means cunning, artfulness, cleverness. Equality was by no means the hallmark of Brazilian society, not even for the free man. The slave had to carve out his own niche using his jeito, his talent for getting things done, for standing on his own two feet, for surviving, for commanding his own self-respect and the respect of others. Part of the slave's jeito was his willingness or refusal to adjust; it was the shrewdness of the survivor, the wisdom born of experience and shaped by the adversity that affected all who lived in Brazil, whether slaves, emancipees, or free men. The clever slave worked to hasten his passage from the mythical lost past through the difficult present toward an idealized future. In everyday life it was jeito that linked past and future, that gave the slave a reason to go on. Imagination was the slave's treasure. Though bought, sold, and ordered about, the slave clung as best he could to independence, humor, and tenderness, and he never stopped dreaming.

The mirage of manumission and, in the late nineteenth-century, the prospect of abolition were tempting hopes, fraught perhaps with dangers. Yet the Brazilian slave was quick to embrace these hopes, certain that thanks to his jeito he would always be able to adapt to whatever fate awaited him in the colorful world of those whom the law was careful not to refer to as free men but rather as manumitted slaves.

SEVEN

The Charter of Freedom

LEGAL DEFINITION AND DESCRIPTION

For the Brazilian slave there was more than one road to much-coveted freedom: flight, death, certain special provisions of the law (in the nineteenth century only), and manumission. The law in Brazil, as in all other slave regimes, provided that the child of a slave mother was born a slave, even if the father was a free man: *Partus sequitur ventrem*. There was one exception to this rule: a child engendered by the master became free after the death of his father, provided the latter recognized him as his child. In the decades prior to the abolition of slavery in Brazil, a few halting efforts were made to legally manumit certain categories of slaves; the 1885 law freeing sexagenarians and above all the law of the "free womb."

The law of 28 September 1871, Law no. 2040 known as the law of the free womb, promulgated by the Imperial Princess Isabelle, regent in the absence of her father Dom Pedro II, granted freedom to children born in Brazil to a female slave. Since it was by then illegal to import slaves from Africa, this meant that there would henceforth be no young slaves to replenish the slave stock, so that slavery would gradually vanish from Brazil. But the law was in reality far less liberal than it appears. The liberty granted to newborns was hedged about with appalling restrictions, such as the stipulation that the minor child remained under the joint authority of the master and its mother, who were supposed to raise it together until it reached the age of eight. After that, the mother's owner had two options. He could accept an indemnity of 600,000 reis from the government or he could use the services of the child until it reached its twenty-first year. In the first case the government took charge of the child. It then generally placed him in a charitable institution, where he was put to work until he reached the age of twenty-one. The 600,000 reis were paid to the master in the form of government bonds paying 6 percent over thirty years. When the child reached the age of eight, the master had one month to make up his mind about which procedure he preferred. In almost all cases he chose to retain the child. This resulted in a few form of slavery, since the law did not specify the maximum work day or minimum health and dietary criteria to which the "free slave" should be subject, thus leaving him entirely at the master's mercy. In a society where any dark-skinned individual was immediately identified as a "slave," his life was scarcely different from that of most slaves. Nor was he likely to fare better if sent to a charitable institution by a master who chose to accept the government indemnity. For after a wrenching separation from his mother and from the slave community the child became an anonymous ward of an impersonal government that exploited him in its own way by putting him to work. Since slavery was abolished in Brazil before any children born under the free-womb law reached age twenty-one, their problems were the same as those of slaves freed by means of conditional manumission.

Manumission was a legal procedure. It could be granted with or without formal proceedings, directly or indirectly, explicitly, tacitly, or presumptively, by contract between living persons or by will of the deceased, under private seal or sworn before a notary, verbally or in writing. In the absence of a written document, witnesses were required to certify that manumission had taken place. Generally manumission was granted by written document, however, signed by the master or by a third party upon request of an illiterate master. To avoid disputes the document customarily was registered with a notary in the presence of witnesses. Several years often elapsed between the grant of liberty and its registration with a notary. Many manumissions were granted by will or at baptism. The owner voluntarily renounced his *manus* on the captive, who became a free man "as if free from birth," as manumission documents often expressed it.

Children who in the eyes of the law have no will of their own therefore could not liberate their slaves. Tutors or guardians of minors were not allowed to dispose of the property of their wards without express authorization of the courts. Similarly, persons possessing slaves "in usufruct," insane persons, "prodigal sons," and slaves who owned another slave were not legally entitled to sign manumission papers. A married woman could sign only with her husband's authorization, except on her death bed, when she became her spouse's equal. Finally, in the nineteenth century, laws were passed authorizing the manumission of so-called national slaves, slaves belonging to the nation as a whole, becaue they had been smuggled in after the abolition of the slave trade in 1831. These slaves were seized and set free at once. The law, in its far-sightedness, even declared that dead slaves would be resurrected as free men, a Christian view often embroidered upon in pastoral homilies. A more tangible measure here below was a law liberating any slave legally married to a free spouse. Finally, all foundlings were presumed free (and it was quite common to abandon newborns). As mentioned earlier, any slave who found a large diamond (more than twenty carats) was immediately freed, but the government, which received the diamond, paid the master an indemnity of 400,000 reis. Slaves who denounced their masters for smuggling or dealing in commodities on which the government had a monopoly (gold, diamonds, Brazil wood) was also liberated and received a reward of 200,000 reis. Any slave belonging to the confraternity of Saint Benedict who paid the redemption price was immediately set free. A slave who managed to cross the borders of the empire gained his freedom, even if he returned to Brazil. Military service brought manumission: many slaves won their freedom in this way during the war with Paraguay (1864–1869). Through inheritance it was common for a slave to become the property of more than one owner. If any one of these masters decided to grant the slave his freedom, all the others were obliged to go along. Finally, if a slave offered his master the sum required for manumission and the master refused to accept it, the slave could ask for the protection of the courts through an intermediary, a court-appointed tutor or guardian (this was necessary since the slave himself possessed no legal personality). After 1831 a slave whose master asked an exorbitant amount for his manumission could be set free by court order, but such judgments were not always easy to acquire.

Some fifteen years prior to abolition, an imperial regulation established a so-called manumission fund. The fund consisted of duties paid on slaves, taxes on transfer of slave ownership, subscriptions, donations, and bequests. The actual endowment was never sufficient. Between 1873 and 1882, 70,183 slaves are said to have been liberated through this fund. To put this figure in perspective, recall that during the same nine years 132,777 slaves died in captivity. It was frequently impossible to call a meeting of the *juntes* who were supposed to decide what slaves were to receive the benefits of the fund, and when they did meet they often gave in to pressure from slave owners: for example, the juntes of São Paulo state met in 1886, two years before the abolition of slavery, and declared that newly freed slaves must faithfully and diligently serve their former masters for five years after receiving their manumission papers.

The law of 28 September 1885, the so-called sexagenarian law which set free all slaves above sixty years of age, also stipulated that the freed slave was required to indemnify his master. If he was unable to do so in cash, he must work for three more years if he was between 60 and 62, or else until he was 65. Now, we know that in the state of São Paulo, only 2,553 slaves were liberated as a result of this law in 1887, and that 2,503 of these were freed under contracts whose terms imposed much longer periods of service than required by the law. Thus the generosity of the laws and regulations was more apparent than real. More than anything else, the laws testify to the efforts of certain masters to delay, by whatever means were available, the inevitable abolition of slavery, upon which they depended for essential manpower.

Slaves were generally unaware of the laws. They rarely benefited from favorable laws unless they had the support of free men. Such support was hard to come by, especially in the countryside, where slaves lived in a closed world and the law was in the hands of their lords and masters. Sometimes manumission cost nothing, either by dint of legislative act or thanks to a generous slave owner. But more often it was costly. Slaves had to pay for their freedom in hard cash, metal coin or paper money, either in a lump sum or by installments. Some slaves redeemed themselves by giving another slave to their masters. If a master's will stipulated the price of a slave's freedom, then the master's heirs had to abide by that price without question, even though it was generally below the slave's actual market value.

Regardless of whether manumission was bought or granted free of charge, it could be revoked. Therein lay one of the ambiguities of the law as well as of actual practice. The grounds for revocation that slave owners were entitled to present were entirely subjective. If a master suddenly discovered "ingratitude" in his former slave, he could annul his manumission as easily as he granted it. Not until 1865 did the courts declare this procedure unacceptable. Despite this judgment, however, the revocation of manumission on grounds of ingratitude, authorized by Title 13, Book 4 of the Philippine Ordinances of the seventeenth century, remained officially legal. Brazil did not adopt a civil code of its own until 1917. Another ambiguous aspect of manumission was that many documents contained restrictive clauses, specifying time delays or suspensive conditions which in practice nullified manumission. The slave was then nominally free but actually prevented from making use of his liberty. In other words, his liberty was conditional. Only a slave who managed to secure complete and un-equivocal manumission, with no second thoughts and no restrictions, really became a "free" citizen.

Still, as we shall see later, even this free citizen did not enjoy full civil rights. But at least he could dispose of his own property as he saw fit. If he died childless and intestate, his inheritance went to his wife or other heirs. If he died unmarried, his property, like that of all free men without heirs, reverted to the state. The slave's former master became his *patrono* after manumission, but the patronage relationship had nothing in common with that of ancient Rome, which imposed numerous obligations on the freed slave. In Brazil the freed slave owed his patron nothing more than the respect had loyalty of a grateful son. The one restriction was that, in order to bring suit against his *patrono*, he required special authorization from the court.

Manumission charters are moving documents. Based on models that changed little over the centuries, they recount the sufferings of an entire people desperate for the favors of masters who often showed themselves to be more calculating than generous. Below are the complete texts of two such charters, chosen from among thousands—two brief and quite ordi-nary examples. Innumerable others are genuine sagas, full of complicated twists and turns. But the simplicity of the two documents cited here shows how little slaveowners were required to justify their actions:

> I, Joaquina de Sant'Anna, hereby declare that among my property is a *cabra* slave by the name of Luciana, daughter of the slave Ines of the Angola nation, now deceased, who also belonged to me; and, further, that the said slave Luciana is from this day forth, by virtue of the good service she has rendered me and for the love of having raised her and for value received, the sum of 100,000 reis in cash, free from this day forth and forevermore, as if she were born of free womb, and my heirs shall have no claim, for which I beseech the justice of His Royal and Imperial Majesty. And if in this charter of freedom some clause is lacking, I consider it as having been expressed.
>
> And because I can neither read nor write I have asked Mr. Aleixo Antunes to prepare this document, which he has signed in my place and as witness and in the presence of other witnesses. Bahia, 15 March 1814, Joaquina de Sant'Anna, and as witness and drafter of this act Aleixo Antunes de Carvalho, and the following witnesses:

Manoel Domingos dos Santos Siloa Cavalcanti, Caetano Alberto de Barros Vianna, Francisco Albergaria. Behia, 16 March 1814, Simões. I recognize my own writing: Marcelino Soares de Albergaria, Bahia, 22 March 1814.

His Excellency, Doctor and Chief of Police,
Registered
30 December 1875
Antonio João Damasio
I, the undersigned, hereby grant liberty as if he were born of free womb to my slave Ramiro, age 19, of creole color [sic], son of my deceased slave Julia, which liberty my aforesaid slave may enjoy from this date forth and forevermore. I beseech the authorities of His Majesty the Emperor to warrant my decision. Bahia, 2 April 1874, signed Maria Custodia. I recognize the above signature. Antonio João Damasio (notary). Bahia, 30 December, 1875.

Generally, manumission charters include such details as the name of the slave to be freed, country of origin, parents if known, color, the reasons for liberation, whether manumission was free, paid for, or conditional, the names of witnesses, and the date of registration with the notary. Occasionally one also finds information about the master's occupation, his place of residence, and the age or occupation of the slave to be freed. Quite clearly, these documents are mirrors in which we see reflected the lives of that privileged group among slaves, those who were destined to be freed. Particularly valuable are the indications of the reasons that led to the grant of freedom as well as the various restrictions that might be imposed on the freed man's liberty. These records give us a vivid and poignant picture of the hopes and illusions of so many men and women who set out to overcome the innumerable pitfalls on the road to freedom.

WHO PURCHASED FREEDOM?

Though manumission existed in Brazil almost as long as slavery itself, many barriers, some legal, some circumstantial, persistently hindered its development. The law prohibited manumission in four situations. First, some slaves had been sold under contracts that explicitly stipulated they could never be freed. On the other hand, some contracts contained clauses providing that the slave would eventually be set free or could be set free if obliged to engage in prostitution by the new master. Second, manumission could not be granted to the detriment of the master's creditors. Now, a slave who knew nothing of his master's legal incapacity may well have paid out all or part of the sum necessary for his manumission, only to find himself legally barred from recovering any of it. Third, manumissions granted by will were held to be null and void if granted in contravention of the law: a master could use only the "disposable third" of his property in liberating slaves, for example. If he made a mistake in evaluation, a slave liberated in good faith might find himself once more a slave when the heirs succeeded in proving "fraud." The last and most interesting case involves slaves mortgaged or given as collateral. As movable property like any other, useable as collateral without restriction, slaves who were mortgaged could never purchase their freedom. These legal restrictions clearly show that, in the eyes of their masters, slaves were first and foremost commodities, sources of profit. To be sure, masters could not ask a slave to engage in illicit or immoral acts, but their only duty to the slave was to provide food, clothing, and medical care in case of sickness. The master could rent, loan, sell, give, alienate, bequeath, mortgage, or grant a life interest in the slave. Not until 1864 did a law prohibit the mortgaging of slaves belonging to an agricultural enterprise, though they could still be used as collateral. Mortgage and collateral documents were notarized acts, just like any other donation *inter vivos* or for *causa mortis*. Five witnesses were required.

The slave was in fact a commodity. That is why government and religious authorities tried in vain to combat prostitution of slaves as a source of profit for their masters. Indeed, a law inherited from Roman law, which declared free any slave obliged to work as a prostitute, seems never to have been enforced. A slave needed substantial support to gain freedom in such conditions. As late as 1871, a Rio de Janeiro court refused manumission to a female slave compelled to engage in prostitution, "because article 179 of the Constitution of the Empire guarantees ownership in the full sense and because the hypothesis of Roman law invoked here is not applicable."

Some of the circumstances that could prevent a slave from achieving freedom have already been mentioned. The cost of manumission was the most obvious of these. It was fixed by mutual verbal agreement, and many freedom charters stipulate that "the price was decided by both parties." Hence it was a contractual price, but based on an evaluation made by the master: "He was liberated at his proper price," writes the all-powerful master. In the nineteenth century, if agreement between master and slave proved difficult, either because the master was reluctant to free his slave at all or because he felt the price offered was insufficient, the slave could seek out a godfather to take his case to court. The courts usually found in favor of the slave. But how many slaves were able to make use of this procedure? With our current information we cannot answer this question. In any case, most manumission documents proclaim to all and sundry that the slave has been granted his freedom "freely and spontaneously, without compulsion of any kind." There is no reason not to accept this at face value, since no earthly power could "compel" a master to grant freedom to his slave against his own judgment and interest. Thus the redemption price was a contractual price based on the local market price, which, as we saw earlier, depended on the slave's health, age, sex, and qualifications. The evaluation of a slave also depended on another very important factor, whose influence is difficult to gauge: the relationship between master and slave. The degree of intimacy between servant and master was important; such feelings are hard to quantify. The cost of freedom was affected by feelings that ranged from friendship to indifference. One can speak of a sort of secondary market, in which a slave's price declined if his master was inclined to favor manumission and rose otherwise. An esteemed slave could have his freedom for less than the market price.

It was not in the master's interest to free a slave unless he could replace the freed worker with a new slave bought on the open market. He might, for example, wish to purchase a younger slave to replace an older one, worn out by years of work. For the master, then, the price of manumission was a true surplus, a supplementary profit on the capital invested in the slave. Quite commonly a slave would begin making payments as much as six, seven, or eight years prior to actual manumission, which increased the master's profits still more. Many slaves purchased their freedom on the "installment plan," paying part of the cost over a number of years. After 1850, by which time the slave trade had been abolished for almost twenty years, the slave market became very tight and the price of slaves rose. Here again the master stood to benefit. He was entitled to ask a high price for freeing an elderly slave because of the high cost of buying a replacement worker. Other circumstances favored manumission. Repeated crises in the sugar industry, which deeply affected northeastern Brazil in the nineteenth century, encouraged masters to free workers who had become a burden. The first to be freed were the elderly and those in poor health. Unfortunately, the basic research needed for further analysis has yet to be done. Masters certainly were always interested in increasing their income, and manumission provided a way of converting capital into cash that could be reinvested at a higher rate of return. After 1850, for example, it was tempting and even fashionable in Salvador to buy real estate, bank stock, and government bonds. The sale of a freedom charter providing ready cash might have seemed a favorable arrangement to both master and slave.

The reality was certainly more complicated than it may seem, for manumissions were not paid for only in cash. Little is known about the question: for information about certain aspects of manumission contracts we have only three studies of freedom charters in Salvador between 1684 and 1889 and one study of manumissions granted in Paraty (Rio de Janeiro province) between 1789 and 1822 to go on. In Salvador, it seems that paid manumissions at no time exceeded 48 percent of the total, whereas in Paraty the corresponding figure was only 31 percent. We cannot begin to answer the question without further study of conditional manumissions, of which there were more (43 percent) in Paraty than in Salvador. Were such manumissions really "free," as some masters liked to claim, given that they required the slave to remain a slave during the lifetime of the master or his son or his sister or some other family member? Conditional manumissions were dearly bought, in fact, since they could be revoked at any time and made the slave even more dependent than ever, knowing that the slightest quarrel, the slightest provocation of the master could wreck well-laid plans for freedom. In Bahia, conditional charters accounted for only 18 to 23 percent of the total, depending on the period, compared with the 43 percent just mentioned in Paraty. But in Paraty there was a large proportion of creoles and half-breeds and hence more women and children. Now, creoles, half-breeds, women, and children were always heavily represented among the liberated in all parts of the country. In Bahia these categories accounted for 80 percent of the slaves freed from the late seventeenth century until the middle of the eighteenth century. Only in the nineteenth century did this proportion drop appreciably, to about half of all manumissions. During the eighteenth century the city of Salvador changed dramatically: as activities related to sugar declined, the city became an important commercial center, a way station for imported merchandise. The growth of trade led to an expansion of the middle class, in which creoles and half-breeds found their place. Moreover, newly arrived Africans were primarily sent to the mining regions, where their prices were higher than in Bahia or Rio. All these circumstances favored the manumission of Bahian creoles. By contrast, when agriculture picked up in the second half of the eighteenth century and even more in the nineteenth century, African slaves were in greater demand. They arrived in large numbers until the abolition of the slave trade in 1831. After 1820 the sugar engenhos experienced periods of crisis alternating with comparative prosperity. The ratio of freed Africans to creoles then increased, to 52 percent in Paraty and to nearly 80 percent in Bahia.

In regard to manumissions of women and children, we have the results of studies carried out in Rio de Janeiro, Salvador, and Paraty. Manumissions of women outnumbered those of men in the three cities by two to one. But in the slave population as a whole, men outnumbered women by the same factor. In other words, manumissions were much more readily granted to women, who generally lived in greater intimacy with the master or worked as itinerant merchants. Women also cost less to replace than men and aged more quickly. Thus women were precious commodities if they knew how to please and rapidly depreciating commodities if they didn't and found it relatively easy to gain freedom for themselves and their children. The precentage of freed children was relatively high until 1745 in Bahia and even higher in Paraty. The ensuing decline (1779–1850) occurred in areas where the number of creole slaves did not increase; creoles had more children than Africans, and it was easier for the children of creoles to gain manumission.

Thus masters were more willing to liberate women and children than men. What about elderly slaves? A vast literature in Brazil describes abandoned old people left to beg at church doors, along with invalids of every stripe, blind people, cripples, and others reduced to living on charity. Substantial research has shown, however, that the elderly and disabled nowhere accounted for more than 10 percent of all manumitted slaves. Most masters did not cast useless slaves out into the street, and in any case people died young in yesterday's Brazil, and younger still if they worked as slaves.

In summary, two-thirds of manumitted slaves were women. For the rest, variations in the conditions of manumission were due mainly to economic circumstances and to differences in the composition of the slave population. But everywhere the majority of manumissions—66 to 75 percent of them—were granted either in exchange for payment or under conditions that profited the owner. The freedom charter was usually a commercial document and rarely a record of generosity.

IMMEDIATE FREEDOM

Why was it easier for ganho and domestic slaves to obtain their freedom than it was for their brothers in captivity? Can a fuller appreciation of the

TABLE 9.
Distribution of Freed Slaves in Brazil by Age and Sex

	A Salvador 1684–1745 (N = 1,160)	%	B Salvador 1779–1850 (N = 6,635)	%	C Salvador 1813–1853 (N = 686)	%	D Salvador 1819–1888 (N = 12,799)	%	E Rio de Janeiro 1807–1831 (N = 1,319)	%	F Paraty 1789–1822 (N = 325)	%		%
Male	384	33.1	2,543	38.3	225	32.7	5,126	41.1	479	36.3	112	34.5		
Female	776	66.9	4,092	61.7	461	67.3	7,673	59.9	840	63.7	213	65.5		
Adult	818[a]	70.5	6,305	88.9	551	80.3	11,430	86.7	1,143	87	213[1]	65.5	156[b]	58
Child	342	29.5	784	11.1	135	19.7	1,697	13.3	176	13	112	34.5	123	41

Source: James Patrick Kiernan, "The Manumission of Slaves in Colonial Brazil," Diss. New York University, 1976, p. 87. Unpublished data from the study, "A carta de alforria como fonte, . . ," pp. 149–163, have been added in column D.
[a] Slaves of unknown age included.
[b] Slaves of unknown age not included.

extremely subtle relationships that developed between masters and slaves be gained by looking at the process of manumission? Indeed, understanding this process can, I think, help us to understand what "being a slave" really meant. For the condition of the freed slave can be grasped only through comparison with the condition of the slave himself. Just as there were many ways of being a slave, so too were there many ways of being a freed slave. The process of liberation and the conditions under which it was achieved can shed a good deal of light on everyday life under slavery.

Obtaining freedom was usually a question of money, since the slave was a commodity with a market value. In freedom charters purchased for cash, it is striking that many preconditions had to be met before any cash could change hands. These conditions have a ritual air and tell us much about master-slave relations. What themes, what litanies recur frequently in manumission documents? The two key formulas are the following: "For having served me well" and "For the love that I bore him (or her) because I raised him (her)." Very few charters fail to contain one or the other of these formulas. To be freed, then, one must have been a hard-working, loyal, and obedient slave. In other words, masters wished to make it clear that the slave deserved his freedom in order to justify their decision to free him. For society had to be reassured, had to be told that the freed slave would become a good citizen and not a public burden in a country where charity was the responsibility of private individuals. Thus freedom was a reward, even when payment was required, and for many years it was dangled before slaves as an incentive to good behavior. To be sure, it was not enough merely to dangle the carrot of freedom: the slave was not a donkey. Nor was he simply a commodity, an object to be bought and sold, or a mere laborer whose initiative could be ignored. The slave was in fact a complex human being, in the master's view somewhat like a difficult child in need of education and guidance in order to become a functioning adult. The language of the charters says much about the moralistic and paternalistic attitudes, more petty than generous, of slave owners toward slaves.

With morality and custom duly taken care of, the charters usually went on to say that the master was freely granting the slave his liberty, without coercion of any kind. But we know that in the nineteenth century some slaves were obliged to seek the help of "godfathers." In 1825, for example, a mulatto woman named Domingas became an object of antipathy to a person acting as guardian for minors whose parents' will stipulated that Domingas should be freed in exchange for a "sum corresponding to her value." The guardian had obtained an evaluation far in excess of the slave's true value. But Domingas successfully called upon the services of the new master to whom she had been hired out, Karl-Gustav Waiss, the Salvadoran vice-consul representing the Hanseatic city of Hamburg, who went to court and obtained a second evaluation favorable to the slave. In this case the promised manumission had to be secured through all-out battle, but this was the exception and not the rule.

Somewhat more numerous were the slaves freed by masters obliged to liquidate their capital in order to survive. Such slaves were set free with great reluctance, and their masters justified their actions to both themselves and their slaves in such passages as the following:

In 1796 Faustina de Santa Teresa de Jesus, widow, freed her slave Theodoro Joaquim de Sant'Anna, half-breed, cobbler by trade, "not only because he aided her, through his trade as a cobbler, in her poverty but also because on various occasions when she had urgent need of money he gave her the sum of 100,000 reis."

João, a creole carpenter, was set free in 1836 by Ana Joaquina de Sacramento, also a widow, for the sum of 380,000 reis, "because, abandoned as she was by her relatives, as is notorious public knowledge, he provided her with food and served her with humility and charity, seeing to it that she wanted for nothing."

The slave Amancio, son of a creole, mulatto, was liberated in 1862 because his master "found himself in a state of great necessity and needed this money to cure his ailments and contribute to his upkeep."

In 1877, Maria Augusta Mendes da Silva was obliged to liberate a young creole named Maria, age nine, because she found herself "utterly abandoned and in complete poverty after being cast out by her husband . . . and in need of money to live on."

These four examples show us that some masters experienced genuine hardship and explain how slaves could, in certain circumstances, help to support their owners' families, serve with zeal and even affection, and earn enough money through outside work to support an entire household.

Stories like these lead us to raise three questions: How did slaves come by the money required for manumission? In what way were payments made? And finally, if manumission was not paid for in cash, what reasons did the masters give to explain why they were granting it?

Mainly the slaves who shared their daily earnings with their masters are the ones who managed to accumulate enough money to buy freedom. Yet no law ever guaranteed that slaves could freely dispose of what they earned. Strictly speaking, slaves possessed nothing of their own. It was up to the master to decide whether or not to allow the slave to hold on to part of his earnings. By verbal agreement it was settled between master and slave that the slave must pay the master a set sum of money every day or every week. What the slave earned beyond this sum then belonged to him. In other words, the master tacitly deemed the slave capable of owning property, which explains why slaves were allowed to possess not just money but even other slaves, and why some slaves went so far as to draw up wills even though they had no legal personality or right to own property. Customary practices were quite contradictory: it was recognized that slaves were entitled to inherit property and to receive gifts and that masters should not appropriate savings amassed by slaves out of allowances for food, lodging, and clothes. Masters also usually respected money awarded to slaves as indemnity for injuries.

None of these rules had any real basis in law, but, tacitly accepted, they acquired a practical social value that helped the slave work his way out of slavery. It was then up to the slave to earn the necessary money, or obtain a loan, or receive a bequest or donation, or persuade his master to grant him his freedom for nothing, which came to the same thing, since free manumission was a form of gift. These practices, of benefit mainly to urban slaves, domestic slaves, and slaves working in the mines, worked against the vast majority of slaves: the field hands.

How long did it take for a slave who worked outside the master's home to amass the sum needed for manumission? The question is not easy to answer. Take two examples: workers in Salvador and Paraty, that is, in large cities of the northeast, and workers in a small town in southern Rio de Janeiro. In Paraty between 1791 and 1815, a slave's daily wage was 160 reis. In an as-yet-unpublished thesis, the American historian James Kiernan has calculated that it would have taken seven long years for a slave to earn the average sum required for manumission in this period (94,584 reis) — assuming that he did not spend a single real in all this time and that the master authorized him to keep all his earnings. If we consider not the average price of manumission but the average market price of slaves during this period, we find that it would have taken twelve and a half years to earn the 167,776 reis paid for the average slave on the Paraty market.

Now, even when slaves purchased their freedom on the installment plan, the payments were never extended over such a long period. In Salvador the average daily wage of a male slave was 160 reis in 1805, compared with 130 reis for a female slave (the figures are for unskilled slaves working in construction, a trade in which work was halted during the winter and the rainy season). It was customary in Salvador for slaves to pay one-third of their earnings to their masters. Assume that the slave spent nothing of what was left to him. Since the average price of manumission was 100,000 reis for men and 80,000 reis for women, it would have taken four years of work for these slaves to purchase their freedom, and five to six years to save an amount equal to their price on the slave market.

It is hard to compare figures that are not really comparable. The criteria used for the Paraty calculations were not exactly the same as those used in the case of Salvador. One must be careful not to generalize on the basis of this type of example, which could easily lead to distortions. Yet the slave's savings must in general have stimulated productivity, and masters must have authorized and even encouraged slaves to save only when their work capacities began to diminish. We have virtually no information about the age of freed slaves. It is unlikely that slaves could begin to work immediately on their own behalf, especially in Salvador in the nineteenth century, where the number of newly arrived Africans was large. The new arrivals did not speak Portuguese, and it would have taken some time for them to learn a trade and win the confidence of their masters. After a period of time, however, a thrifty, hard-working slave could hope to earn enough at work to purchase freedom. Consider the case of one barber, a "black named Albano" (his master must not have known much Latin to have given him such a name), who was liberated in 1811 for the round sum of 250,000 reis, and whose manumission papers state that he was highly skilled at working with his hands. Or Ana Joaquina, adept at embroidery, originally from Guinea, to whom Francisco Amoroso de Castro sold her freedom for 180,000 reis in 1809. Precisely because these prices are high masters took great care to praise the merits and virtues of the freed slaves. Slaves with no particular skills with which to earn what they needed for manumission could be freed by a family member or godparent or even a friend or workmate. Some were not required to pay the full price of manumission, because their masters took pity on them and decided to help them along the hard road to freedom.

From a thousand examples, I have chosen a few slaves' stories to present. All are Bahian. Some are sordid, others moving, a few comical or surprising in what they reveal of the ins and outs of a practice whose details varied widely from case to case.

In 1855, Francisco Antonio Pereira da Rocha inherited the slave José Joaquim, itinerant fruit and vegetable merchant, whom he set free for just 25,000 reis "because of services rendered to his family for a very long time."

From Fabricio, a Nago, his master declared that he had received in 1857 "only" 400,000 reis and that he "forgave him the rest so that he could trade and earn his living, since he is old."

In 1879, the creole Eugenia, an excellent cook and laundress who worked in the home of her owner in Alagoinhas, a small town in the Bahian *agreste*, obtained her freedom for 1,000,000 reis, although she had been evaluated at 1,200,000 reis.

In 1825, Joaquim Valentin, a mulatto carpenter, had to pay 100,000 reis for his freedom, even though he had lost one arm on the job.

In most cases, if the master seemed willing to grant manumission to a slave who could not amass the required sum, the slave's father, mother, grandparents, sisters and brothers, husband, or godmother hastened to help out as much as they could. The opportunity could not be allowed to pass. It is easy to imagine how eagerly the master's words were scrutinized for the slightest sign that he was willing to free this or that slave on such and such terms. As in the African bush drums beat out the news, which spread as fast as the wind could carry it. In the cantos and confraternities and senzalas, and across the fields, the rumors spread, blood ties were revived, humble savings were pooled, and all sorts of allegiances were called upon for help.

In 1751, Jeronyma da Conceição, a widow, freed Marcelianno, a mulatto aged two or three, for the sum of 30,000 reis paid by his father, the adjutant Floriano Alvares Pereira, who must have been a free man.

In 1866, Maria Joaquina de Jesus, in exchange for the sum of 800,000 reis, granted freedom to her creole slave Tomasia, age twenty, and to her daughter Cassiana, age eleven months. The father of little Cassiana, a freed African by the name of Pompeu de Barros, had made a cash down payment of 400,000 reis to secure the two women's freedom. The rest was to be paid in twelve months with an interest of 2 percent on the guarantee of another freed African by the name of João Thomaz.

João, a slave born in Portugal, had his freedom purchased by his mother, who substituted for him an African slave from Mina. The master agreed to set him free "because he suffers from asthma and has crises at every quarter of the moon, which prevents him from serving well, and also because one of his eyes is cloudy."

In 1819, Sister Maria Clara de Jesus, professed nun of the convent of Santa-Clara-do-Desterro, freed a newborn creole for 20,000 reis, payed by his mother of the Gégé nation.

At age seventeen, the slave Emiliana had a daughter, Agostinha. She purchased the child's liberty for 100,000 reis but continued to work as a slave.

A grandmother might wish to liberate her infant grandchild and yet not wish, or be unable, to liberate the child's mother, still a slave. More grandmothers than grandfathers paid for the manumission of their grandchildren, but in one will, dating from 1766, we find the curious case of Felix de Andrade dos Reis, who made the following declaration:

> Among the goods that I possess, there is a granddaughter, daughter of my son-in-law Ignacio de Souza, whom I bought for 70,000 reis from Jeronimo Ferreira, who had purchased her at the auction of the property of the fathers of the Company of Jesus and of their *fazenda* at Campinas. My granddaughter is named Clara de Jesus de Andrade Souza, she is mulatto, and I hereby set her free for the sum of 70,000 reis received from her father.

In other words, the child's father paid his father-in-law for the child's freedom; the grandfather set her free, but he did not do so free of charge.

Families tried whenever possible to gain the freedom of newborns prior to baptism. In 1866 a young creole named Alberto and his freedom purchased by his African grandmother Josefa, "so that he could be baptized a free man." His owner added this further declaration: "I did not have him baptized sooner, before the sum at which he had been evaluated was completed, so that he would not receive this sacrament as a slave."

Of 16,403 freedom charters examined in Bahia, none pertained to the purchase of a husband's freedom by his wife. A very few referred to the freeing of a wife by her husband. In 1806, Pedro Alexandrino de Souza Portugal, owner and master of the São Gonçalo sugar engenho, freed his creole slave Felipa "because of her marriage to Bartolomeu de Costa Pinto, a manumitted male mulatto, who will sacrifice his wages as overseer and bookkeeper of his engenho in order to pay the sum of 60,000 reis per year for two years."

Many charters were purchased by close relatives: a son paid for the freedom of Joana, a black woman from Angola, who was set free in 1839 after twenty years of faithful service, during which she raised her master's child. The 100,000 reis were earned during two voyages that Joana's son made from Pernambuco to Angola. The young creole Rosa was set free in 1855 when her elder sister paid her owner money she needed to pay taxes on her late husband's estate. In these official, registered, and notarized documents we witness a parade of relatives and friends coming forward to offer their assistance, sometimes in the most unexpected forms. Especially in the cities slaves found the community ready to support them in many ways. This support was so effective that it sometimes astonished masters, who indicated that the slave's freedom had been purchased by an "unknown" person. And consider this interesting item from the *Jornal da Bahia* for 23 January 1855:

An Act of Philanthropy

The Chief of Police [Innocencio Marques de Araujo] has just performed a praiseworthy act of philanthropy. Having learned that the master of a slave who last September won a 400,000 reis prize in the lottery had taken the money and, after punishing the slave, sold him, even though he had promised to set him free in three years, the chief of police summoned this individual together with the person who had purchased the Negro. After confirming the accuracy of the reports, he had the 400,000 reis returned to the slave and persuaded his new master to set him free for the sum of 1,200,000 reis. The slave had only the 400,000 reis of his prize, but thanks to the efforts of the police he soon found someone who loaned him 800,000 reis, which he will pay off with six years of labor.

To fully appreciate this story we should remember that from the 1830s on various abolitionist and even ordinary patriotic groups (such as veterans' organizations and holiday organizing committees) as well as political parties, student groups, and merchants' organizations contributed to the manumission of slaves. For some time many people had been persuaded that slavery, though an institution good for all who profited from it and indispensable to the economic life of the nation, should normally lead to manumission. To free a slave became a meritorious act, something to boast about. In 1865, for example, the society União e Segredo (Union and Secret) freed Isabel, a two-year-old mulatto child, "not yet baptized, daughter of the black slave Lima." The president of the society paid the girl's mistress 150,000 reis. Similarly, the owner of Maria, age eleven, received 600,000 reis from the treasurer of "the commission which, in the name of the commercial class, will today go to the Public Theater to pay homage to the talent of the illustrious Brazilian maestro, Antonio Carlos Gomes," author of the opera *Le Guarany*, which tells the edifying story of a proud Indian.

Manumission was never a solitary venture. Many different allegiances were called into play. Endless negotiations were held. Procedures of compensation were fixed, promises were made and kept. And various precepts and conventions were followed—reflecting notions of what was "just" and "usual" in the context of Brazilian society. In the second half of the nineteenth century it became quite fashionable to free slaves in homage to a person or in honor of a birthday, a religious holiday, a diploma earned, an unexpected success: manumission became a kind of ex voto, an act of piety, of gratitude, of edification. The Viscount Pedroso e Albuquerque, for example, freed the slave Telesonia in 1879 "in commemoration of this day, the day of the sacred death and Passion of Our Lord Jesus Christ." On Christmas Eve in 1870, the day he "received the rank of doctor of medicine," Frederico Augusto da Silva Lisboa freed the creole José, age nine; "I am also doing this," the young doctor added, "out of respect for my mother."

Thus family, friends, and neighbors all contributed in fundamental ways to the purchase of manumission. But when freedom was granted free of charge, masters invoked a thousand and one different and unexpected reasons for their decision. What were the real motives behind these displays of "generosity"? Much subtlety is called for in the interpretation of the sources. Once again, let us consider a few examples in order to restore balance to a portrait that might otherwise seem unduly colorful or hopelessly bleak.

Luis, a black Gégé, was freed in 1766 by Francisco Marcellino da Gou-veia, a member of the Ultramar council: he had served faithfully for seven-teen years.

In 1786, Mariana Pires de Miranda freed the creole Joana, because of the "loyalty and love with which she has served for a very long time and be-cause she supported [her mistress] in her infirmities, which was more than her husband ever did."

Luis, an Angolan black, was freed in 1813 after twenty-five years of good and loyal service.

Marcelina, a mulatto woman, was freed in 1819 after fifty years of loyal service.

All the documents refer to service for periods in excess of ten years, and many mention much, much longer periods. Furthermore, the sources do not discuss the slave's future: Will he or she remain with the master or strike out on his or her own? After fifty years of service even a slave who had first come to work as a child was well advanced in years. There are, however, a few noteworthy exceptions to this general lack of concern about the future. Consider, for example, the trading firm Gonçalves Costa e Companhia, which in 1870 set free its African slave Paulo with the following declaration: "Because he has served several years and is now tired, we have decided to set him free but, instead of abandoning him, to offer all that is necessary for his upkeep, provided that he wishes to remain with our company." Similarly, Pedro Cerqueira Lima freed Paulina in 1875 with the following words: "I give her her freedom free of charge in return for the good service she has given me for more than forty years. She leaves me of her own free will, seeing as I would have liked to keep her so that she would want for nothing in her old age. But since she wishes to live with her nephew, I give her permission to do so."

But for every caring, generous master, how many showed the hardness of their hearts by liberating sick slaves no longer able to work? Consider, for example, Maria Madalena Alvares de Jesus, who in August of 1805 lib-erated free of charge poor Antonio Villela, more than seventy years old, of whom his mistress declared with undisguised cruelty that he was "full of diseases, because of which no one who saw him would pay much of any-thing for him." Richard Hogg, an English merchant, was a man of some-what more tender sensibility: in 1859 he freed his black slave Benedicta, who was on her deathbed, "so that she would have the pleasure of dying free." Another master freed Francisco, age seventy, in 1866, saying that he was unable to work because of chronic ailments but that he could remain in the house rather than live in the streets.

Hospitals did take in indigent freed slaves free of charge, as João Pires de Carvalho explained in 1859 in granting freedom to his slave Antoine, a native of Benin. Listen to his sad story: "Since he was already fairly old when I bought him and since his mind was disturbed, I had him treated on 22 February 1858 by a physician. But this did not result in any improvement. [The slave] fled into the forest, and each time I had him brought back, he fled again. Since I did not want him to die of hunger, seeing that he is now in the city, I set him free so that he could go to the hospital for free treatment." Some sick slaves did not even go to the hospital in search of illusory cures: in 1866, for example, a mistress wrote of her African slave Caroline that "being ill she asked me to give her her freedom so that she could have herself treated with the native remedies of her own country, since no other treatment had been successful."

I have dwelt at length on these concrete examples because even though freedom charters were governed by strict laws and registered with notaries, they reveal the sufferings and strivings of both slaves and masters. Lessons in reality, mirrors of behavior, and life histories, each is unique, and yet collectively they reveal subtle differences of behavior and shed much light on people of different ages, characters, and social positions. When all is said and done, doesn't it come to the same thing whether a slave was freed for hard cash or freed simply because one no longer knew what to do with him? To bring our examination of the many kinds and varieties of manumission to an end, let us look, finally, at documents that emphasize the human aspect of the act of liberation, at cases in which the master was directly implicated by ties of blood. Literature and tradition have stressed the stories of bastards born of relations between master and slave. There is abundant proof that such children were generally liberated free of charge while still young. João Telles, who lived in the small town of São Francisco in the Bahian hinterland, in 1765 freed Manoel and Josefa, children of the black slave Victoria, "children that I have always held to be mine and whom I recognize as such." Luzia Nunes de Affonseca, the widow of João de Sà Feire, in 1783 freed her half-breed slave Maria, "not only because I am certain that she is the daughter of my late husband but also because she has always served me with loyalty and because I bear her love and affection from having raised her as my own daughter." Equally touching is the charter granted by Claudina Alberto de Franco, herself a freed African, to the creole Marianne Borges, age six, "for the love of having raised her and for the knowledge that she is the daughter of Domingos Borges da Silva, whom I shall marry."

Note, too, that the law automatically granted freedom to any slave who bore her master seven children. But Maria Joaquina da Costa and her husband Simão Antonio das Virgens, in obedience to the orders of their late father, freed, in 1855, not only Martiniana, "now mad," but also her seven children, four daughters and three sons. And the curate of Jacuipe was moved by holy anger in 1762 when he freed his slave Josefa Antonia, a native of São Thomé, "provided she leaves my home and never shows herself to me again nor sets foot in my house for she has a bad character and ill treats the members of my household."

What similarities were there among charters issued to slaves who served as replacements in the army, those issued to a sister or a son, and those sold to highly skilled slaves? All followed the same conventions: masters freed slaves when they wished and because they wished, because they found it in their interest to do so, or because they felt they were acting out of justice or charity. The curate who was irritated by the stubborness of Josefa Antonia was certainly more generous than the master who sold his recalcitrant slave to a new master thousands of kilometers away, far from the community he had created for himself. But in any case manumission charters are a good index of the attitudes of masters, who is this slave society had no need to justify their grant of freedom but liked to convince themselves that they were acting equitably and according to law. This ambiguity becomes even more striking when we attempt to answer the following essential question: Did the freed slave become a full-fledged citizen? Was being liberated the same thing as being free? Was conditional liberation the same thing as being a slave? What outlook did freed slaves have? And did the attitudes of freed slaves and slaves who hoped to be freed vary as much as did the conditions placed upon freedom and the avowed or unavowed reasons for granting it?

The Mirage of Freedom

Very few slaves saw their dreams of freedom come true. Though their numbers were minuscule, these former slaves played an important social role, which depended on locale and period: the life of a freed man in Bahia was quite unlike the life of a freed man in São Paulo, even if, legally speaking, their rights and obligations were the same. Any attempt to describe freed slaves as a group merits subtlety of interpretation. As we have seen, moreover, the slave was not always declared free immediately. Sometimes conditions were imposed on his freedom. Those conditions, which also varied widely, delayed, sometimes for long periods, the slave's full enjoyment of liberty. The attitudes of those "awaiting freedom" were no longer those of slaves but not yet those of the manumitted. Was freedom a mirage or a reality? The slave awaiting freedom, the "freeable" slave, was no longer a "thing" and already in some respects a "person," recognized as such by the state and by public opinion. But was he a free man? What was the status of the slave to whom freedom had been promised in the distant or not-too-distant future? Freeable yet not freed, how did he experience this time of trial, this dreamlike period during which freedom became tangible? We have already had some inkling of the pitfalls that stood between the freeable slave and freedom. The period of waiting was a happy time but also an anxious one. It was a state whose parameters were in the end defined by the ruling classes. Some of the bonds of slavery extended beyond the time of captivity. The liberated slave was not entirely a free man. Let us examine his condition. Let us measure to what extent emancipation was a sham and whether it was worth sweating blood to win the good graces of masters whose generosity was rarely sincere or freely given. For masters generally acted in their own best interest, having fully calculated the costs and benefits.

WAS BEING LIBERATED THE SAME AS BEING FREE?

It has often been asserted that former slaves—whether mulattoes or blacks, Africans or creoles—always bore the stigma of "manumission," even if their manumission papers proclaimed that freedom, like a second baptism, made them identical to their Brazilian brothers "born of a free womb." What exactly was a freed slave? Did he possess full legal rights? And did society as a whole recognize him as a free man or treat him as separate? If we are to understand the structure of Brazilian society in all its geographical and historical diversity, these questions must be answered. For even though the law at one point did grant to all freed slaves the same rights, former slaves found white society more accessible in the northeast than in the region of São Paulo. We must allow for the existence of several "Brazils" if we wish to appreciate the many varieties of "freedom" accorded to freed and "freeable" slaves and to their children.

The Brazilian constitution, granted by the royal government in 1824, for this first time clearly set forth the legal status of the freed slave. In article six, paragraph one, it declares that any freed slave born in Brazil is a Brazilian citizen "by birth." Thus the freed creole, either black or mulatto, immediately acquired Brazilian citizenship without having to engage in any special procedure. All that was required was proof of birth in Brazilian territory, and such proof was contained in the emancipation papers, which were required to state the origins of the slave being freed. Slaves born in Africa, however, had to undergo a lengthy naturalization procedure, the same as for any foreigner wishing to renounce his nationality to become a Brazilian citizen. Paragraph five of article six of the constitution of 1824 was felt not to be clear or stringent enough, so that it was clarified by additional laws passed in 1832, 1843, 1850, 1855, and 1860. Initially, then, the African slave was at a disadvantage compared with his creole comrade. Many remained foreigners throughout their lives. No study has yet been done of naturalizations of freed African slaves. Documents do exist, however, even if they are not very numerous. As far as the state of Bahia is concerned, for example, we do find, for the second half of the nineteenth century, applications for naturalization by freed African-born slaves. Generally speaking, however, Africans were not even informed of their rights. If by some chance they were informed, why would they hasten to acquire naturalization from which they had little to gain, whose importance must have seemed hazy to them, and which, assuming they remained emotionally tied to their homelands, may have struck them as nothing short of treason?

In fact, the legal rights of freed slaves who became citizens, whether Brazilian born or naturalized, were quite limited. To be sure, the freed slave regained the right to have a family, own property, and pass what he owned on to heirs. He was like a minor fully liberated from paternal governance. He could even be chosen as ward or guardian of persons deemed civilly incapacitated. But a series of restrictions deprived him of his political rights. In Brazil, an electoral system based on property qualification endured almost as long as slavery; the first direct elections were held in 1881, seven years before the abolition of slavery. Under the Brazilian system freed slaves could vote only in primary elections, elections held in the parishes to chose the major electors who in turn chose deputies and senators. Only municipal councilors could be chosen from among the electors in the primary assemblies. What is more, to become a primary elector a Brazilian had to demonstrate an annual income of 100,000 reis from land, work, trade, or other employment. Few freed slaves enjoyed such incomes, particularly after spending all their savings to purchase their freedom. Slaves who had to borrow the price of manumission usually took many years to repay their debt. We have no idea how many freed slaves managed to rise to the humble status of primary electors—informed, property-owning voters. How many had sufficient income to vote and thus to attract the attention of political candidates in a society much given to clientele relations, to protective paternalism? We know of no freed slave who became a municipal councilor, and it seems likely that few would have seen the point of exercising such limited political rights as they possessed. Freed slaves also had the right to serve in the army, the navy, and the national guard, but only as private soldiers. Any slave who enlisted automatically became free. But he could not become an officer. Once again, the freed slave bore a lifelong stigma. It is true that in the old captaincies of the northeast, all ranks in the militia were open to blacks and mulattoes. But this was the exception that confirms the rule, that a country as vast as Brazil is bound to reveal sharp contrasts.

Assimilation took many forms. When society was able to overlook the background of a freed slave, assimilation was easier than when demographic or economic conditions made that background hard to overlook. The status of the freed slave depended on his location: the established society of the northeast differed from the newer society of the south and the regimented society of the mining regions. Let us first consider freed slaves in rural areas, whose history remains rather mysterious, particularly as there were so few of them. In the old agricultural regions of the northeast, these former slaves mingled with a relatively sparse population of small farmers. Tradition has it that the land and its use were controlled by the large landowners. But of these, some quickly developed the habit of entrusting a portion of their holdings to free sharecroppers. Where were these sharecroppers recruited? Who were they? When did their numbers increase and when did they decrease? Demographic and economic factors must have played a role about which we still know very little.

In the Reconcavo, or Bahian hinterland, where there was a long tradition of sugar planting, we find, in addition to the owners of the great sugar mills, several categories of farmers, sharecroppers, and small rural landowners. Many of them were undoubtedly former slaves. Accurate figures are not available, but we do know that Portuguese-born whites refused to farm the land. Contemporary accounts are unanimous in complaining of this situation. Moreover, after the cholera epidemic of 1855–1856, which decimated the population of Salvador and its Reconcavo, it was suggested that all unemployed freed slaves be put to work as agricultural laborers. Whites refused to work the soil because they knew that they could never acquire enough acreage to become powerful *senhors de engenho*, especially since few properties were for sale. For the freed slave, however, even sharecropping was a good thing. It enabled him to supply his own needs and to sell his surplus crop on the market. The freed slave who was allowed to remain on his master's land had his future guaranteed and his fear of the unknown dispelled. He felt safe. Yet for the immediate future his freedom was quite precarious, economically and socially. He remained within the closed world that revolved around his former master, who remained a model, a protector, a buoy in a storm. The freed slave stood at the bottom of the agrarian hierarchy, barely distinguished from the mass of slaves, because even though he was free he still owed his former master the same obedience, the same humility, the same tolerance as before, at least if he wished to live in peace and keep his hard-won earnings. In order to escape from his former owner and gain true independence, he had to move far away from his old plantation and cut all the ties that bound him to the world of slaves. Very few did so, and masters, delighted to retain men and women ready to render a thousand little services, were careful not to make such prospects known. The newly freed slave depended economically on the good will of his former owner, who bought his crops or served as an agent for selling them on the open market.

The freed slave in the rural Reconcavo of Bahia therefore needed the support of his former master or, if he settled on the lands of a new engenho or fazenda, of a new master. Tied to the land, men became its prisoners. This system left the freed slave in the northeast little more than a serf subject to all the afflictions of slavery, upon whom the master could call at will. It was considered so degrading in the northeast to work another man's soil that no European colonist would agree to take the place of slave labor. In the south, however, in São Paulo state, agricultural jobs were divided between slaves and free workers who labored in the hope of soon buying some of the still abundant virgin land, but sugar-mill owners turned away free colonists for fear of losing their landed property. They saw the freed slave as much less of a threat. They knew that, in the short run at least, the former slave would not be able to break the habits that had made him, and would continue to make him, dependent on his one-time owner. European farmers, who arrived with a different background and different ambitions, were determined to fight for success. Freed slaves, on the other hand, felt that they had already succeeded, since they had been able to purchase their freedom; they had to be helped along and their tenuous achievement protected. Freed men did not see how their new status, free yet dependent, left them on the fringes of the power structure. Forced to compete in the south with European settlers who came to grow coffee, freed slaves eventually found it difficult even to find work. Those who received a bit of land found it impossible to work that land as "capitalists" and were quickly forced to sell. They then came to the cities, where they swelled the ranks of a rootless population of the starving unemployed, who lived on occasional odd jobs and depended heavily on the wealthy classes, on the very people who had once been their masters.

Freed slaves who had to contend with harsh competition in the cities did not fare much better than their rural counterparts. They had to contend with competition from free laborers and new immigrants from Europe, sometimes both, depending on the location and the period. Here, it is important once again to distinguish between older, established cities and cities which, though founded at an early date, did not really become important until the nineteenth century. By focusing on one example, Salvador, we can gain a better idea of the structure of the urban job market and the problems faced by the freed urban slave.

Salvador, capital of the colony, always had a small white population and large numbers of freed slaves. It was a city of half-breeds: only a quarter of the population was white at the beginning of the nineteenth century. The only Europeans who came in large numbers were the Portuguese. Few people came from other countries, even when there was a flood of immigration to the southern provinces of São Paulo, Parana, Santa Catarina, and Rio Grande do Sul. The few thousand white settlers who wished to become farmers were given land in the south and in remote interior regions of Bahia, where there were few Africans. The few Europeans who settled in the capital worked in new, unfamiliar trades: watchmakers, glovemakers, hatmakers, milliners, and artists. In these trades there was no competition. Thus freed men in Salvador competed only with slaves, but the latter had the backing of their masters. In other words, freed slaves traded security of employment for what turned out to be an illusory freedom, for socially and economically they continued to be lumped together with the slaves but on the whole received no help from masters. When markets tightened, the freed men were the first to suffer. To be sure, there were some slaves who, once freed, rapidly climbed in the social hierarchy. For example, Felix de Sant'Anna, a barber and orchestra leader, died in 1811, leaving a handsome fortune and a reputation for having been an excellent captain of the city's black militia. A creole, born to an African mother and an unknown father, he was in many ways the typical freed slave and succeeded thanks to the strength of his personality and the luck of knowing a useful trade. He had been owned by four different masters, the penultimate being a Benedictine monk and the ultimate Captain Felis da Costa Lisboa, who sold him his freedom for 130,000 reis. A widower, he remarried but had no children by his legitimate wives. As a bachelor, however, he had a daughter who remained a slave of the wife of his former owner, Felis da Costa Lisboa, until her father died. To her Felix de Sant'Anna left a handsome legacy of slaves, furniture, silver, and cash.

In Salvador, where there was little competition from industrious whites, a former slave could truly hope to conquer his place in the sun and enter without too much difficulty into the population of an open, rapidly expanding city. But it was as an individual that the freed man succeeded, aided by circumstances and above all by communal support. Though Salvador was a city in which much of the population was of mixed race, it behaved like a white society, and to be accepted one had to assimilate its values and behave according to one's station. Even in the nineteenth century former masters often—very often—required their freed slaves to "show eternal respect of gratitude" or risk becoming slaves once again. Freedom charters could even require freed slaves to be obedient and polite not only to their former owner but to his children as well. Felix de Sant'Anna left his daughter in slavery with his former master. This token of dependence was not without its quid pro quo, since first the former master and then his widow raised the child and taught her a trade. After the death of Felix de Sant'Anna, the heiress, finally freed from slavery, became a good marriage prospect, and her father's will required her to mary. Thus she passed from the power of a master to the power of a husband. In the judgment of her father, the freed slave Felix de Sant'Anna, this was best for his daughter's welfare.

To be freed was therefore not to become free all at once. It was not until the second or third generation that the dream of complete freedom came true. It is as if Brazilian society, which used manumission much more freely than other slave societies in the New World, did so in full awareness, even certainty, that the distinction between slave and freed man was in the end a sham, a matter of semantics, a gold star awarded to good workers. Freed men behaved in much the same way as slaves. If they became wealthy, they adopted attitudes as close as possible to those of the master class, especially toward their own slaves. But they continued to owe obedience, humility, and loyalty to the powerful. Among the powerful were the former slave's former master and all those who shared the masters' mentality. Like the slave, the freed man had to work, and to work in trades and jobs reserved for inferior social groups. His success would be of benefit only to his descendants, full-fledged citizens who adapted to the white model. The freed slave himself was forced to be content with having made the first step and with the respect that his liberation earned him in the black community. Was he aware of the price he had paid for his precarious freedom in terms of adaptation to his environment? As the law said, manumission was naturalization, which recognized that the former slave, still close to his African homeland, was a man capable of becoming a full-fledged Brazilian; yet it consigned him to purgatory for at least a generation before he could be fully accepted into society. Thus the machinery for moving from slavery to freedom, well oiled as it was, moved very slowly indeed.

Without any doubt liberated slaves on the whole were fully aware of the pitfalls of freedom. They knew that they ran the risk of dying free but poor, yet they preferred freedom under such conditions to slavery with all its protections—and bear in mind that freed men had been relatively well "protected" as slaves, for otherwise they would never have been able to gain their freedom. The liberated were people who had made their mark on both the black and white communities prior to manumission. Those who were freed in infancy or childhood had been able to call upon the necessary intercessors. In any case, the freed slave accepted freedom with open eyes, prepared to face its risks and perils.

To us, in the late twentieth century, such freedom seems entirely hypothetical, the same as the manumission granted in 1888 (when slavery was abolished) to thousands of men and women whose joy at regaining their freedom was quickly tempered by fear of a homeless, breadless tomorrow. But that is another story.

WAS CONDITIONAL MANUMISSION STILL SLAVERY?

Up to this point we have focused primarily on manumissions (free of charge or for payment) that resulted in immediate "freedom." Though this freedom was, in our judgment, highly precarious in the end, it was nevertheless recognized as freedom. The freed slaves enjoyed a new prestige, and their freedom held out hope for their children. But it was also very common for manumissions granted "free of charge" to come with delays and restrictions. Masters who granted manumission free of charge were proud of their generosity, but their slaves actually paid a high price for their freedom—a payment in kind rather than money. In this section I look at the way in which delays and restrictions created a group of people who were neither free nor slaves, whose legal position in the community was unique.

In Roman law, the slave to be freed after a specified period of time, *in diem* or *ex die*, had a different position from that of the slave; he was known as a *statuliber*. In Brazil this conditionally emancipated slave was always considered a free man in the eyes of the law. He regained his legal personality. Full employment and complete exercise of his freedom were delayed, however, until all the restrictive clauses in his manumission document had been satisfied. The Brazilian *statuliber* slave was treated legally in the same way as an unemancipated minor. He could therefore acquire property and was exempt from corporal punishment and other penalties reserved for slaves. In the courts he was not judged as a slave. He could not be sold, alienated, or mortgaged. Nor could he be threatened with punishment and induced to return to slavery, for he was a person in the full legal sense. We shall see, however, how masters circumvented this as-

pect of the law. If a statuliber committed an offense, he could reply personally and directly to the charges. His children were born free. His work was
not even considered servile labor.

Legally, then, the status of the statuliber would seem quite close to that
of the manumitted slave who had been set free without any conditions or
restrictions. In practice, however, the freedom of the statuliber was limited
by the restrictions specified in his manumission documents. The most
common such restriction was a stipulation that the slave would become
free only after the death of his lord and master. This clause is repeated like
a refrain in many manumission documents. A delay linked to the owner's
death was an unpredictable delay, a sort of game to see who would die
first. How old was the slave and how old the master who entered into such
agreements? Generally speaking, we do not know. Many possible combinations are readily imaginable. It may be that this type of manumission
was often granted to middle-aged slaves who were likely to die before their
masters and thus to remain minors until their death. Many charters stipulated that the future free man must not only serve his master but, further,
that after the death of the master he must continue to serve his master's
wife or children or some distant relative for a specified number of years.
Clauses of this type are often found, too, in purchased manumission, but
in such cases the time of service imposed never exceeded seven years. In
the 1880s this custom was shrewdly exploited by slave owners aware that
the slave system was in its death agony and certain that once slavery was
abolished they would never get the indemnities they were asking. The
sharper operators therefore abruptly liberated their slaves "free of charge"
but on condition that they remain on the plantation as paid agricultural laborers. There were a thousand and one ways to avoid paying such laborers
their wages. Thus the old structure was maintained at little or no cost.

Clauses that established very lengthy waiting periods before the statuliber obtained complete freedom were a wonderful way of both slaking the
slave's thirst for freedom and satisfying the slave owner's desire to hold on
to a good worker. Documents have been found showing that periods of
fifteen, twenty, and even thirty-five years elapsed between the time conditional manumission was granted and the death of the slave's owner. If the
slave was to benefit from his freedom, he had to be liberated while still
very young. The mature or elderly slave who had spent his entire life
watching others decide for him and act in his behalf, the slave who had always followed orders, must have found it difficult to be truly independent.

This is not to say that the slave was passive or lacking in courage, or that he did not enjoy autonomy within the zone of security created by the master. Such a slave was likely to remain tied to his master by bonds of familiarity rather than affection, however, just as many wives remain bound to their husbands for fear of having to struggle to survive on their own. Force of habit and the feeling that society, however receptive it may have seemed, was ultimately hostile to newcomers led the conditionally manumitted slave to accept a hybrid status, half-slave and half-free. His position was above that of other slaves, and yet the master maintained control over him and was confident of being well served, generally for life. Consider, for example, one tragicomic, not to say macabre, manumission of 1831, in which Mathias Baptiste de Carvelho promised freedom to the mulatto Isidoro Baptista, son of the freed slave Eusebia, for "one hour prior to his death," because of "the friendship he bore her" and because Isidoro was light-skinned. This master probably wanted to carry with him to the grave the charitable merit of having freed his slave during his lifetime.

Besides the time restrictions just mentioned, many other restrictive clauses can be found in the manumission documents. Most common were clauses providing for cash payments. A certain sum of money was specified as due to the master or a third party. For example, in 1856, the Nago Esperança was freed by her owner on condition that she pay 600,000 reis to a certain Marcelina, to whom the owner owed that sum. If Esperança failed to pay, her manumission would be canceled. Nevertheless, she would not be entirely free until the death of her owner, Maria Antonia Teixeira. Thus Esperança continued to live in a semicaptive state, goaded by the mirage of liberty, for in 1856 600,000 reis was a truly enormous sum. To have amassed that amount in two years, the slave would have had to kill herself with work. An even more difficult obstacle confronted the slave who had to earn a certain sum of money outside of normal working hours. All sorts of arrangements were concocted by needy and clever masters. Sometimes the slave was lucky: his interests and the master's coincided. This was the case with Eusebio, a black African beyond the age of fifty, a farmer on a plantation belonging to the Count of Pedroso e Albuquerque, one of the wealthiest men in Bahia, whose fortune derived from the slave trade and from passing counterfeit copper coin. In 1881 Eusebio was offered his freedom on condition that he pay 240,000 reis per year in services for almost five years. A contract of this type allowed the slave to remain on the premises and probably to continue to be maintained by his master.

Quite similar was the situation of the conditionally liberated slave who was forced to pay for freedom by serving some other master as a domestic. The employer paid the slave's owner the wages earned by the statuliber. The slave worked as an unpaid domestic servant for a specified period. One example is the service contract signed by Marie Carolina Mendes Dias: in 1876, she freed her mulatto slave Flora for the sum of 1,150,000 reis, paid by Ubaldina Pedrosa de Lacerda, who obtained Flora's services for a period of seven years. Flora was obviously better off than other slaves who were forced to borrow to pay for manumission. The period for which she was obliged to work was clearly stated. But many documents limited themselves to the vague statement that the statuliber had to work until his owner "was eventually indemnified," which left the door open to all sorts of double-dealing and gave the master control over the slave for an indefinite period of time.

When a child was liberated, the custom was that full enjoyment of freedom did not begin until age twenty in the case of a female and age twenty-five in the case of a male. Masters were generally guided by prudence, occasionally by affection. The delay was intended to allow for the child's upbringing and training, as we see in the following manumission document from 1755: "I, Teresa de Souza Rabello, hereby declare that among the goods I possess and which have been awarded to me on the death of my father Domingos de Souza Rabello, there are my two brothers on my mother's side, Crispim and Simão, whom I set free from this day and forever more, on condition that they be subject for three years to my agent Luiz Goncalves dos Santos and my cousin Dionizio de Campos da Costa, so that they may learn their trades, Crispim that of tailor and Simão that of carpenter." The story is on the one hand edifying and touching—a woman freeing her half brothers—and on the other hand cruel, for it shows that a person could own his or her own close relatives. Quite often, noble sentiments were mixed with more or less openly avowed self-interest. A conditionally freed slave, trained in a good craft, was an owner's dream, an ideal source of income. Note, too, that many conditionally freed slaves were excellent artisans and skilled domestics.

Let me add two additional "cases" to our already long list of manumitted slaves. Angela Ferreira, a midwife of mixed race, was freed in 1755 for the handsome sum of 160,000 reis but required to continue serving as midwife on the engenho of her former master. And Manoel, liberated free of charge in 1789 by Teresa Maria de Jesus, was a half-breed and overseer of his fazenda. He was freed on condition that he stay on as overseer. This type of condition was commonly imposed on slaves who held specialized positions with an engenho or fazenda. Masters used whatever means were available to hold on to skilled workers, who were hard to replace.

It is exciting to decipher conditional manumission documents, because doing so helps make clear exactly how the slave system worked: the slave was dependent on the master, but the master was also dependent on the slave. The men and women who owned slaves knew that they could not survive without the help of their servants. Some concealed this fact with clever formulas, while others admitted it openly, declaring, for example, that a slave could have his freedom only after the master had found the replacement needed to run his business, farm, or home. Antonio Lourenço Gomes, who owned a large bakery, in 1839 freed his black slave Joaquim (who was by then sixty years old, incidentally), on condition that Joaquim teach the art of baking to the other employees of the bakery. Joaquim agreed to continue to run the business for a salary of 4,000 reis per month. Thus the slave and the freed man needed the master to earn a living and to rise in the social hierarchy, but the master also needed the slave who had been intimately involved in every aspect of his life, as business partner, breadwinner, and domestic servant—indispensable in every way.

This interdependence colored all relations between dominator and dominated, greatly complicating the picture of this slave society, seething with life, in which the jeito of each man meshed with the jeito of his neighbor and everyone tried to avoid losing face. Each person shrewdly calculated how best to accommodate his desires to this interests, how to protect himself, how to exploit his advantages. Ties that developed on the job were so personal, so intimately associated with the patriarchal slave system, that they tended to make even the manumitted slave something of an indispensable child to be educated and used, especially when his income was necessary for his former master's survival. Liberated slaves continued to cultivate their masters' gardens, to run their masters' factories, to train disciples, to market goods. Beyond freedom, which brought moral satisfaction, a sense of rebirth, and newfound dignity, the ex-slave could hope to be paid a "just wage" for his labor. From now on he would be paid for his work, even if that pay was to be used to purchase his freedom.

We still do not know, however, what this just wage was, nor by what criteria it was deemed to be "just." Wages were paid only to valued slaves in any case, and then only if the master realized how useful the slave was. All indications are, however, that few masters were aware of the exact value of their slaves. Human nature is such that often we do not realize the value of what we have until we must do without it. As long as slave labor was abundant, slave owners could ignore, or pretend to ignore, their dependence on their slaves. The conditions imposed on freed slaves show the many kinds of services that masters expected their slaves to perform. Some had to accompany their masters on journeys, others to take care of the children or relatives, still others to accept service as domestics in Portugal, where slavery was abolished in the middle of the eighteenth century. Nothing was too much to ask of a conditionally liberated slave. Freedom was priceless and the slave would give anything for it: it was an enchanting mirage that receded as one drew near, like the vision of an oasis in a desert.

The examples given above are far from exhaustive, but it would be tedious to enumerate all the different situations that a slave awaiting liberation might face. Psychologically speaking, conditional liberation improved the slave's situation. He regained some of his human rights. He became a member of the master's community. The "freeable" slaves, slaves on the road to freedom, formed an "aristocracy" among slaves—an aristocracy of limited numbers, to be sure. But the freeable slave, like his brother the freed man, remained what official documents and common parlance alike referred to as the *forro*, or manumitted slave. He had a well-defined place in the social hierarchy, nearer to that of the slave than to that of the free man. The slave population of Brazil thus consisted of three groups: slaves, conditionally manumitted slaves, and manumitted slaves. The latter two groups were held up as models of behavior to the mass of slaves. They constituted an influential minority among the slave population, precisely because of this exemplary role.

ATTITUDES OF FREEABLE AND FREED SLAVES

In describing the range of conditions to which the former slave's freedom was subject, we have seen how the rules of the game were set by the master, who attempted to maintain close ties with the slaves whom he freed, who were generally judged to be humble, loyal, and obedient, indispensable and excellent workers. Let us take the analysis one step further. Was the slave owner the sole arbiter of the rules, as indicated in the manumission documents? In reality, the slave was not like the mouse with which the cat plays prior to devouring it. Once raised from the prostration of captivity, he showed good sense in not accepting all the principles and practices of white society. The ludicrous image of the slave as a passive, indolent, and irresolute character should be consigned to the dustbin of history. This image was the work of people in too much of a hurry to disavow the slave system; in their haste they relied on poorly chosen arguments. In fact, slaves remained free to challenge or reject those demands of their masters which were offensive to their dignity. We have already discussed the importance of individual and collective rebellion, ineffective though it usually proved. Some rebel slaves went so far as to draw up "treaties" that they tried, unsuccessfully, to force their masters to sign: in the Ilheus region in the late eighteenth century, for example, rebel slaves killed the overseer of their engengho and offered the master terms concerning their clothing, recreation, leisure time, culture, fishing to supplement their diet. Their program, worthy of a twentieth–century trade union, tells us much about the slaves' attitudes. Compelled by need, coerced by force, slaves in white society obeyed the rules only insofar as was necessary to ensure their survival. They had to play the game in order to live, yet they never sacrificed their dignity as individuals. What was imposed upon them from the outside never affected their inner being, fostered by the black community, which offered compensations and satisfactions not found in the fields, the mine, the streets, or the master's household. For the slave, submission and acceptance were tactics, one side of the dialectic that governed his double life.

The freed slave ran the risk of being seen as a traitor, as one who had betrayed the slave community and gone over to the enemy. There was the stereotype of the "good servant deserving of reward," the good servant whom the master manipulated by holding out the prospect of eventual liberation, the good servant who took care of his master, insinuated himself into his master's good graces, became his confidant, and earned the money necessary to purchase freedom. We have seen how the clever worker made the master appreciate his qualities. Slaves knew that they had to cross the dividing line between slavery and freedom all alone, and that once freed they would have to take their distance from the slave community. That community was in any case not homogeneous: some had lighter skin and less curly hair and less flat noses that others. The candidate for manumission knew perfectly well that freedom would set him apart, not only from his erstwhile brothers but also from free whites. His opportunities would depend on the color of his skin and on his facial features. This makes it easier to understand why so many slaves accepted the relatively privileged status of conditional manumission, even if they were under no illusions as to their ultimate prospects and knew perfectly well that they could never fulfill the conditions required for complete manumission. They knew that immediate freedom was not in the cards in any case and that only their children could hope to make their legal status coincide with the concrete realities of Brazilian society. Still, the freeable slave could make use of his privileges to ensure the survival of black culture and black society. To the freed slaves fell the task of preserving the African heritage by adapting it to life in Brazil. That heritage made itself felt in the sometimes dramatic efforts of slaves to escape from the subordination of captivity. Freeable slaves served the black community in individual as well as collective ways. They were the natural intermediary between masters and slaves. They assumed a leadership role and took advantage of their opportunities. Without abdicating the past, they accepted the present in all its complexity. Later on we shall see the relations that developed among freed slaves, conditionally freed slaves, slaves, and free individuals. Historians and sociologists have exaggerated the hostilities that may have existed among these different classes of people.

There can be no doubt that the behavior of freed slaves depended on the composition of the larger society. The more cut off that society was from white cultural influence, the easier it was for the freed slave to integrate. If the receiving society was open to white influence, the chance of integration decreased. Integration—social adaptation—also depended on certain economic realities. Space does not permit us to go into detail about the various degrees and nuances of this social adaptation. Let us therefore consider, once again, two models: the freed slave in Bahia state and the freed slave in the south.

Here again, Salvador presents an extreme case: it was almost totally closed to white immigration. The Portuguese who came seeking their fortunes were almost all males. What is more, Salvador was not only the major slave port, it was also an important center for the use of slave labor. A population of mixed race quickly developed. The intermediate levels of the social hierarchy consisted mainly of former slaves, both half-breeds and blacks, and their descendants. People were quick to forget the skin color of a successful half-breed, all the more because freed slaves sought deliberately and systematically to *limpar o sangue*, to "cleanse" their blood by having children whiter than themselves. For them this was a way of assimilating to the white model. Slave owners needed these intermediate social groups to perform numerous indispensable services, to work as artisans, or in transport and navigation. A sign of the situation was the way in which encumbering racial regulations were circumvented. The ordination of black priests was forbidden, for example. Yet at all times we find large numbers of mulattoes and blacks among the priests of Salvador, as their wills make clear. Even the Company of Jesus, theoretically closed to men of color, counted among its most illustrious members of grandson of a mulatto woman, Father Antonio Vieira, defender of the Indians, indefatigable writer, and influential apostle whose work left a deep mark on seventeenth-century Portugal as well as Brazil. A superior of the company and counselor to the king of Portugal, he abandoned his distinctions to return to Brazil where he wished to die and where he spent the next sixteen years preaching and leading a religious life before passing away at a ripe old age. As an amusing sidelight Brazil at this stage was reputed to be a most healthful country, where people lived long lives. The background and skin color of the child of a freed person no longer mattered. When color had to be recorded, it was often a matter of some confusion: the same person might be marked down as white or mulatto in different official documents. The only rule of the game insisted upon social and economic "bleaching." Evidence from Bahia (a sample of 471 wills of freed slaves) suggests that manumitted slaves preferred to marry women of the same color as themselves. Thus the free slave kept faith with his own world, and the bleaching process did not begin, it seems, until the next generation. Popular tradition and older writers like to tell the story of black women, creole or African, who sought to bear the master's children and were proud of their mulattoes. I am not so sure that pride was what they felt. In my view, the manumitted slave in Bahia did not need to make any fundamental change in his behavior, because he continued to live a double life, in part within an African community adapted to Bahian ways, in part within a European community that established the criteria for social and economic success. In the long run the freed slave had two options: either remain in Salvador and see his children assimilate completely and gradually abandon the black world of their ancestors, or else return to Africa. But it was impossible to go back in time, and those who returned to Africa had adaptation problems of their own, about which I shall have more to say later on. In any case, the freed man who stayed in Bahia had no further sacrifice to make. His attitudes remained the same as those of the freeable slave. But the freed man who wished to return home to Africa had to pay dearly, not only in cash for the voyage but in human terms as well, for friends and relatives were left behind and old habits broken. Some Africans even returned from Africa to Bahia: João de Oliveira, who was arrested in Salvador in 1770, for example. He was wrongly accused of smuggling in merchandise from Africa, where he had been in business for thirty-eight years. He had returned to Salvador to die "among Catholics." His lawyer prepared a fine petition in which he praised both João's Christian sentiments and the services to Portuguese commerce at Porto Novo and Lagos rendered by a man who, though sold to a Pernambuco slaver as a child, had "always been the greatest protector of the Portuguese" and always maintained "the complete purity of his Catholic faith."

Quite different was the situation of the freed slave in areas where there was significant white immigration, where the stigma of slavery tended to persist for a long time. White society rejected him as an inferior being. Slaves were not introduced into the states of southern Brazil until quite late. What is more, they arrived at the same time as white immigrants. In the south there was also an indigenous population of Indians, who played an important role in the process of racial mixing, whereas in the north, mixing with Indians occurred only in the inland sertão of the northeast or the captaincies of the far north, to which few Africans came. In areas where there were large numbers of Indians and whites, freed blacks had a much harder struggle than in the northeast or Minas Gerais or even Rio de Janeiro. In the south, the bleaching and acculturation process was obligatory. But society, dominated by the white model, tended to be static. It reacted vigorously against racial mixing between whites and blacks; Indians were considered to be nobler. The freed slave was rejected and made a social and economic outcast. Hence he adopted ambivalent attitudes. He was forced to make large concessions. Former slaves and even their children ultimately formed a social group that was sharply differentiated from the rest of society both by color and employment. They lacked the support necessary for real social and economic progress. Where such progress did occur, it was extremely slow. Here the mulatto was seen as black by whites but not by Africans. He developed hostility to both whites and blacks, and the ambivalence of his situation extended over several generations, again in contrast to what seems to have been the case in Bahia. We shall gain a better idea of these problems by describing the development of social relations in Brazilian slave society.

NINE

The Manumitted Slave as Social Intermediary

Diverse by skin color, origin, and training, manumitted slaves influenced all aspects of Brazilian society. The masters who profited from their labor had little notion of the vast human riches to be found in the makeshift dwellings occupied by men and women whose only treasure was their hard-won, reluctantly granted, and shrewdly manipulated freedom. Like his brother the slave, the freed man was acutely aware of his dignity as a human being and of the value of his labor. In some respects the gods of his ancestors set him free. He experienced his newfound liberty in a society that was far from homogeneous. His responses were as varied as the situations with which he had to cope. To examine the social relations that developed between freed slaves and free men and between freed slaves and slaves is to perform an autopsy on Brazilian slave society. This is no simple task, owing to the baffling complexity of that colorful and vibrant society, by turns sad or happy, rigid or flexible.

SOCIAL RELATIONS BETWEEN MANUMITTED SLAVES AND FREE MEN

Just as the African captive and Brazilian-born creole had to adjust to and suffer harsh apprenticeship in two different worlds, one white, the other black, so, too, was the freed slave forced to walk a tightrope between the world he had left behind and the new world he had only recently entered. In the northeast and center this new world was predominantly black, whereas in the south, more recently settled and predominantly white, complete assimilation was correspondingly more difficult. It may be somewhat misleading to contrast these two "ideal types," for the reality was a good deal more subtle than so sharp a contrast would suggest. Yet provided we refrain from superficial generalization, this schematic distinction will help us to grasp certain essential differences between the societies of the north and south.

Throughout much of the foregoing discussion it has been assumed that predominantly black society was more open and receptive to the slave than predominantly white society. Does this assumption hold good over a period of more than three centuries? Let me once again draw a contrast between Salvador and São Paulo, the two poles or centers of Brazilian development, windows onto more obscure parts of the country which borrowed customs and ideas from these major cities and adapted them to local circumstances. Salvador, the jewel of the Portuguese colony, a city whose population was predominantly of mixed race as early as the seventeenth century, was totally different from its daughter in the south, the white and Indian city of São Paulo, which became, in the nineteenth century, the dynamic coffee capital of Brazil. The life of a freed slave in Bahia was different from the life of a freed slave in São Paulo. Patterns of social mobility were also different, as we have already seen. But now we must press our investigation further. Black slaves had been arriving in Salvador from the second half of the sixteenth century on. By the seventeenth century they constituted a majority of the population. There was relatively little white immigration. The native Indian population had been driven as far from the coast as possible. Near the cities there remained only a few *aldeamentos,* or Indian villages run by Jesuits, who acted as the Indians' guardians. When the Jesuits were expelled from Brazil in 1759, the government was no longer able to protect the indigenous population. Mixing of white and Indian blood had already begun. It is difficult to say when white men, European settlers or their children, began to show a preference for black women over Indians. But clearly by the seventeenth century Salvadoran society was racially quite mixed: the fact is attested by travelers' accounts and by regulations imposing various restrictions on the mulatto population of Salvador (whether artisan, itinerant merchant, or senhor de engenho). In vain the dominant society sought to defend itself by all available means against any change in its self-image: that of a white society transplanted from the mother country to American soil. But in Brazil one found few European-born women, and sexual needs could not be denied. Bahian society was a society of many colors. The industrious mulatto made himself officially white, especially if he was lucky enough to be born with light skin and to be freed. The dominant society, which did everything it could to stay white, established barriers to social mobility, but these proved vain. In theory, the colored man, even if manumitted, was barred from holding certain offices, including all positions of authority, and could not enter the priesthood. He was even required to wear dark clothing to set him apart from whites. As of 1708 captive and freed Negro males were not allowed to wear silk. Freed mulatto women could line their clothing with taffeta or wear silk stockings. Mulattoes, males and female, free or not, were not allowed to wear gold or silver braid or buttons. They could be carried through the streets only in open hammocks. The opulent curtained palanquins were for whites only.

These harsh regulations cannot obscure, however, the great changes that were taking place in Bahian society. It became increasingly difficult for whites to prevent what they considered scandalous changes in individual relations. Mulattoes ultimately gained acceptance—though not all of them. It is difficult to judge what criteria governed their slow but steady rise, since the breakthroughs were made by individuals, not groups. But so many individuals did break through that finally society itself was altered. A mulatto seeking new privileges had to rely on the help, support, and solidarity of others. The mixed-race son of a powerful senhor de engenho or a wealthy Portuguese merchant could, even if his mother was an African or creole slave, obliterate his origins, silence gossips, and take steps to protect himself against anyone who might consider contesting his whiteness.

To see what criteria were at issue, consider the entry requirements for the illustrious and exclusive confraternity of Santa-Casa-da-Misericordia of Bahia. Candidates had to prove that they were honest and capable of earning a living. In addition, they were required to be of "pure" blood. This meant that they must not be "new Christians," that is, of Jewish origin, and must not have colored ancestors or spouses. But in fact this regulation was only sporadically enforced. If the candidate was a personage of some repute, the confraternity "forgot" about his origins—though the question could subsequently be raised if some cabal wished to expel a member considered for some reason to be "undesirable." In 1679, Domingos Roiz, a confectioner, petitioned for membership in this very powerful confraternity. He was rejected because his wife was Teodora Barbosa, a mulatto, daughter of a black woman, and because he himself could neither read nor write. Some years later, in 1709, the headmaster and members of the confraternity's directorate rejected the membership applications of Joseph dos Reis de Oliveira and his brother-in-law, the goldsmith Joseph de Almeida Pacheco, for "defects of blood." These two names do not figure in the lists of Bahian "new Christians" for this period, when it would have been quite extraordinary for the Inquisition to have overlooked anyone in its persecutions. Indications are, therefore, that the problem with the two men was a black ancestor in their family. In 1714, however, the directorate decided to accept this same Joseph de Almeida Pacheco, "having determined the purity of his wife's blood through her dowry contract." Thus the confraternity overruled itself five years after the first decision: the petitioner was suddenly awarded a certificate of "whiteness." Since his wife and his ancestors had not changed in the interim, he must have found the kind of support needed to bestow legitimacy upon any transgression.

In Bahia, once beyond the generation of manumission, color no longer counted compared with individual success and the support of powerful allies. If an institution recognized a mulatto as being of "pure blood," that person's whole family became white, notwithstanding possible protests. African blood deeply marked the Bahian population: foreign travelers in the seventeenth, eighteenth, and in nineteenth centuries do not bother to conceal their surprise at finding signs of it in the faces of the city's leading families. Skin color was an obstacle to social ascendancy only if the person who aspired to become fully assimilated was not accepted by the dominant social group. On the other hand, it did not count if a colored individual's relatives and friends were powerful enough to acknowledge their ties. Consider the case of the four bastard sons of Cristovão da Rocha Pita, a leading senhor de engenho. He died in 1808, leaving all his property to these four sons. All were children of Vitoria da Fonseca, an unmarried mulatto women. Cristovão da Rocha Pita had had his sons legitimized before his death, but his will was immediately contested by his "white" nephews. It took thirty-six long years for the legitimated children to win their case and themselves become true senhores de engenho. From that point on, their origins were forgotten, as were their facial features and hair. The Bahians, in fact, were the inventors of the lovely term branco da terra, white of the land. Success was the surest means of "purifying" the blood. One did not have to be the son of a major sugar planter, moreover. Any kind of success would do, and anyone could be helped, encouraged, and legalized. One poor Portuguese who came to Salvador as an adolescent worked in a bakery kept by a mulatto, the son of freed slaves. He married their daughter and made a fortune. Having become leading grain merchants, Mr. and Mrs. X were ennobled. No one dreamed of challenging the purity of the blood of the Viscountess of R.

One has only to examine family portraits, yellowing nineteenth-century photographs, and travelers' drawings to convince oneself that Bahian society, so proud of being white and European, actually has deep roots among the faceless people who arrived from Africa on slave ships. These roots go unavowed, or else they are concealed, if necessary, with the fiction of an Indian ancestor. But no one is deceived, unless it be the blind entourage of those brancos da terra who reject Africa's racial as well as cultural contribution to Brazilian society and who will, if pushed to the wall, exalt the Indian contribution to the Brazilian people, but no other.

To sum up, then, Bahian society in the colonial period (1500–1822), unable to maintain its "whiteness" and forced in daily practice to violate its own prohibitions, seemed gradually to evolve an ideology of purification. This ideology had two aims: to make purification relatively simple and to force the new "white" to break all ties with his original ethnic group and to cut himself off entirely from black culture, religion, customs, and friends. Hence Bahian society, despite or perhaps because it was predominantly black, was profoundly imbued with its European origins. The mulatto who aspired to assimilate adopted a lifestyle as similar as possible to that of Europe; he accepted the culture of the white man. The problem of mixed blood did not arise as such, since anyone who was successful and willing to assimilate could win acceptance. Thus it was an open society, a society willing to welcome successful individuals with open arms, especially since each success was in fact a tribute to the white ideal inspired by the dominant groups within the society.

With the coming of independence and the loosening of the ties between Brazil and Portugal, the white mother country (or at any rate a mother country thought to be white, even though it, too, had known slavery and racial mixing), Bahians suddenly found themselves frightened. Everything possible had to be done to ensure that the new independent Brazil would be a "European" Brazil. Theirs was an alienating realization: amazed Bahians looked with new eyes at the world around them and rejected whatever seemed at odds with the mythical European model. The result was a whole range of scornful attitudes toward anything that recalled the colony's original sin: slavery, "primitive" crops, dark skin. Bahia's beauties took care not to expose their white skin to the sun for fear of being mistaken for mulattoes. The upper classes armed themselves with prejudices and closed ranks, especially after manumissions began to increase the numbers of free African workers. "Dark-skinned" became a synonym for "lower class." Yet in 1775 the population of Salvador was only 36 percent white. This percentage feel to 27.81 percent in 1807 and 22.37 percent in

1824 before rising once more to 35.2 percent in 1872, where it remained practically unchanged until 1940. It was chiefly the mulatto population that grew in Bahia, from 20 percent in 1807 to 44.3 percent in 1872.

"Purification" became the only course open to the colored man who wished to erase the "stain" of his African origin, rise in society, and obtain economic influence. But the first effect of the new attitudes was to isolate the well-defined mulatto group. Rejected by whites, who gravitated toward those whiter than themselves, and also rejected by blacks, who considered them traitors, the mulattoes tried to adapt in every way to the white model. Bear in mind that the battle cry of Bahian black rebels throughout the first forty years of the nineteenth century was "death to whites and mulattoes." Remember, too, that the police forces used by the whites to control the African population were composed mainly of mulattoes. Mulattoes were promised the world on condition that they strive to make Salvador more "white": only foreign travelers loved the city's exotic, iridescent colors; locals did all they could to make it conform to Europe's frigid lackluster. Mulattoes, in alliance with whites, dreamed that their children and grandchildren would quickly become good Europeans. Hence they quickly became the white man's aides, encouraged by the many examples of success, by more or less light-skinned brothers, brancos da terra, who had become illustrious doctors and lawyers, excellent preachers, indispensable schoolteachers, brilliant professors. It was in no way extraordinary in nineteenth-century Bahia, proud of its humanist culture and of its position as the liberated child of the Portuguese mother country, to see a black professor enjoying friendly collegial relations with the sons of great sugar planters who had also taken jobs as professors in urban schools. But all mulattoes who held positions of importance, including high government posts, behaved like whites, thought like whites, and served in the white administration, courts, legislature, and diplomatic corps. A white woman might well complain that some beautiful mulatto was stealing her son; she could do nothing about it. "Purification" was irreversible; it enriched a society which, though it wished to remain closed, never managed to find a way to refuse the new blood constantly offered by a social group whose only ambition was to disappear: the mulattoes.

How did recently freed Africans and creoles react to this flight of mulattoes toward the world of the white man? Did blacks imitate mulattoes, succumb to the blandishments of the wealthier classes, and seek to forget their "blackness"? The reactions of creoles in fact were different from those of Africans. These differences reveal the speed with which creoles born in the mild and receptive climate of northeastern Brazil could forget the lands of their ancestors. The liberated creole, born and raised in the bosom of a Brazilian family, had a totally different view of the world from his African brother; his former masters felt that he was much closer to their world, much more reliable, adaptable, and manageable than the African. The special favors that creoles enjoyed were embodied in legislation in the nineteenth century, in discriminatory right-to-work laws. To cite one example from among a hundred: in 1850, a provincial decree prohibited African sailors from docking their boats. Henceforth this was a privilege reserved for Brazilians. Growing animosity, in some cases stirred up deliberately by powerful whites, separated Africans and creoles in competition for work. It was an unequal struggle: the African got no help from hostile and wary employers in a market where labor was overabundant. Though creoles and Africans were of the same color, they were treated very differently by a society frightened by a rash of slave rebellions, rebellions which, though harshly put down, had left lingering suspicion of all who refused to assimilate. Of the creole, on the other hand, people believed and even expressed views similar to this one, which I heard expressed not so long ago by a grand lady who was manifestly a branca da terra: "He's black but has the soul of a white man." In conformity with the expectations of white society, the creole separated from his black African brothers and tried to acquire a white soul. He offered his services to the rulers—all his services, especially against the constant threat posed by slaves and certain freed men. He felt secure only in the company of Brazilians like himself, who had no living memory of Africa. Brazil, his native land, was also his protector. She allowed him to have his own confraternities and organizations. She gave him work and placed in him her trust, that most precious commodity.

Such trust did not always prevail between freed Africans and the masters who had nevertheless granted them freedom, because the African retained visceral memories of his ancestors across the sea. Manumission changed nothing. The sad words of the African's work shanty are all too true:

> Vida de negro é dificil
> E dificil como quê . . .

> The black man's life is hard
> Hard to know nothing more . . .

Did the freed Bahian African continue to live, as in the time of slavery, according to both the teachings of his Brazilian community and the legacy of his ancestors? Or did he, like the creole black, seek as quickly as possible to efface his family's culture and customs? Was his adaptation to two structures and two communities sufficiently complete and profound for him to go on being a man of two religions, two educations, and two complementary families? As we have seen, his son the creole was in general unable to relate to his African origins; like a moth drawn to a candle, he was transfixed by the promise of a better life if he joined the white man's world. But the African's native land was not Brazil. As the lost, far-off homeland, Africa glowed with memories of childhood and youth. Actually, several different attitudes coexisted in the large African community, whose ranks were of course replenished by the constant arrival in Bahia of new slaves. A minority sought to emulate the behavior of freed creoles. They forgot Africa, or at any rate behaved as though they did. This was the reaction of fear in the face of a hostile society, clearly visible particularly during periods when insurrection and ensuing repression sowed terror in the African community. Police documents show us frightened Africans who claim to be "well known to all the whites on the street" and who describe their quiet lives, boast of their creole children, and point to their unblemished work records. They are trying to keep from being arrested, of course, at a time when every freed African was viewed with suspicion. But clearly these attitudes were characteristic of a segment of the black community which had made up its mind to fight to protect its hard-won freedom, to run no risks, and to accept the friendship of whites and the help of their creole children as the best way to win total acceptance in Bahian society.

Still, many freed Africans, like the slaves they had been only a short while before, continued to straddle two communities, two worlds that seem incompatible only to us, too blind to see the reality. But for the African, who placed so much value on gestures, rituals, and on the realm of spirituality and religion, there were riches to be had in both communities. He consulted both witch doctor and physician. He demanded Catholic baptism so that he could join the confraternity devoted to praying to his orisha. He asked for protection from his ancestors as well as the Virgin Mary. He adopted Saints Benedict and Iphigenia as his own. Though he learned to eat in the European style, he did not forget his delicious African dishes. He lived a double life, gathering in small circles to practice, far from prying white eyes, the religions and customs of the Nagos or Fons of Dahomey. Freed blacks were held together by the fear they inspired in the white community. The African retained his identity. He sought to pass on his cultural riches to his creole children.

It is to African slaves freed in the nineteenth century that Bahians are indebted for the preservation of the peculiar and novel social structure of the black community, a legacy of the time of slavery when European and African cultures coexisted in perfect harmony.

What happened, though, if a liberated African, impelled by an irresistible desire to return to his native land, decided to go back to Africa? And what about those sentenced to deportation by the Brazilian courts? The black who returned to Africa was a man deeply changed by his stay in Brazil. In Dahomey and Nigeria, Brazilians—as others were quick to call them—proclaimed their loyalty to a way of life they had abandoned. They felt affection for their Bahia, a gay, prosperous city which they remembered for its markets and for the friends they had left behind. Having fled the hostility of some segments of white society, they became sailors or artisans, coopers or barbers aboard ships engaged in the Atlantic trade, and they brought news, gifts, and religious objects from Africa. Some helped fugitive slaves to stow away. They settled in cities on the Bay of Benin, such as Agoué, Ouidah, Porto-Novo, and Lagos, and there helped to spread Brazilian traditions. Today many families—Catholic, Protestant, and Muslim—descended from those Brazilian returnees continue to worship the African gods of their ancestors and to speak a language that is a mixture of Portuguese and African words. Pierre Verger tells the story of one freed slave who returned to Africa in 1842 to found the first Catholic church in Agoué, dedicated to Our Lord the Good Jesus of the Redemption, honoring the church of the same name in Salvador. When French missionaries came to Agoué thirty years later, they found a Catholic community more than eight hundred strong. Whenever a priest of any nationality visited Agoué, the "Brazilians" of the city hastened to ask him to say mass. Returnees continued to have their children baptized and to teach them Portuguese, which was a marvelous tool with which to earn a living through trade with the former land of exile. Catholicism was the bond that held together social structures inherited from white society, just as African religion had proved indispensable for maintaining African culture and beliefs in Brazil.

Up to now we have focused on the complex process of adaptation that freed slaves in northeastern Brazil had to undergo. In what ways did the northeast differ from, say, São Paulo, where free society was truly white and those of dark skin were in the minority? In attempting to answer this question we may rely on the thorough work of Roger Bastide and Florestan Fernandes. African workers did not begin to arrive in São Paulo in large numbers until after the abolition of the slave trade in 1830, which coincided with a large influx of European immigrants. As time passed São Paulo became increasingly white: in 1804, 46.31 percent of the population was white, in 1818, 48.85 percent, in 1886, 79 percent. By 1940, the city had a population of 1,326,261, of whom 1,203,111, or 90.71 percent, were white. At that point Salvador was only 33 percent white. Thus the "bleaching" of São Paulo is undeniable. Black slaves were very costly and few were freed, because labor was in great demand on the coffee plantations. Immigrant Europeans rather than blacks or mulattoes reaped the benefits of the city's growth. In Rio de Janeiro and the Minas, freed slaves and their children were apparently able to monopolize certain lines of small business and transport, much as their Bahian brothers did. But in São Paulo these jobs often passed directly from Indians to European immigrants, probably because white workers were in the majority and did not refuse jobs that the few Portuguese who came to Bahia deemed unworthy of them. In any case, in Bahia there were too few Europeans to perform all such jobs. By contrast, in São Paulo it was the colored population that was marginalized. Negroes received the worst paid and most difficult jobs. In the south blacks were not even allowed to compete with whites in agriculture: witness the great exodus that occurred when slavery was abolished and blacks were forced to leave the plantations and either go to the cities to live in poverty or make the long trek northward in the company of others as wretched as themselves. They returned to Bahia, from which they had been uprooted years earlier to work the coffee plantations. In the nineteenth century, in São Paulo even more than in Bahia, skin color became the symbol of a person's social position. The dominant white society placed a thousand and one obstacles in the way of blacks who wished to integrate and assimilate. Antagonisms between masters and slaves festered, and social relations were cold and stiff. In São Paulo freed men were required to behave like slaves, to show respect and modesty in their language, restraint in their gestures, circumspection in their voices and manner of expression. Free blacks and mulattoes were supposed to behave as humbly as slaves: they had to hold themselves erect without swaying, speak only when spoken to, ard perform even the most unpleasant tasks cheerfully and without protest. The terms *senhor, senhora,* and *dona* were used only in addressing whites, never blacks. Blacks had to walk in the middle of the road, where the mud was usually thickest and filthiest. And they were not allowed to dress like their former masters.

Faced with such exigencies, freed men rebelled and became unreliable workers. The freed slave trusted no one but his former master, who knew and respected him, who protected him against the hostility of the rest of society and to whom, out of habit and gratitude, he showed the respect that he refused to show to whites in general. Generally speaking, then, the freed slave in São Paulo became a true dependent. His world revolved around that of his former owner. Even mulattoes rarely obtained positions open to people of mixed race in Bahia. What is more, the numbers of the liberated were small. It was therefore difficult for them to safeguard their African heritage. Mulattoes and blacks alike were objects of the white man's disdain. Few light-skinned creoles managed to "pass" for white, yet they served as models for all their brothers, who dreamed of assimilation, of "purification," much more than they dreamed of returning to Africa or asserting themselves as Brazilian blacks.

SOCIAL RELATIONS BETWEEN FREED MEN AND SLAVES

What was the attitude of the freed man toward his former companions in captivity, as he attempted to strike a difficult balance between the world of servitude and the world of freedom? How did white influence affect relations between freed men and slaves? What common interests, class consciousness, or other factors united freed men and slaves? What issues divided them? These questions are complex and obviously could have many different answers, not all of them very clear, for research has hitherto focused primarily on master-slave relations, secondarily on relations between masters and manumitted slaves, and very little on relations between slaves and freed men. Some Bahian historians, however, have attempted to explore this new area. Hence this account will once again focus primarily on Bahia in the nineteenth century. Though limited, this approach remains valuable as an example and suggestive for our understanding of the process by which people moved from one status to another over the course of three centuries of slavery.

Three centuries of slavery and three centuries of manumission. Three centuries during which social relations never stabilized, adapting instead to changing times. Three centuries of widespread illiteracy affecting almost every segment of the population. Still, there are sources to which the resourceful researcher may turn: oral sources, administrative and judicial records, wills and estate inventories, and police reports of insurrections or other disturbances. The following account is based on reasonably reliable information drawn from such sources. What is more, the Salvadoran archives have been found to contain hitherto unsuspected riches: information concerning colored confraternities as well as 471 freed men's wills registered with notaries between 1790 and 1890. One of these, included in its entirety as an appendix to the present work, may be taken, for the firmness of its affirmations *in articulo mortis* and for its rich expression of human desires, as exemplary. It will give some idea of one freed Bahian's views of his place in the social hierarchy, and the way in which he situated himself in relation to his world.

Hostilities within the black community complicated the relations between freed men and slaves—their own, those of others, and those, in particular, of their former masters. Toward the end of the eighteenth century, as we saw earlier, the slaves of the Sant'Anna engenho rebelled, killed their overseer, and offered their master peace terms, which included a demand that creole slaves be exempted from the difficult job of deep-sea fishing: "Let the Minas do that kind of work," they said. Ethnic and religious hostilities were carefully fostered by slave owners and naturally influenced freed slaves, who were not always above such feelings. Some freed men continued to feel not only the hatreds they had learned in Africa but others that were taught or fomented in Brazil. Two examples from the records of the police investigation that followed the uprising of 1835 illustrate the nature of these hostilities. João Ezequiel, a freed Nago, was called to testify against Cornelio, also a Nago but still in slavery. He lambasted the accused as a Muslim who "had tried to convert him" and "ate no pork." Now, the man had been called as a witness because the authorities suspected the two Nagos of being friends. But João Ezequiel denied this. Islam, which for the slave Cornelio was a religion of freedom, a refuge, was for the freed man João—eager to enter white, Christian society—a dangerous trap. Similarly, Feliciano, a Nago slave and palanquin bearer, was arrested at his job. Interrogated by the police about the activities of "relatives" suspected of having taken part in the insurrection, he answered that the other blacks told him no secrets because he was not of the same religion. Feliciano had been working in Salvador for only seven months, before which he had been in Jiquiriça, a small inland town. His former master, Antonio Rodriges Ribeiro, had used him to pay off a debt to his new master in Bahia. Seven months' time was not long enough for him to win the trust of his "relatives." The black community had its own structure, its own norms, its own hierarchies. Prior to 1850, the constant influx of new slaves to Salvador made it possible for different "nations" not only to preserve their identitites but also to cultivate inner divisions and rivalries. Nagos all spoke the same language but as we saw a moment ago did not all practice the same religion. "Though all Nagos, each has his own country," said another witness at the 1835 trial. This same witness went so far as to maintain that he did not know the Nagos who inhabited the ground floor of the house of which he occupied the balcony. Pierre Verger recounts the story of João Duarte da Silva, a freed Gégé, a ship's cook who lived in the São Miguel quarter in the same house as José, another Gégé, ambassador from Agoumé (present-day Abomey). He stated that he did not speak Nago because the Nagos "are the enemies of the Gégés." The Hausas also defended themselves in this trial by testifying that they did not understand the language of the insurgent Nagos and detested people of that nation. One manumitted Hausa, João Borges, tells how, as a slave, he had been stabbed twice by a Nago companion who wanted to "force" him to take part in one of the first Nago uprisings against the whites. He claimed to be outraged and said he wanted nothing to do with the Nagos. Though he lived above an ill-tempered Nago who was always picking fights with his wife, he never went down to see him. Was this just a talkative witness or was his testimony sincere? How much of what he said was bluff? What hostilities were merely private affairs? The question remains open.

Among Africans in Bahia, differences and disputes, loyalty and devotion had nothing to do with social status. The black elite did not consist solely of freed slaves. There were parallel black hierarchies totally independent of the white authorities. A slave might be the Koran teacher of a freed man, another the "holy mother" of a cult practiced by both freed men and slaves. The memory of old Pacifico Licutan, the pious *alufa,* or master, of the Salvadoran Muslim community, survives even today: he was a slave. His master twice refused to set him free, despite the pleas of his followers. He served time in prison for a debt incurred by his master—a sum of money owed to a convent of Carmelites. His cell was crowded with slaves and freed men who came to ask for his blessings and prayers. Quite often it was the lowliest of slaves who held the highest rank in the African community. The least integrated slaves were the ones who, through trances, communicated most easily with other world. The less assimilated the African was, the less he wished to forget his own cultural heritage, the less fascinated he was by the culture of the masters, the more likely he was to wield influence in the black community. The clandestine priest of a terreiro was first among his brothers even if he was last in the eyes of his master. Social relations between freed men and slaves therefore depended mainly on their cultural role. There was no fixed hierarchy according to which freed men stood above slaves, even though all slaves hoped to gain their freedom, to secure the illusory civil liberties available through manumission. Freed men served as advisers and exerted real influence over slaves through the religious confraternities and lay mutual aid organizations, whose importance we saw earlier.

Solidarity among blacks also developed in everyday contacts. Consider the affection of freed men for their own slaves and the slaves of others. Of the 471 freed men's wills found in Bahia, 200 have been submitted to exhaustive analysis, 100 for the period 1800–1826, 100 others for the period 1863–1890. Of the first group, 20 are the wills of liberated creoles, whereas of the second group none is. Why? No doubt because after the independence of Brazil, the liberated creole became a full-fledged citizen of Brazil, while the African still had to undergo naturalization in order to acquire citizenship. Thus it was imperative for the African to ensure that his rights were recognized, to obtain such recognition in writing, to file the document with a notary, and in short to secure every possible guarantee that his wishes would be respected. The African developed a real passion for official documents, owing to an understandable wariness shared by all foreigners living in Salvador. Creoles and Bahians alike evinced little interest in such proceedings, for which they did not feel the necessity.

Most freed slaves were slave owners. In the 1800–1826 sample (of 100 wills), 53 Africans and 12 creoles owned slaves. Of the Africans 25 freed their slaves when they (or, if married, their wives) died. Three others authorized their slaves to purchase their freedom for minimal, almost symbolic, sums. But only 1 of the 12 creoles freed his slaves upon his death. This fact says a great deal about the behavior of creoles: they acted like whites. Those Africans who freed some but not all of their slaves chose to grant freedom to slaves who belonged to the same ethnic group as themselves. Gégés freed Gégé slaves, Nagos freed Nagos. Furthermore, very few Africans owned creole slaves, but creoles generally owned only African slaves. Only 24 of the 100 freed Africans in the sample for the period 1863–1890 owned slaves; 11 freed their slaves when they died, 3 required their slaves to indemnify their heirs in order to obtain their freedom, and 5 freed one or two slaves belonging to their "nation."

Is it therefore correct to say that creoles and African blacks had different attitudes toward slavery? Certainly. The African, born free, was more sensitive to the evils of slavery than the creole, to whom the institution seemed natural. This fundamental divergence of views explains some of the animosity between Africans and creoles. The freed African was closer to his slaves, more strongly tied to his old community. Not only was he more disposed to manumit his own slaves, but he also exhibited greater solidarity with the slave community as a whole. One sees this in the wills, in numerous legacies to godchildren and others in the slave community. The households of these freed Africans must have been quite animated with the games and work of protégés. Many slaves would not have been able to purchase their freedom had it not been for bequests from a freed relative or friend. Some freed men placed their newfound wealth at the disposal of their brothers, making many small loans to friends in need and helping those who were sick. When a freed man died, he almost always left his work tools to his slaves or money for the training of the young. Cases are known in which a freed man and his slave became joint owners of a house. Freed men often held the savings of slaves, which they invested or simply kept safe from thieves. They were always willing to lend the paltry ten or fifty reis that a slave would not have dared to ask of his master. Freed men and women also served as godparents to slave children; more surprisingly, slaves were also chosen as godparents for the children of freed men, which again demonstrates that the social hierarchies established by whites did not coincide with those established by blacks. A friend's personal qualities were more important to the black man than his connections in the white community. Patriarchal relations developed at all levels, within the black as well as the white community, and also in relations between blacks and whites.

Over the three-hundred-year existence of Bahia's small slave community the freed African served as the hub of new social relations. He was the essential intermediary, the crucial link in the chain that joined the slave to the community of truly free men. From his days as a free man he retained inner riches, despite the depredations of his masters—the riches of the poor man, the man so clever and so good at his work as to have made himself indispensable. The riches of the illiterate as well as of the Islamic scholar, of the men whose memories preserved and passed on secret rites, myths, songs, and prayers. The slave knew suffering but also knew the relief of his brothers' affection. He made his own a Christianity that was at first imposed, then possessed, finally mastered and set easily alongside the cult of the orishas. The slave survived. He learned how to please his masters. Eventually he became a free man, no longer a beast of burden but a person. Dignified and proud, he still bore a fraternal resemblance to the erstwhile slave. He used his experience and wisdom to help relieve the anguish of a subjugated people. For him the cardinal virtues continued to be labor and loyalty: loyalty to his elders, to his nation, to his masters black and white, to his companions in captivity. Loyalty above all to the two cultures that were henceforth his: the maternal culture, frequently clandestine yet vital and life-giving, and the other, the foreign yet still fascinating culture of the white man. Freed creoles and mulattoes were surely more likely to yield to the fascination of white culture than were their African comrades, yet all remained staunch allies of the slave community, indispensable intermediaries between the world of the free man and the world of the captive. Hence their social role was ambiguous, a catalyst around which crystallized the various antagonisms engendered by slavery. The freed men were the linchpins of the dual society of predominantly black Bahia.

The freed slave who did not reject the African world obviously was less welcomed by white society than the creole or mulatto. True for Salvador, this statement holds good also for the rest of Brazil, where there was no need to eliminate African rebels by force or deportation. Blacks were in the minority, and their actions had little effect in a society where all privileges were for whites only. In some areas whites ultimately came to feel that it was not impossible to do without slave labor.

AFRICA FORGOTTEN OR NEW AFRICA

Law No. 3353 of 13 May 1888
Declares slavery in Brazil to be extinct

The Imperial Princess Regent, in the name of His Majesty the Emperor Lord Dom Pedro II, announces to all subjects of the Empire that the General Assembly has decreed, and His Majesty has sanctioned, the following law:

Article 1: As of the date of this law, slavery in Brazil is declared to be extinct.

Article 2: All contrary measures are revoked.

All authorities charged with notification and execution of the aforementioned law are hereby ordered to uphold it and to see that it is obeyed and that its contents are observed.

The Secretary of State for Agricultural Affairs, Commerce, and Public Works and Acting Secretary for Foreign Affairs, Attorney Rodrigo Augusto da Silva, member of the Council of His Majesty the Emperor, is hereby ordered to enforce, publish, and distribute this law.

Given in his Palace at Rio de Janeiro, 13 May 1888, 67th year of the Independence of the Empire.

Imperial Princess Regent
Rodrigo A. da Silva

Charter of the law whereby Your Imperial Highness orders the execution of the Decree of the General Assembly that Your Highness has deemed worthy of sanction and that declares slavery in Brazil to be extinct as specified herein.

Supreme Chancellery of the Empire
Antonio Ferreira Viana
Received 13 May 1888
José Julio de Albuquerque Barros

For the eyes of Your Imperial Highness.

Thus, in its entirety, reads the law abolishing slavery in Brazil. A few cold, impersonal words sufficed to put an end to an institution that had endured for more than three centuries. Abolition came at a time when the slave system was showing visible signs of exhaustion. It freed the productive classes of the country from an outdated mode of labor whose profitability had dwindled. It also freed the consciences of those who had sincerely fought to rid Brazilian society of what people at the time called the stigmata of slavery.

On 13 May 1888 there was not a single slave, creole or African, black or mulatto, who did not sing and dance at the good news. To be sure, the Brazilian-born creole, brought up speaking Portuguese, knew nothing of the free man's life but what he had heard from others who came from Africa as slaves and what he had seen of the lives of freed men. But Africans believed they had regained a lost paradise. For all slaves, from the most rebellious to the most assimilated, the thirteenth of May was a day of rejoicing. Despite the rigors of the system, the slaves had fulfilled their mission, and a great mission it was. They had created wealth by cultivating the earth, working the mines, treating, manufacturing, and selling their products. Anyone who gives his sweat, his strength, his life, his friendship, and his affection to a job feels himself tied to the finished product, especially when the work is done, as it generally was in Brazil, with loyalty, dignity, pride, and a spirit of invention. In the end, very few slaves managed to buy their own freedom. For the rest, the Golden Law, as the law of 13 May 1888 was known, seemed to inaugurate a new era.

The rejoicing was short-lived, however. Freedom that is nothing but the freedom to remain poor and indigent is not true freedom. Listen to A., an old female slave on a sugar plantation on the island of Itaparica, whose mango trees dominated the entrance to the Bay of All Saints. For three days and three nights, she says, the former slaves of the engenho sang, danced, and were beside themselves with joy. Sounds of drums filled the island. On the fourth day the overseer had the former slaves assembled and informed them of their dismissal. All had to leave the plantation immediately. There was no longer room for them. Then began a life of wandering and misery, with no overseer to hand out food, no master to provide clothing and medical care. For the first few days the freed men of the island offered food to the former slaves. But gradually they were forced to disperse. Many crossed the bay, took refuge in the big city, and joined the ranks of the poor and unemployed. For the abolition of slavery brought no guarantee of economic security, no special forms of assistance intended to help the thousands of freed slaves. However golden the Golden Law, it left the newly freed slaves to cope on their own, shifted the terms of exchange in the labor market in favor of the former masters, and disrupted the mechanisms of social adjustment which had developed over the three centuries of the slave system. Field hands became rural wage earners, exploited and living in poverty, attached to the meager plots of land that they had been given but could never cultivate rationally. Other slaves looked to the cities for jobs that were not always there: in the northeast there was unemployment owing to a crisis in the sugar industry, and elsewhere there was an oversupply of labor aggravated by European immigration. Slaves with small, badly run plots were forced to sell their land. The abolitionists had thought only of freeing the slaves, not of integrating them into the society and the economy.

Blacks and mulattoes were henceforth excluded from white society. This was true even in Salvador, where during the era of slavery there had been bridges between the white and the black communities. After 1888, Bahian society stabilized and closed its ranks. The upper classes became acutely conscious of everything that separated the white man from the black man and mulatto. Skin color, once "forgotten," now established an unbreachable divide between rich and poor. Unsuccessful whites were lumped together with blacks. The old families, bankrupt or not, prided themselves on their supposed all-white ancestry, despite all the evidence to the contrary. Everywhere there was racism, and everywhere it was denied. "Purification" became a necessary prerequisite for upward mobility. In relations between individuals, the imperatives of humility, obedience, and fidelity were even stronger than they had been during the time of slavery.

Did the dual structure of the old Brazilian society survive the coming of a new social order with capitalist and unifying tendencies? There can be no doubt that the answer is yes. The African heritage was too rich to be effaced, too deep to be forgotten. Africa was not lost. Like a growing plant it flourished anew—in solidarity among black men and women who shared the same miserable fate and in African religions that preserved the cultural heritage of the homeland—and solidarity and religion together preserved the characteristic qualities of the Brazilian slave: dignity, pride, and courage.

APPENDICES

A. Will of Francisco Nunes de Moraes

B. Glossary

C. Currency Tables

A. WILL OF FRANCISCO NUNES DE MORAES[1]

Registration of the will and codicil left at his death by the Black Francisco Nunes de Moraes, deceased 13 January 1811. The executor is his wife, Efigenia Marie da Trinidade, who lives in the Pillar (the street after the seaside warehouse).

In the name of the Lord, amen. I, Francisco Nunes de Moraes, ill but still standing and perfectly sound in mind and understanding, yet fearing death and wishing to take the precautions necessary for my salvation, order that my will be written down as follows:

"I obey the law of God and have lived since my baptism in the same religion of which I have made profession, and it is in this religion that I wish to die, for outside of this religion there is no salvation.

"I was born on the Mina coast and baptized in the bosom of the Church as a true Christian, and I was a slave of the late Captain Major Antonio Nunes de Moraes, who freed me upon his death for the sum of two hundred fifty thousand reis, which was paid in cash to his executor Francisco Rodriguez Vianna.

"I am married to Efigenia Marie da Trinidade, a creole woman, from which marriage no son or daughter has issued up to now, and as a bachelor I had no children either, and anyone who claims otherwise speaks a falsehood for in conscience I have never had a child.

"The property that I possess has been acquired by myself and by my companion Efigenia Marie da Trinidade, who, after paying my funeral expenses and any debts I may owe, is instituted by me as residuary legatee of all that I possess and shall possess, for such is my true will once the provisions specified below have been carried out.

"I leave my funeral and burial to the care of my aforementioned wife, for I have confidence in her love, and because of the mutual confidence we have always enjoyed I know that she will act for me as I would act for her if I were to survive her.

"As executor of this will I therefore name in the first place the aforesaid spouse Efigenia Marie da Trinidade and in the second place José Pacheco Nunes, and in the third place Captain Domingues Rodrigues Vianna. I ask them in the service of God and from good will toward me to accept this charge, and I give them all power to do whatever is necessary in regard to any agreement or convention that

[1]Translated into English from the author's French translation, as originally published—Trans.

may be necessary. In the fourth place I also call upon Francisco Gomes Pereira as executor, and to whoever my executor may be I grant three years to render an accounting.

"Because I took pity on the motherless orphan creole Maria, I generously offered her freedom and had her live with me, in the hope that she would grow up decent enough for my wife and me to find her a husband, for such was our intention. But our wish was not fulfilled, for she dishonored herself with someone quite her inferior and she now has two children, a son and a daughter. Since I still feel pity for her, owing to the affection I felt for her as a child, I have decided to leave her in one payment fifty thousand reis and forty thousand to each of her children, who are named Custodio and Vicencia, in the hope that by this legacy [some words are illegible] to my executrix before the time that I have granted to close all accounts, and if the contrary occurs said legacies shall be lost by them and in that case revoked: as it often happens that people upon whom one wishes to bestow the abundant love of God will then argue, as is customary here, that they are the testator's children, I declare that she is not my daughter and that if she claims otherwise and says as much publicly the gifts to her and her children shall be eliminated.

"Because of the good service that she has rendered me and because she is my godmother, the Black Anna do Gentio da Costa, my slave, has been evaluated (*coarctada*) at my behest at thirty thousand reis, which she shall pay to my executrix in the two years following my death, which sum is to be paid in weekly payments, so that she may acquit all of them while continuing to spend her nights in the home of my executrix.

"Among the other slaves that I own there is a creole named Francisco, to whom I taught the trade of barber and musician capable of playing several instruments: it was part of my intention to free him entirely from slavery, but since he has behaved very badly toward me by leaving my house without case or reason and solely out of his predilection for vagabondage, I find myself obliged and I wish that he should remain for five years in the company of my heiress. At the end of that time, if he has behaved well, she shall grant him his letter of manumission. However, if my wife remarries, he should be freed immediately, with this will serving as his title and proof of his liberation, but if he does not behave well he shall remain a captive.

"I do not list the property that I own because it is known and my wife, executrix, and heiress knows everything on this subject.

"I leave to the confraternity of Our Lady of the Rosary in Lower Shoemaker's Street, which I served as a most unworthy judge, an alms of twenty-five thousand reis in one payment, destined to be used for whatever Our Lady requires.

"Everything that is listed in an account book that I possess and that is due me according to these writings need not be reregistered by my executors, for I so decide.

"I desire that my executrix enjoy a credit of four thousand reis to meet any obligations or debts that I may have toward anyone I have forgotten for the moment.

"I leave twelve thousand eight hundred reis to Alcandro da Conceção who lives in Plama in gratitude for his work in teaching several of my slaves their trade as rebec players.

"I leave one thousand two hundred reis for six masses to be said at two hundred reis each for the soul of my former master.

"And for the salvation of my soul my executrix and heiress will have said four times fifty masses of the same price and twenty-five for the souls of my deceased slaves and another twenty-five for the souls plunged in the fires of Purgatory under the invocation of My Lord Jesus Christ.

"My wife and heiress shall distribute my used clothing to my slaves.

"I consider my will terminated and I have asked and beseeched Francisco da Cunha e Araujo to write it at my behest and it is I who sign with my usual sign, asking His Majesty's Justice to see that it is fully executed as herein specified. Bahia 7 September—we say six September 1790. Francisco Nunes de Moraes, written upon his request by Francisco da Cunha e Araujo."

REGISTRATION

Be it known that this last and true testament has been publicly registered in this city of Salvador da Bahia de Todos os Santos in the year One Thousand Seven Hundred Ninety after the birth of Our Lord Jesus Christ. In my notarial offices there appeared Francisco Nunes de Moraes, Black Gégé, standing and apparently in good health and in full possession of his faculties as he appeared to myself, as notary, and to the witnesses enumerated below, all of whom have signed after hearing the answers that he made to questions posed by me before these same witnesses. And by his hands into mine he then submitted to me these three sheets of paper written on six sides and the last ends where the registration begins, saying to me that this was his last and true testament and that he had had it drawn up by Francisco de Cunha e Araujo, who after writing it read it to him, the testator, word for word. Because he found it to his liking and faithful to what he had dictated, he signed it with his usual sign, and the aforesaid Francisco da Cunha e Araujo also signed it, witnessing that he wrote it at the behest of paid testator, and that by this testament he revokes all other testaments and codicils made previously, for he wishes this one to be executory and to remain in force as representing his last and true will, and he asks His Majesty's Justice to enforce the observance and to execute his will as he requested by this writing. And I, as notary, register this will after having examined it and found it proper, without flaw or erasure between the lines and containing nothing dubious or suspicious in any way whatsoever. That is why I have marked it with my seal, which is *Campello.* I have registered it as I am obliged to do by my office.

DECLARATION

I, as testator, declare that I leave as alms to Our Lady of the Pillar of the Beach twenty-five thousand reis in one payment and that is all that I have to declare before witnesses: Pedro Alexandrino Monteiro, Florencio Pereira Pimentel, Miguel Luis Soares, Manoel Paulo Ferreira da Silva, Manoel Marques de Souza Porto, who have also signed after this was read to them.

I, Manoel Antonio Campello, notary, have written this. The public seal is affixed hereto as a mark of authenticity.

Manoel Antonio Campello, Francisco Nunes de Moraes, Manoel Paulo Ferreira da Silva, Florencio Pereira Pimentel, Manoel Marques de Souza Porto, Pedro Alexandrino Monteiro, Miguel Luis Soares.

ATTESTATION

Will of Francisco Nunes de Moraes approved by myself, the undersigned notary, sealed with five seals of red wax on the side and sewn in five points with red thread. Bahia seven October one thousand seven hundred ninety. Manoel Antonio Campello.

CLAUSE

There is one codicil that I, as notary, registered on 2 December one thousand eight hundred ten. Mata Bacellar.

OPENING

Done without reason for nullification and without prejudice to any third party. Bahia, thirteen January, one thousand eight hundred eleven. Cogominho.

ACCEPTANCE

I agree to sever as executrix and heiress with all rights reserved in case of prejudice on my account. Bahia twenty-three January one thousand eight hundred eleven. At the request of Efigenia Marie da Trinidade. Bernardo de França Burgos.

NOTIFICATION

Registered at Bahia twenty-three January one thousand eight hundred eleven. Simoens.

STAMP

Number six hundred eighty-five. Paid two hundred forty reis for stamping of six half sheets. Bahia, twenty-three January one thousand eight hundred eleven. Tavares.

TESTAMENT (CODICIL)

In the name—I mean by the name of the Lord—

"I Francisco Nunes de Moraes, sick and on my death bed from pains suffered by the will of God but perfectly sound in mind, wishing to seek the means that might lead to my salvation, order that the codicil be drawn up as follows.

"In my will I named as executrix my wife and others who are deceased and today I approve and ratify the choice of my wife as primary executrix and in the second place Captain José Teixeira de Souza, in third place Antonio Perira da Fonseca, whom I ask for the love of God and as a service to me to please accept my will and if my wife is not executrix whichever of the others is will receive as compensation for his labors one hundred thousand reis in a single payment and may take up to six years to render an accounting.

"I leave free my black slave Gonçallo Nunes de Bonfim because he is the oldest and has remained with me and has suffered from my ill temper, and if he wishes to remain with my wife and executrix she shall treat him as she wishes but she shall in any case give him his letter of manumission.

"The slaves named José-Gégé, Joam-Gégé—I mean João-Mina—Leandro and Domingos, all of whom practice the trade of barber and musician, must accompany my wife until her death and two months after her death each will have to pay sixty thousand reis to be used as she decides, and if she specifies no use this sum shall be used to pay for a mass for my soul and the souls of my wife and our slaves and for the souls in Purgatory who have nobody to worry about them and also for the souls of all those with whom we have done business and whom I may have injured in some way without knowing it and each mass will be for one pataca.

"If these slaves should lose their merit by evil dealings authentically proved by my executors, the kindness that I offer them shall be without effect. Viricimo remains captive to serve his mistress.

"The black Thereza Angolla to whom I gave Rosa whom I raised and who was married to Fellis Antão has come back into my possession after the death of the two aforementioned persons; she shall be liberated and should be given her letter of manumission.

"The creoles Custodio and Manoel have been liberated and I have given them their letters of manumission and they shall have charge of themselves.

"If the creole Patornilha [*sic*] behaves well and marries a person of good behavior my executrix shall give her her trousseau and out of her entitlements a lump-sum payment of one hundred thousand reis. To Bonifacia, daughter of Domingos Vianna, I give on the same terms twenty-five thousand reis. To Maria Amorim and to all her children, I have already given charters of liberty and declare free her grandchildren who shall receive their charters from my executors. All instruments necessary for the profession of barber and musician shall remain the property of my wife, so that the slaves may use them, and upon her death they shall be divided among them, taking account of the merits of each one. And I ask them urgently and beg them because it is my will to accompany Our Good Lord whenever he is in the streets and they have no other pressing work. Also, six months should be added to the six months I allowed my slaves to free themselves by paying the sum of sixty thousand reis or suffer the loss of the grace granted them after the death of my wife.

"I hereby declare ended my codicil, which is part of my will, and to validate it I beg and ask the Justice of His Royal Highness to cause it to be executed in all of its parts.

"It was written at my behest by Bernardo de França Burgos, and I have signed it with my usual sign at Bahia, on 2 December one thousand eight hundred ten."

Francisco Nunes Moraes. Written on demand. Bernard de França Burgos. [The usual registrations follow.]

—*Archives of the State of Bahia*, Judicial Section, ser. "Livro de Registros de Testamentos," blk. 3, fol. 34–39.

B. GLOSSARY

Agregado: man or woman, black, white, or mulatto, free or manumitted, who lived under the protection of a family.

Agreste: region of sparse vegetation, midway between the dry *caatinga* and the damp forest.

Alfandega: customs in Portuguese. The word is of Arabic origin.

Alvarà: document issued by the courts or governmental authorities approving, confirming, or authorizing certain specified acts or rights. Formerly granted by the sovereign, often temporarily.

Arrobe: measure equivalent to 14.745 kilograms.

Avença: license issued by the contratador of the assiento to an individual who, in exchange for payment, fitted ships for the slave trade.

Bagasse: solid residue of sugar cane after milling.

Banzo: fatal nostalgia of African blacks shipped as captives to Brazil.

Big house: in the northeast, the *casa grande* was the plantation owner's house. In the south the term used was *morada*, which means dwelling simply.

Bossale: a slave born in Africa, as opposed to a creole born in Brazil. The term was applied in particular to newly arrived slaves from Africa, not yet able to speak Portuguese. Bossale was also a synonym for "hick."

Brazil wood: precious wood that grows naturally in Brazilian forests. Brazil's major export product prior to sugar cane. The scientific name of this tree is the *caesalpina echinata*. It was shredded to manufacture a red dye.

Brigantine: a small, two-masted ship, similar to a brig but of smaller tonnage. It was not used after the first half of the nineteenth century.

Cabocle: a person of mixed white and Indian blood, with copper-colored skin and straight hair.

Cabra: the child of a mulatto and a black, quite light-skinned. Same root as the French *cabri*. Could sometimes pass for white.

Cafuzo: person of mixed Indian and black blood. Generally black with smooth hair.

Canto: a small square or street corner where slaves and freed men of a particular ethnic group waited for clients wishing to employ them.

Caravel: the Portuguese claim to have been the first to design this type of ship. We know little about the caravels of the fifteenth century. They were apparently rigged with lateen sails (like the Niña of Columbus). In the sixteenth century the *caravela redonda* was fitted with four masts plus a bowsprit. The caravel had finer lines than the carracks, galleons, howkers, and other ships of the period and was certainly a good ocean vessel.

Colonial exclusive: a privilege granted to certain companies granting exclusive rights to trade with overseas possessions.

Comadre: godmother in Portuguese.

Compadre: godfather in Portuguese.

Constitution of 1824: first constitution of independent Brazil. Slavery was abolished in Portugal, but in Portugal only, in 1773. The Constitution of 1824 defined the position of the slave in the new empire, ameliorating among other things his status vis-à-vis punishment.

Cowries: shells long used as money in eastern Africa, Chad, and even Asia, usually strung together in bracelets or necklaces.

Creole: black slave born in Brazil.

Crusado: see currency table in Appendix C. Equivalent of 400 reis.

Engenho: cf. sugar mill.

Frazenda: rural property for farming and raising of livestock.

Fazendeiro: owner of a fazenda.

Freedom charter: a document, usually notarized, by which a master granted freedom to a slave. It specified both parties' particulars and the conditions under which liberation was being granted. These conditions varied widely. Also known as a letter of manumission.

Ganho: a slave de ganho was one who carried palanquins or merchandise.

Grão Para: state in northeast Brazil, straddling the lower Amazon. Capital Bélem.

Guardian: person requested by a slave to plead for him with his master or with the courts. Often appointed by the courts.

Hausa: black from the Niger region. The Hausas interbred extensively with the Peuls. They were influenced by Islam from the fourteenth century.

Half-breed: person of mixed white, black, Indian, or even oriental blood.

Independence: Brazil separated from Portugal in 1822.

Jeito: art, skill, resourcefulness, cleverness. *Dar um jeito* was to attempt something rather complicated. *Jeito* was in a sense know-how.

Ladino: slave who spoke Portuguese, knew something about the Christian religion, and had acquired the rudiments of a trade or office.

Lançado: mulatto or white who lived at the court of an African king or native chieftain. He lived in a hut like the blacks, was Christian, and took it upon himself to sell the chief's slaves.

Malembo: a friend from the first hours of captivity.

Manioc flour: added to liquid dishes to give more consistency.

Manumission: emancipation, from the Latin *manumissio*, the term for the freeing of a Roman slave.

Maranhão: coastal state of northeastern Brazil, 332,000 square kilometers, capital São Luis.

Mato Grosso: state of western Brazil, along the border with Bolivia and Paraguay, 1,265,000 square kilometers, capital Cuiabà, which replaced Mato Grosso, founded in the seventeenth century but abandoned because of the unhealthy climate.

Maxambula: mule cart, used to carry slaves to the coffee fields.

Mina: black people of western Africa, from the region of present-day Togo, along the coast and in lower Dahomey. Of Ashanti origin, the Minas were often fishermen and known for their aptitude for domestic work.

Minas Gerais: state in eastern Brazil, 583,000 square kilometers, capital Belo Horizonte.

Moleque: child; the feminine was moleca, diminutives molequinho, molequinha.

Mucama: an especially valued slave who raised the master's children. She might also be a nurse and raise both her own child and the master's.

Mulatto: generally a person of mixed black and white blood.

Nago: a Yoruban black from the Sudan. Groups of Nagos settled in Ifé in the thirteenth century and later in Oyo. Archeological research suggests an advanced culture.

Nankeen: a yellow cotton fabric used for umbrellas and parasols.

Orisha: African spirit, also called a voodoo.

Pataca: 320 reis. See currency table in Appendix C.

Patrono: term used to refer to a former master.

Pernambuco: like Bahia, Pernambuco is a state of 98,000 square kilometers in northeastern Brazil. Its capital and principal port, Recife, is often called Pernambuco.

Pombeiro, or pumbeiro: term applied to those who went into inland Africa, especially Angola, in search of captives, for whom they traded merchandise. The same term was applied in Brazil to those who traded with the Indians.

Quilombo: a fugitive slave hideout (house or community, sometimes of considerable size).

Quimzumba: African songs.

Real: see currency table in Appendix C.

Recife: see Pernambuco.

Reconcavo: the hinterland of Salvador. The word means "bay shore," but the Bahian Reconcavo included not just the coastal zone but also the plateaus of the sertão and the neighboring agreste.

Resgate: goods bartered or sold in exchange for "slave pieces."

Salvador da Bahia de Todos os Santos: Bahia is the name of one of the states of the Federal Republic of Brazil as well as of one of the old captaincies of the colonial era. It has an area 561,000 square kilometers (slightly larger than France). The capital, Salvador, is usually called Bahia, because it is located on the "bay of all saints" (Bahia means "bay" in Portuguese). Salvandor was the capital of Brazil until 1763.

Senzala: building housing the slaves of a plantation or religious establishment.

Serão: work done by slaves after nightfall.

Sesmaria: royal concession of uncultivated land, given to a *sesmeiro* to farm.

Sertão: brushland, generally dry.

Slave piece, or Indies piece: a measure defined in 1678 as "a Negro fifteen to twenty-five years of age; or eight to fifteen years of age; or twenty to thirty-five years of age, the three together counting as two. Below age eight and from thir-ty-five to forty-five, two count as one. Children at the breast accompany their mother without being counted." Those who were more than forty-five years old or sick were evaluated by appraisers.

Sova: native chieftain.

Stern post: stout piece of wood attached to a ship's keel and extending it toward the rear.

Sugar factory: sugar mill with steam-operated machinery and concentrated capi-talist production.

Sugar mill: in the narrow sense, the sugar mill was a machine for grinding and crushing sugar cane. But by extension the term was used to refer collectively to the properties where cane was grown and then treated. In Portuguese the term was engenho (referring to both the cane plantation and the factory where dif-ferent grades of sugar were manufactured), and the owner was called the senhor de engenho.

Sumaca: small two-masted ship, used mainly in South America. Derived from the Dutch *schmake*.

Tangomau: slave recruiter in Guinea.

Triangular trade: the three vertices of the triangle were Europe, Africa, and America.

Trunk: an instrument of torture consisting of a tree trunk with holes bored in it, into which the victim's ankles or neck were inserted and crushed by the weight of the wood.

C. CURRENCY TABLES

CURRENCY	VALUE (IN REIS)
Monies of account	
Conto de reis	1,000,000
	(or 2,500 crusados)
Thousand crusados	400,000
Dobra or dobrão	12,800
Crusado	400
Real (plural: reis)	1
Portuguese gold coin	
Gold piece	4,800
New crusado	480
Brazilian gold coin	
Gold piece	4,000
Half gold piece	2,000
Quarter gold piece	1,000
Silver coin	
Tostão	100
Pataca	320
Half pataca	160
Brazilian copper coin	
4 vinténs	80
2 vinténs	40
1 vintén	20

Source: Based on R. C. Simonsen, *História Econômica do Brasil 1500–1820* (São Paulo: Editora Nacional, 1967), p. 464.

FLUCTUATIONS OF EXCHANGE RATE OF REAL			
Date	Value	Date	Value
1808	72.0	1849	25.8
1809	73.6	1850	28.7
1810	71.7	1851	29.1
1811	73.6	1852	27.4
1812	76.6	1853	28.5
1813	86.5	1854	27.6
1814	76.1	1855	27.5
1815	64.0	1856	27.5
1816	57.0	1857	26.6
1817	72.3	1858	25.5
1818	66.1	1859	25.6
1819	57.8	1860	25.8
1820	51.5	1861	25.5
1821	50.0	1862	26.3
1822	49.0	1863	27.2
1823	50.7	1864	26.7
1824	48.2	1865	25.0
1825	51.8	1866	24.2
1826	48.1	1867	22.4
1827	35.2	1868	17.0
1828	31.6	1869	18.8
1829	24.6	1870	22.6
1830	22.8	1871	24.3
1831	25.0	1872	24.3
1832	35.1	1873	26.9
1833	37.8	1874	25.7
1834	38.7	1875	27.2
1835	39.2	1876	25.3
1836	38.4	1877	24.5
1837	29.5	1878	22.9
1838	28.6	1879	21.3
1839	31.6	1880	22.9
1840	31.0	1881	21.2
1841	30.3	1882	21.1
1842	26.8	1883	21.5
1843	25.8	1884	20.6
1844	23.1	1885	18.5
1845	25.4	1886	18.6
1846	26.9	1887	22.4
1847	28.0	1888	25.2
1848	25.0	1889	26.4

Source: Westphalen, Bach and Krohn, *Centenário 1828–1928* (Bahia, 1928), p. 87.
Note: These figures are annual averages given in English pence.

	PARITY OF REAL IN GOLD	
Date	Weight in grams	Carats
1500	0.009	23.75
1550	0.008	22.625
1600	0.007	22.125
1650	0.003	22
1700	0.002	22
1750	0.002	22
1800	0.002	22

Source: Mircea Buescu, *Evolução econômica do Brazil* (Rio de Janeiro, 1974); p. 217.

BIBLIOGRAPHIES

ABBREVIATIONS

The following abbreviations are used in the bibliography.

A	*Africa*
AA	*Afro/Asia*
AAEB	*Anais do Arquivo do Estado da Bahia*
ACDA	*Atti del XLI Congresso degli Americanisti*
AH	*Anais de História*
AMP	*Anais do Museu Paulista*
ASNPUH	*Anais do VI Simpósio Nacional dos Professores Universitários de História*
CAL	*Cahiers des Amériques Latines*
CEA	*Cahiers des études africaines*
CEE	*Ciência e cultura*
EH	*Estudos Históricos*
HAHR	*Hispanic American Historical Review*
IHEAL	*Institut des Hautes Etudes de l'Amérique Latine*
JAH	*Journal of African History*
JEH	*Journal of Economic History*
JHSN	*Journal of the Historical Society of Nigeria*
JSA	*Journal de la Société des Americanistes*
JSH	*Journal of Social History*
PA	*Présence Africaine*
RAMS	*Revista do Arquivo Municipal de São Paulo*
RBE	*Revista Brasileira de Economia*
RH	*Revista de História*
RIGHS	*Revista do Instituto Histórico e Geográfico de São Paulo*
RIEB	*Revista do Instituto de Estudos Brasileiros*

MAIN BIBLIOGRAPHY

Following is a bibliography of sources used. Notes have not been given in the text so as not to overburden the narrative with references that are in any case well known to specialists. The interested reader will find answers to his questions in the glossary or the works cited. Information from the sources cited here has been supplemented or refined with the aid of newly studied materials. A supplementary listing of sources published since 1979 follows the main bibliography.

A. MANUSCRIPT SOURCES

These are indicated only for the State of Bahia, where a study has been under way for ten years. This study has been conducted for the past two years under the auspices of the Brazilian National Council for Scientific and Technological Development (C.N.Pq.). Its purpose has been to carry out a systematic search of public and private archives for materials relating to slavery. After abolition, the minister Ruy Barbosa ordered systematic destruction of all documents concerning slavery, a practice henceforth considered shameful, of which the government wished to suppress all traces.

Below are listed only the principal bodies of documents studied up to the present.

1. Archives of the State of Bahia

Judicial section: three main series of documents have been investigated:
Freedom charters: 1684–1888. These are found in the notaries' books entitled *Livros de Notas e Escrituras*.
Estate inventories: A good series of these exists, but unfortunately for the nineteenth century only (1800–1890).
Wills: A collection of 64 books contains the wills of persons who died in Salvador. It is called the *Livros de Registro de Testamentos* and covers the period 1805–1892. There are major gaps in the documentation.

2. Municipal Archives of Salvador

The series is entitled *Escrituras de Escravos*. It covers the period 1827–1889 and consists of documents concerning the sale, hiring, mortgaging, and donation of slaves, along with a fair number of freedom charters. There are 120 books numbered 66.1 to 82.20.

B. SOURCES: UNPUBLISHED THESES

Below are cited only those unpublished theses that add new information to our understanding of the slave system in Brazil:

Andrade, Maria José de Souza, *A mão de obra escrava em Salvador de 1811 a 1860: Um estudo de História quantitativa.* Universidade Federal da Bahia, 1975 (Masters).
Karash, Mary, *Slave Life in Rio de Janeiro, 1808–1860.* University of Wisconsin, 1972 (Ph.D.).
Kiernan, James Patrick, *The Manumission of Slaves in Colonial Brazil: Paraty 1789 – 1822.* New York University, 1976 (Ph.D.).
Reis, João José, *Slave Revolt in Bahia 1790–1835: Economy, Society, Demography.* University of Minnesota, 1977 (Masters).

C. PRINTED SOURCES AND BIBLIOGRAPHY

This bibliography, though not exhaustive, is intended to be fairly complete. Insofar as possible, I have attempted to indicate English or French translations of works first published in Portuguese.

1. The Contemporaries of Slavery

Historians

Antonil. *Cultura e opulência do Brasil por suas Drogas e Minas.* Text of the original edition of 1711, French translation and commentary by A. Mansuy. Paris: IHEAL, 1968.
Benci, Jorge S. J. *Economia cristã dos senhores no governo dos escravos (Livro brasileiro de 1700).* São Paulo: Editorial Grijalbo, 1977.
Cincinnatus (pseud.). *O elemento escravo e as questões econômicas do Brazil.* Bahia: Typographia dos dous mundos, 1885.
Coutinho, J. J. da Cunha Azeredo. *Obras econômicas.* São Paulo: Ed. Nacional, 1966.
Couty, Louis. *Le Brésil en 1864.* Rio de Janeiro: Faro et Livio Editores, 1884.
——. *L'esclavage au Brésil.* Paris: Guillaumin, 1881.
Dialogos das grandezas do Brasil. Introduction by Capistrano de Abreu. Rio de Janeiro: Officina Industrial Graphica, 1930.
Gandavo, Pero de Magalhães. *Tractado da provincia do Brasil.* Rio de Janeiro: Instituto Nacional do Livro, 1965.
Marques, Xavier. *O Feiticeiro.* Rio de Janeiro: Liv. Leste Ribeiro, 1922.
Mendes, Luiz Antonio de Oliveira. *Memória a respeito dos escravos e tráfico da escravatura entre a Costa d'Africa e o Brasil.* Porto: Publicações Escorpião, 1977.
Nabuco, Joaquim. *O Abolicionismo.* Petropolis: Editora Vozes/INL, 1977.

Oliveira, J. M. Cardoso de. *Dois metros e cinco: Aventura de Marcos Parreira (Costumes brasileiros)*. Rio de Janeiro: Liv. Briguiet, 1936.

Pereira, Nuno Marques. *Compêndio narrativo do peregrino da America*. 6th ed. 2 vols. Rio de Janeiro: Academia Brasileira, 1939.

Pitta, Sebastião da Rocha. *História da America Portugueza*. Bahia: Imprensa Econômica, 1878.

Salvador, Frei Vicente do. *História do Brasil (1500–1627)*. São Paulo: Melhoramentos, 1965.

Souza, Gabriel Soares de. *Tratado descritivo do Brasil em 1587*. São Paulo: Ed. Nacional, 1971.

Southey, Robert. *História do Brasil*. 6 vols. São Paulo: Obelisco, 1965.

Varnhagen, Francisco Adolfo. *História general do Brasil*. 5 vols. São Paulo: Melhoramento/INL/MEC, 1975.

Vilhena, Luis dos Santos *A Bahia no século XVIII*. 3 vols. Bahia: Itapuã, 1969.

Travelers

Agassiz, Elizabeth C. C., and J.-L. R. Agassiz. *Viagem ao Brasil, 1865–1866*. São Paulo: Liv. Ed. Nacional, 1938.

Alincourt, Luis d., *Memórias sobre a viagem do Porto de Santos à Cidade de Cuiabá*. São Paulo, 1853.

Assier, Adolphe d'. *Le Brésil contemporain: Races, Mœurs, Institutions, Paysages*. Paris: Durand et Lauriel, 1867.

Ave-Lallemant, Robert C. *Viagem pelo norte do Brasil no ano de 1859*. Rio de Janeiro: Instituto Nacional do Livro, 1951.

———. *Viagem pelo sul do Brasil no ano de 1858* (First Part), Rio de Janeiro: Instituto Nacional do Livro, 1953.

Barbinais, Sieur Gentil de la. *Voyages*. Paris, 1729.

Bennet, Frank. *Forty Years in Brazil*. London, 1914.

Beyer, Gustav. *Ligeiras notas de viagem do Rio de Janeiro à capitania de São Paulo, no Brasil, no verão de 1813*. RIHGS. São Paulo, 1907.

Biard, Auguste François. *Dois anos no Brasil*. São Paulo: Ed Nacional, 1945.

Canstatt, Oscar. *Brasil, A terra e a gente, 1871*. Rio de Janeiro: Pongetti, 1954.

Codman, John. *Ten Months in Brazil*. Boston, 1867.

Dampier, William. *Voyages (faits en 1699)*. Amsterdam, 1705.

Davatz, Thomas. *Memórias de um colono no Brasil*. São Paulo: Liv. Martins, 1941.

Debret, Jean-Baptiste. *Viagem pitoresca e histórica ao Brasil*. São Paulo: Liv. Martins/EDUSP, 1972.

Denis, Ferdinand. *Lettres familières et fragments du journal intime de Ferdinand Denis à Bahia (1816–1819)*. Edited and commented by L. Bourdon. Coimbra, 1957.

Dugrivel, A. *Des bords de la Saône à la baie de San Salvador, ou promenade sentimentale en France et au Brésil*. Paris: Librairie Lecour, 1843.

Duncan, John. *Travels in Western Africa (1845–1846)*. 2 vols. London, 1847.

Eschwege, W. L. von. *Diário de uma viagem do Rio de Janeiro a Vila Rica, na Capitania de Minas Gerais*. São Paulo: Imprensa Oficial do Estado, 1936.

Ewbank, Thomas. *A vida no Brasil*. Rio de Janeiro: Editora Conquista, 1973.

Expilly, Charles. *Le Brésil tel qu'il est.* Paris: E. Dentu, 1862.

Frezier, A. F. *Relation du voyage de la mer du sud (1712–1714).* Amsterdam, 1717.

Froger, le Sieur. *Relation d'un voyage . . . de M. de Gennes (1695–1697).* Paris, 1698.

Graham, Maria. *Diário de uma viagem ao Brasil e de uma estada nesse país durante parte dos anos de 1821, 1822 e 1823.* São Paulo: Ed. Nacional, 1956.

Isabelle, Arsène. *Viagem ao Rio Grande do Sul (1833–1834).* Porto Alegre: Secretaria Educação e Cultura, 1946.

Kidder, Daniel P. *Reminiscência de viagens e permanência no Brasil (Rio de Janeiro e província de São Paulo).* São Paulo: Liv. Martins/EDUSP, 1972.

——. *Reminiscência de viagens e permanência no Brasil (Províncias do norte).* São Paulo: Liv. Martins/EDUSP, 1972.

Koster, Henry. *Viagem ao nordeste do Brasil.* (Travels in Brazil). São Paulo: Ed. Nacional, 1942.

Lamberg, Maurício. *O Brasil. A terra e a gente.* Rio de Janeiro: Typographia Nunes, 1896.

Latteaux, D^r. *A travers le Brésil: Au pays de l'or et des diamants.* Paris: Ailland Alves, 1910.

Lindley, Thomas. *Narrativa de uma viagem ao Brasil.* São Paulo: Ed. Nacional, 1969.

Luccock, Juhn. *Notas sobre o Rio de Janeiro e partes meridionais do Brasil.* São Paulo: Liv. Martins, 1951.

Mathison, Gilbert Farguhar. *Narrative of a Visit to Brazil, Chile, Peru, and the Sandwich Islands, 1821–1822.* London, 1825.

Mawe, John. *Viagens ao interior do Brasil principalmente aos distritos de ouro e dos diamantes.* Rio de Janeiro: Liv. Valverde, 1944.

Pohl, João Emanuel. *Viagens no interior do Brasil (1817–1820).* 2 vols. Rio de Janeiro: Instituto Nacional do Livro, 1948.

Pradez, Charles. *Nouvelles études sur le Brésil.* Paris, 1872.

Principe, Adalberto. *Travels of Prince Adalbert of Prussia.* 2 vols. London, 1849.

Prior, James. *Voyage along the Eastern Coast of Africa to Mosambique, Johanna and Quiloa, to St. Helena, Rio de Janeiro, Bahia, Pernambuco; in the Nisus Frigate.* London: Richard, Phillips, 1819.

Pyrard de Laval, François. *Voyages . . .* Paris, 1679.

Ribeyrolles, Charles. *Brasil pitoresco.* 2 vols. São Paulo: Liv. Martins, 1941.

Rugendas, João Mauricio. *Viagem pitoresca através do Brasil.* São Paulo: Liv. Martins, 1967.

Saint Hilaire, Augusto de. *Segunda viagem do Rio de Janeiro a Minas Gerais e São Paulo.* São Paulo: Ed. Nacional, 1938.

——. *Viagem à província de São Paulo.* São Paulo: Liv. Martins/EDUSP, 1972.

——. *Viagem ao Rio Grande do Sul.* Belo Horizonte: Ed. Itatiaia/EDUSP, 1974.

——. *Viagem pelas provincias do Rio de Janeiro, e de Minas Gerais.* Belo Horizonte: Ed. Itatiaia/EDUSP, 1975.

Scully, William. *Brazil: Its Provinces and Chief Cities.* London: Murray, 1866.

Spix, J., and K. F. Ph. Martius. *Através da Bahia.* São Paulo: Ed. Nacional, 1938.

——. *Viagens pelo Brasil (1817–1820).* São Paulo: Ed. Melhoramentos, 1961.

Stewart, C. S. *Brazil and La Plata*. New York, 1856.
Suzannet, Conde de. *O Brasil em 1845*. Rio de Janeiro, 1957.
Tollenare, Louis François de. *Notas Dominicais*. Salvador: Liv. Progresso, 1956.
Turnbull, John. *A Voyage round the World*. London: Maxwell, 1813.
Wetherell, James. *Brasil. Apontamentos sobre a Bahia, 1842–1857*. Bahia: Banco da Bahia, 1972.
Wied-Neuwied, Maximiliano (Principe de). *Viagem no Brasil nos anos de 1815 a 1817*. São Paulo: Ed. Nacional, 1958.

2. Our Contemporaries

Historians, Anthropologists, and Sociologists: General Studies

AFRICA

Balandier, Georges. *La vie quotidienne au royaume du Kongo du XVIᵉ au XVIIIᵉ siècle*. Paris: Hachette, 1965.
——. *Sociologie actuelle de l'Afrique noire*. Paris: PUF, 1963.
Beachey, R. W. *A Collection of Documents of the Slave Trade of Eastern Africa*. London: R. Collings, 1976.
Boxer, Charles R. *Salvador de Sá and the Struggle for Brazil and Angola (1602–1685.)* London, 1962; reimpression Westport, Conn.: Greenwood Press, 1975.
——. *Race Relations in the Portuguese Colonial Empire, 1415–1825*. Oxford, 1963.
Coquery, Catherine. *La découverte de l'Afrique*. Paris: Julliard, 1965.
Cornevin, Robert. *Histoire de l'Afrique*. Vol 2: L'Afrique précoloniale. Paris: Payot, 1976.
Curtin, Philipp D., *The Atlantic Slave Trade: A Census*. Madison: Univ. of Wisconsin Press, 1969.
Davidson, Basil. *Mère Afrique*. Paris: PUF, 1965.
Deschamps, Hubert. *Histoire générale de l'Afrique noire*. Vol. 1: Des origines à 1800, 1970; Vol. 2: De 1800 à nos jours, 1971.
——. *Les religions de l'Afrique noire*. Paris: PUF, 1977.
Ducasse, André. *Les négriers*. Paris: Hachette, 1948.
Emmer, P., et al. *La traite des noirs par l'Atlantique: Nouvelles approaches*. Paris: Société Française d'Histoire d'Outre-mer, 1975.
Gaston, Martin. *Nantes au XVIIIᵉ siècle. L'ère des négriers (1714–1774)*. Based on unpublished documents. Paris: Librairie Felix Alcan, 1931.
Hallet, Robin. *Africa to 1875*. Ann Arbor: Univ. of Michigan Press, 1970.
Herscovits, Melville J. *The Economic Life of Primitive Peoples*. New York and London: Alfred A. Knopf, 1940.
Holas, J. B. *L'Afrique noire*. Paris: Bloud et Gay, 1965.
——. *Changements sociaux en Côte d'Ivoire*. Paris: PUF, 1961.
Lacroix, Louis. *Les derniers négriers*. Paris, 1952.
L'esclavage en Afrique précoloniale. Seventeen Studies Presented by Claude Meillassoux. Paris: François Maspero, 1975.
Mannix, D. P. *Black Cargoes: A History of the Atlantic Slave Trade*. New York: Viking Press, 1962.

Maquet, Jacques J. *Afrique, les civilisations noires*. Paris: PUF, 1962.

Mauro, Frédéric. *L'expansion européenne (1600–1870)*. Paris: PUF, 1964.

Monteil, Vincent. *L'Islam noir*. Paris: Seuil, 1964.

Oliver, Roland, and J. D. Fage. *Breve história de Africa*. Madrid: Alianza Editorial, 1972.

Parrinder, Geoffrey. *La religion en Afrique occidentale*. Paris: Payot, 1950.

Paulme, Denise. *Les civilisations africaines*. Paris: PUF, 1974.

Race and Slavery in the Western Hemisphere: Quantitative Studies. Ed. L. Engerman and Eugene D. Genovese. Princeton: Princeton Univ. Press, 1975.

Rinchon, Dieudonné. *La traite et l'esclavage des Congolais par les Européens*. Bruxelles, 1929.

Roncière, Charles de la. *Nègres et négriers*. Paris: Editions Portiques, 1933.

Suret-Canale, Jean. "Afrique noire: Occidentale et centrale," *Géographie, civilisations, histoire*. Paris: Editions Sociales, 1973.

Tindall, P. E. N. *Race Relations in Western Africa in the Slave Trade Era*. Salisbury: The Central Africa Historical Association, 1975.

Trimingham, J. S. *Islam in West Africa*. Oxford: Oxford Univ. Press, 1959.

PORTUGAL AND BRAZIL

Abreu, João Capistrano de. *Caminhos antigos e povoamento do Brasil*. Rio de Janeiro: Liv. Briguiet, 1960.

——. *Capítulos de História colonial*. Rio de Janeiro: Liv. Briguiet, 1954.

Alden, Dauril, ed. *Colonial Roots of Modern Brazil*. Berkeley: Univ. of California Press, 1973.

Andrade, Manuel Correia de. *A terra e o homem no nordeste*. São Paulo: Brasiliense, 1963.

Azevedo, J. Lucio de. *Epocas de Portugal econômico*. Lisbonne: Liv. Clássica, 1947.

Azevedo, Thales de. *Classes sociais e grupos de prestígio*. Bahia: UFBᵃ, 1959.

Boxer, Charles R. *The Dutch in Brazil (1624–1654)*. Oxford: Oxford Univ. Press, 1957.

——. *The Golden Age of Brazil*. Berkeley: Univ. of California Press, 1962.

Buescu, Mircea. *História econômica do Brasil: Pesquisas e analises*. Rio de Janeiro: APEC, 1970.

——. *Evolução econômica do Brasil*. Rio de Janeiro: APEC, 1974.

——. *300 anos de inflação*. Rio de Janeiro: APEC, 1973.

Calmon, Pedro. *História social do Brasil*. 3 vols. São Paulo: Ed. Nacional, 1940.

Calogeras, J. Pandiá. *Formação histórica do Brasil*. São Paulo: Ed Nacional, 1957.

Carreira, Antonio. *As companhias pombalinas de navegação, comércio, e tráfico de escravos entre a costa africana e o nordeste brasileiro*. Porto, 1969.

Dias, Carlos Malheiro, *et al. História da colonização portuguesa no Brasil*. 3 vols. Porto, 1924.

Diegues, Jr. Manuel. *Etnias e culturas no Brasil*. Rio de Janeiro: Civilização Brasileira/MEC, 1976.

Fernandes, Florestan. *Mudanças sociais no Brasil*. São Paulo: Difel, 1960.

Freyre, Gilberto. *Nordeste*. Rio de Janeiro: Liv. José Oympio, 1961.

——. *Ordem e Progresso*. Rio de Janeiro: Liv. José Olympio/MEC, 1974.

Furtado, Celso. *La formation économique du Brésil.* Paris: Mouton, 1972.

Gonçalves de Mello, José Antonio. *No tempo dos flamengos: Influência da ocupação holandesa na vida e cultura do norte do Brasil.* São Paulo: Editora Nacional, 1951.

Graham, Richard. *A Grã-Bretanha e o início da modernização do Brasil.* São Paulo: Brasiliense, 1973.

História general da civilização brasileira. (Ed. Sergio Buarque de Holanda). 6 vols. São Paulo: Difel, 1963–1967.

Holanda, Sergio Buarque de. *Raizes do Brasil.* Rio de Janeiro: Liv. José Olympio, 1976.

——. *Visão do Paraíso.* São Paulo: Ed. Nacional, 1977.

Hoornaert, Eduardo. *Formação do catolicismo brasileiro, 1960–1800: Ensaio de interpretação a partir dos oprimidos.* Petró-polis: Vozes, 1974.

Leite, Serafim. *História da Companhia de Jesus no Brasil.* 10 vols. Rio de Janeiro, 1938–1950.

Magalhaes Godinho, Vitorino. *A economia dos descobrimentos henriquinos.* Lisbonne: Livraria Sá da Costa, 1962.

Marchant, Alexandre. *Do escambo a escravidão.* São Paulo: Ed Nacional, 1943.

Marcilio, Maria Luiza. *La ville de São Paulo: Peuplement et population, 1750–1850.* Rouen: Université de Rouen, 1968.

Mattos, Raymundo José da Cunha. "Chorografia histórica da província de Goyaz," *Revista Instituto Histórico Geográfico e Etnográfico do Brasil,* 37:213–398; 38:1–149. Rio de Janeiro, 1874.

Mauro, Frédéric. *Le Portugal et l'Atlantique au dix-septième siècle (1570–1670).* Paris: S.E.V.P.E.N., 1960.

Maxwell, K. R. "Conflicts and Conspiracies: Brazil and Portugal 1750–1808," *Cambridge, Latin American Studies,* 16.

Mota, Carlos Guilherme. *Nordeste 1817.* São Paulo: Perspectiva SA, 1972.

Pelaez, Carlos Manuel and Mircea Buescu. *A moderna história econômica.* Rio de Janeiro: APEC, 1976.

Petrone, Maria Thereza Schorer. *A lavoura canavieira em São Paulo: Expansão e declínio (1765–1851).* São Paulo: Difel, 1968.

Pinho, José Wanderley de Araújo. *História de um engenho do Recôncavo, 1552–1944.* Rio de Janeiro: Liv. Valverde, 1946.

Prado, Jr. Caio. *The Colonial Background of Modern Brazil.* Berkeley: Univ. of California Press, 1967.

——. *História econômica do Brasil.* São Paulo: Brasiliense, 1963.

Rodrigues, José Honório. *Historiografia e bibliografia do domínio holandês no Brasil.* Rio de Janeiro, 1949.

Russell-Wood, A. J. R. *Fidalgos and Philanthropists: The Santa Casa de Misericórdia of Bahia, 1550–1755.* Berkeley: Univ. of California Press, 1968.

Sanchez-Albornoz, Nicolás. *The Population of Latin America: A History.* Berkeley, Univ. of California Press, 1974.

Santos, Joaquim, Felicio (dos.). *Memórias do Distrito Diamantino da Comarca do Serro Frio.* Rio de Janeiro: Edicões O Cruzeiro, 1956.

Schwartz, Stuart B., *Sovereignty and Society in Colonial Brazil.* Berkeley: Univ. of California Press, 1973.

Simonsen, Roberto. *História econômica do Brasil (1600–1820)*. São Paulo: Ed. Nacional, 1967.

Vianna, F. J. Oliveira. *Introdução à história social da economia pré-capitalista no Brasil*. Rio de Janeiro: Liv. José Olympio, 1968.

———. *Populações meridionais do Brasil*. 2 vols. Rio de Janeiro: Paz e Terra, 1973.

Vianna, Hildegardes. *A Bahia já foi assim (Crônica de costumes)*. Salvador. Ed. Itapuã, 1973.

Historians, Anthropologists, and Sociologists of Slavery

Azevedo, Thales de. *Les élites de couleur dans une ville brésilienne*. Paris: UNESCO, 1953.

———. *Cultura e situação racial no Brasil*. Rio de Janeiro: Civilização Brasileira, 1966.

———. *Civilização e mestissagem*. Salvador: Ed. Progresso, 1951.

Bastide, Roger. *Les Amériques noires: Les civilisations africaines dans le nouveau monde*. Paris: Payot, 1967.

———. *Les religions africaines du Brésil*. Paris: PUF, 1960.

Bastide, Roger, and Florestan Fernandes. *Brancos e Negros em São Paulo: Ensaio sociológico sobre aspectos da formação, manifestações atuais e efeitos do preconceito de cor na sociedade paulistana*. São Paulo: Editora Nacional, 1971.

Bethell, Leslie. *The Abolition of the Brazilian Slave Trade: Brazil and the Slave Question (1807–1869)*. Cambridge: Cambridge Univ. Press, 1970.

Cardoso, Fernando Henrique. *Capitalismo e escravidão no Brasil meridional*. Rio de Janeiro: Paz e Terra, 1977.

Cardoso, Fernando Henrique, and Octávio Ianni. *Cor e mobilidade social em Florianopolis*. São Paulo: Ed. Nacional, 1960.

Carneiro, Edison. *Candomblés da Bahia*. Rio de Janeiro: Edições de Ouro, 1969.

———. *Negros Bantus*. Rio de Janeiro: Civilização Brasileira, 1937.

———. *O quilombo dos Palmares*. Rio de Janeiro: Civilização Brasileira, 1966.

Conrad, Robert. *The Destruction of Brazilian Slavery, 1850–1880*. Berkeley: Univ. of California Press, 1972.

Costa, Emilia Viotti da, *Da senzala a colônia*. São Paulo: Difel, 1966.

Costa, L. A., *O negro no Rio de Janeiro*. Rio de Janeiro: Ed. Nacional, 1953.

Dean, Warren. *Rio Claro: A Brazilian Plantation System, 1820–1920*. Stanford: Stanford Univ. Press, 1976.

Degler, Carl. *Neither Black nor White: Slavery and Race Relations in Brazil and the United States*. New York, 1971.

Dornas Filho, João. *A escravidão no Brasil*. Rio de Janeiro: Civilização Brasileira, 1939.

———. *A influência social do negro brasileiro*. Curitiba: Guaíra, 1943.

Ennes, Ernesto. *As guerras nos Palmares*. Rio de Janeiro: Ed. Nacional, 1958.

Etzel, Eduardo. *Escravidão negra e branca: O passado através do presente*. São Paulo: Global editora, 1976.

Fernandes, Florestan. *O negro no mundo dos brancos*. São Paulo: Difel, 1972.

———. *A integração do negro na sociedade de classes*. 2 vols. São Paulo: Dominus, 1965.

Franco, Maria Silvia de Carvalho. *Homens livres na sociedade escravocrata.* São Paulo: Instituto Estudos Brasileiros-USP, 1969.

Freitas, Décio. *Palmares, a guerra dos escravos.* Porto Alegre: Ed. Movimento, 1973.

Freyre, Gilberto. *Maîtres et esclaves.* Paris: Gallimard, 1975 (out of print).

――. *O escravo nos anuncios dos jornais brasileiros do século XIX.* Recife: Imprensa Universitária, 1963.

――. *Sobrados e Mucambos.* São Paulo: Liv. José Olympio, 1968.

Gerson, *Brasil: A escravidão no Império.* Rio de Janeiro: Pallas, 1975.

Gorender, Jacob. *O escravismo colonial.* São Paulo: Atica, 1978.

Goulart, José Alipio. *Da fuga ao suicídio: Aspectos da rebeldia dos escravos no Brasil.* Rio de Janeiro: Conquista, 1972.

――. *Da palmatória ao patíbulo (castigos de escravos no Brazil).* Rio de Janeiro: Conquista, 1971.

――. *O Regatão.* Rio de Janeiro: Conquista, 1972.

Goulart, Maurício. *A escravidão africana no Brasil (Das origens à extinção do trafico).* São Paulo: Alfa-Omega, 1975.

Gouveia, Maurilio de. *História da escravidão.* Rio de Janeiro: Gráfica Tupy, 1955.

Harris, Marvin. *Patterns of Race in the Americas.* New York: Norton Library, 1974.

Ianni, Octavio. *As Metamorfoses do escravo.* São Paulo: Difel, 1962.

――. *Raças e classes sociais no Brasil.* Rio de Janeiro: Civilização Brasileira, 1972.

Jurema, Aderbal. *Insurreições negras no Brasil.* Recife: Ed. Mozart, 1935.

Lapassade, G., and Marco Aurelio Luz. *O segredo da Macumba,* Rio de Janeiro: Paz e Terra, 1972.

Laytand, Dante de, *Alguns aspectos da história do negro no Rio Grande do Sul.* Rio Grande do Sul: Imagem da terra gaucha; Porto Alegre: Kosmos, 1942.

Luna, Luiz. *O negro na luta contra a escravidão.* Rio de Janeiro: Ed. Leitura, 1968.

Maia Machado, Filho (Aires da), *O negro e o garimpo em Minas Gerais.* Rio de Janeiro: José Olimpio, 1943.

Malheiro, Perdigão. *A escravidão no Brasil: Ensaio histórico, jurídico, social.* 2 vols. Petropolis: Vozes/INL, 1976.

Moraes, Evaristo de, *A escravidão africana no Brasil (Das origens à extinção).* São Paulo. Ed. Nacional, 1933.

――. *A campanha abolicionista (1879–1888).* Rio de Janeiro: Liv. Leite Ribeiro, 1924.

Moura, Clovis. *O negro: De bom escravo a mau cidadão.* Rio de Janeiro: Conquista, 1977.

――. *Rebeliões da senzala: Quilombos, insurreções, guerrilhas.* Rio de Janeiro: Conquista, 1972.

Pereira, João Baptista Borges. *Cor, profissão e mobilidade.* São Paulo: Pioneira, 1967.

Pereira, Nunes. *A casa das Minas,* Rio de Janeiro: Sociedade Brasileira de Antropologia e Etnologia, 1947.

Pierson, Donald. *Brancos e pretos na Bahia: Estudo de contacto racial.* São Paulo: Ed. Nacional, 1971.

――. *O candomblé da Bahia,* Curitiba: Ed. Guaíra, 1942.

———. *Negroes in Brazil.* 2d ed. Carbondale: Univ. of Illinois Press, 1967.

Queiroz, Suely Robles de, *Escravidão negra em São Paulo: Um estudo das tensões provocadas pelo escravismo no século XIX.* Rio de Janeiro: José Olímpio/MEC, 1977.

Querino, Manuel. *Costumes africanos no Brasil.* Rio de Janeiro: Civilização Brasileira, 1938.

———. *A Bahia de outrora.* Bahia: Liv. Econômica, 1916.

Ramos, Arthur. *A aculturação negra no Brasil.* São Paulo: Ed. Nacional, 1942.

———. *O negro brasileiro.* Rio de Janeiro: Civilização Brasileira, 1934.

———. *O negro na civilização brasileira.* Rio de Janeiro: Ed. Casa dos Estudantes do Brasil, n.d.

Renault, Delso. *Industria, escravidão, sociedade: Uma pesquisa historiográfica do Rio de Janeiro no século XIX.* Rio de Janeiro: Civilização Brasileira, INL, 1976.

Ribeiro, João. *O elemento negro: História, folclore, linguística.* Rio de Janeiro, n.s.d.

Rodrigues, José Honório. *Brasil e Africa, outro horizonte (relações e politíca brasileiro-africana).* 2 vols. Rio de Janeiro: Civilização Brasileira, 1961.

Rodrigues, Nina. *Os africanos no Brasil.* São Paulo: Ed. Nacional, 1976.

———. *O animismo fetichista dos negros baianos.* Rio de Janeiro: Civilização Brasileira, 1935.

Salles, Vicente. *O negro no Pará sob o regime da escravidão.* Rio de Janeiro: Fundação Getulio Vargas/Universidade Federal do Pará, 1971.

Santos, Deoscoredes M. dos. *Axé Opó Afonjá.* Rio de Janeiro, 1962.

Santos, Juana Elbein dos. *Os Nagô e a morte: Pàde, Asèsè e o culto Egun na Bahia.* Petropolis: Vozes, 1976.

Sayers, Raymond S. *O negro na literatura Brasileira.* Rio de Janeiro: Edições o Cruzeiro, 1958.

Scarano, Julita. *Devoção e escravidão: A irmandade de Nossa Senho ra do Rosário dos pretos no distrito diamantino no século XVIII.* São Paulo: Ed. Nacional, 1976.

Skidmore, Thomas E. *Preto no branco: Raça e nacionalidade no pensamento brasileiro.* Rio de Janeiro: Paz e Terra, 1976.

Stein, Stanley J. *Vassouras, a Brazilian Coffee County, 1850–1890: The Roles of Planter and Slave in Changing Plantation Society.* New York: Atheneum, 1974.

Taunay, Affonso d'E. *Subsídios para a história do tráfico africano no Brasil colonial.* Rio de Janeiro, 1941.

Toplin, Robert Brent. *The Abolition of Brazilian Slavery.* New York, 1972.

Valente, Waldemar. *Sincretismo religioso afro-brasileiro.* São Paulo: Ed. Nacional, 1955.

Verger, Pierre. *O fumo da Bahia e o tráfico dos escravos do gôlfo de Benim.* Salvador: Centro de Estudos Afro-Orientais da Universidade Federal da Bahia, 1966.

———. *Flux et reflux de la traite des nègres entre le golfe de Bénin et Bahia de Todos os Santos du XVIIᵉ au XIXᵉ siècle.* Paris: Mouton, 1968.

Viana, Filho Luiz. *O negro na Bahia.* Rio de Janeiro: José Olympio, 1946.

Articles

Boxer, Charles R. "Negro Slavery in Brazil," *Race,* 5 (1964).

Brandao, Julio de Freitas. "O escravo e o direito," *ASNPUH,* 1 (1973), 255–283.

Brunschwig, H. "La troque et la traite." *CEA*, 2/7 (1962), 339–346.

Campos, J. da Silva. "Ligeiras notas sobre a vida in[tima, costumes e religião dos Africanos na Bahia." *AAEB*, 29 (1943).

Castro, Helio Oliveira Portocarrero de. "Viabilidade econômica da escravidão no Brasil, 1850–1888," *RBE*, 27/1 (1973), 43–67.

Castro, Jeanne Berrance de. "O negro na guarda nacional," *AMP*, 23(1969), 149–172.

Cerqueira, Beatriz Westin. "Um estudo da escravidão em Ubatuba," *EH*, 5 (1966), 7–58.

Costa, Emilia Viotti da. "Da escravidão ao trabalho livre." In *Da Monarquia a República: Momentos decisivos*. São Paulo: Grijalbo, 1977. Pp. 209–226.

——. "O mito da democracia racial no Brasil." In *Da Monarquia a República: Momentos decisivos*. São Paulo: Grijalbo, 1977. Pp. 227–242.

Dornas, Filho João. "A influência social do negro brasileiro," *RAMS*, 51 (1938), 95–134.

Galloway, J. H. "The Last Years of Slavery in the Sugar Plantations of Northeastern Brazil," *HAHR*, 51/4 (1971).

Graham, Richard. "Brazilian Slavery Re-examined: A Review Article," Institute of Latin American Studies, The University of Texas at Austin (reprint from *JSH*, 3/4 (1970), 431–453.

Ianni, Octávio. "Escravismo e racismo," *AH*, 7 (1975), 66–94.

Ignace, Etienne. "A revolta dos Malês," *AA*, 10/11 (1970), 121–135.

Keith, Henri H. "A tradição não-violenta na história do Brasil: Mito que precisa ser demolido?" In *Conflito e continuidade na sociedade brasileira*. Rio de Janeiro: Civilização Brasileira, 1970.

Kessler, Arnold. *Bahian Manumission Practices in the Early Nineteenth Century,* Communication given at the American Historical Association. San Francisco, 1973 (xerox).

Klein, Herbert S. "The Colored Freedman in Brazilian Slave Society," *JSH*, 3/1 (Fall 1969), 30–52.

——. "The Internal Slave Trade in 19th-century Brazil: A Study of Slave Importations into Rio de Janeiro in 1852," *HAHR*, 51/4 (1971), 567–586.

——. "The Trade in African Slaves to Rio de Janeiro 1795–1811: Estimates of Mortality and Patterns of Voyages," *JAH*, 10/4 (1969), 533–549.

——. "The Portuguese Slave Trade from Angola in the 18th century," *JEH*, 32/4 (1972), 894–917.

Klein, H. S., and St. L. Engerman. "Padrões de embarque e mortalidade no tráfico de escravos africanos ao Rio de Janeiro, 1825–1830." In *Moderna História Econômica*. Rio de Janeiro: APEC, 1976. Pp. 96–113.

Leff, Nathaniel, and Herbert J. Klein. "O crescimento da população não européia antes do início do descobrimento: O Brasil do século XIX, » *Anais de História*, 6 (1974), 51–70.

Lisanti, Luis. « Delta importazione degli schiavi nel Brazile coloniale (1715), » *ACDA*, 4 (1972), 305–307.

Marcillo, Maria Luiza, Marques, Rubens Murillo, and José Carlos Barreiro. "Considerações sobre o preço de escravo no período imperial: Uma analise quantitativa," *AH*, 3 (1971), 179–194.

Mattoso, Katia M. de Queirós. "A carta de alforria como fonte complementar para o estudo da rentabilidade de mão-de-obra escrava urbana (1819–1888." In *Moderna História Econômica*. Rio de Janeiro: *APEC*, 1976. Pp. 149–163.

——. "A propósito de cartas de alforria—Bahia, 1779–1850," *AH*, 4 (1972), 23–52.

——. "Conjoncture et société au Brésil à la fin du xviiie siècle," *CAL*, 5 (1970), 33–53.

——. "Les esclaves de Bahia au début du xixe siècle (étude d'un groupe social)," *CAL*, 9/10 (1974), 105–129.

——. "Um estudo quantitativo de estrutura social: A cidade do Salvador, Bahia de Todos os Santos no século XIX. Primeiras abordagens, primeiros resultados," *EH*, 15 (1976), 7–28.

Mott, Luiz R. B. "A etnodemografia histórica e o problema das fontes documentais para o estudo da população de Sergipe na 1ª metade do século XIX," *CEE*, 29/1 (1976), 3–24.

——. "Cautelas de alforria de duas escravas na Província do Pará (1829–1846)," *RH*, 95 (1973), 263–268.

——. "A Escravatura: A propósito de uma representação a El Rei sobre a escravatura no Brasil," *RIEB*, 14 (1973), 127–136.

——. "Brancos, Pardos, Pretos e Indios em Sergipe: 1825–1830," *AH*, 6 (1974), 139–184.

——. "Pardos e Pretos em Sergipe: 1774–1851," *RIEB*, 18 (1976), 8–37.

Pádua, Ciro T. de. O negro no planalto do século XVI ao século XIX, *RIHGS*, 41 (1942), 127–228.

Paulme, Denise. "Structures sociales traditionnelles en Afrique noire," *CEA*, 1 (1960), 15–27.

Queiroz, Suely Robles Reis de. "Brandura da escravidão brasileira: Mito ou realidade?" 103 (1975), 443–482.

Ramos, Arthur. "Castigos de escravos," *RAMS*, 48 (1938), 79–104.

——. "O espírito associativo do negro brasileiro," *RAMS*, 48 (1938), 105–126.

Ramos, Donald. "Mariage and family in Colonial Vila Rica," *HAHR*, 55/2 (1975), 220–225.

Russell-Wood, A. J. R. "Aspectos da vida social das Irmandades leigas da Bahia no século XVIII." *Bicentenário de um monumento baiano*. Salvador: Ed. Beneditina, 1971.

——. "Black Mulatto Brotherhood in Colonial Brazil: A Study in Collective Behavior," *HAHR*, 54/4 (1974), 567–602.

Ryder, A. F. C. "The Re-establishment of Portuguese Factories in the Costa de Minas to the Mid-eighteenth Century," *JHSN*, 1958.

Santos, Corcino Medeiros dos. "Relações de Angola com o Rio de Janeiro (1736–1808)," *EH*, 12 (1973), 7–66.

Santos, Juana Elbein dos, and Deoscoredes M. dos Santos. "Ancestor Worship in Bahia: The Egun Cult," *JSA*, 58 (1969), 79–108.

Schwartz, Stuart B. "The Manumission of Slaves in Colonial Brazil: Bahia, 1684–1745," *HAHR*, 54/4 (1974), 603–635.

——. "Resistance and Accommodation in 18th-Century Brazil: The Slaves' View of Slavery," *HAHR*, 57/1 (1977), 69–81.

——. "The Mocambo: Slave Resistance in Colonial Bahia," *JSH*, 3/4 (1973), 313–338.

Smith, M. G. "The Haoussa System of Social Status," A, 29/3 (1959), 239–252.

Suret Canale, Jean. "Contexte et conséquences sociales de la traite africaine," *PA* (1964/2), 127–150.

Westphalen, Cecilia Maria. "A introdução de escravos novos no littoral paranaense," *RH*, 89 (1972), 139–154.

SUPPLEMENTARY BIBLIOGRAPHY

A. UNPUBLISHED THESES

Flory, Rae Jean Dell. *Bahian Society in the Mid-Colonial Period: The Sugar Planters, Tobacco Growers, Merchants and Artisans of Salvador and the Recôncavo, 1680–1725*. University of Texas at Austin, 1978 (Ph.D.).

Martins, Roberto. *Growing in Silence: The Slave Economy of Nineteenth Century Minas Gerais, Brazil*. Vanderbilt University, 1980 (Ph.D.).

Mello, Pedro Carvalho de. *The Economics of Labor in Brazilian Coffee Plantations, 1850–1888*. University of Chicago, 1977 (Ph.D.).

Metcalf, Alida Christine. *Families of Planters, Peasants and Slaves: Strategies of Survival in Santana de Parnaiba, Brazil, 1720–1820*. University of Texas at Austin, 1980 (Ph.D.).

Oliveira, Maria Inês Cortes de. *O liberto o seu mundo e os outros*. Salvador, Universidade Federal da Bahia, 1979 (Masters).

Reis, João José. *Slave Rebellion in Brazil: The African Muslim Uprising in Bahia, 1835*. University of Minnesota, 1982 (Ph.D.).

B. HISTORIANS AND ECONOMISTS OF SLAVERY

Almada, Vilma Paraiso Ferreira de. *Escravismo e transição: O Espirito Santo (1850–1888)*. Rio de Janeiro: Graal, 1984.

Bakos, Margareth Marchiori. *RS: Escravismo e abolição*. Porto Alegre: Mercado Aberto, 1982.

Beiguelman, Paula. *A crise do escravismo e a grande imigração*. São Paulo: Brasiliense, 1981.

Cardoso, Ciro Flamarion S. *Agricultura, escravidão e capitalismo*. Petropolis: Vozes, 1979.

——. *Afro-America: A escravidão no novo mundo*. São Paulo: Brasiliense, 1982.

Chiavenato, Julio José. *O negro no Brasil: Da senzala à guerra do Paraguai*. São Paulo: Brasiliense, 1980.

Conrad, Robert Edgar. *Children of God's Fire: A Documentary History of Black Slavery in Brazil*. Princeton: Princeton Univ. Press, 1983.

Conrad, Robert Edgar. *Tumbeiros: O tráfico de escravos para o Brasil*. São Paulo: Brasiliense, 1985.

Costa, Iraci del Nero da. *Vila Rica: População (1719–1826)*. São Paulo: IPE/USP, 1979.

——. *Populações mineiras: sobre a estrutura populacional des alguns nucleos mineiros no alvorecer do século XIX.* São Paulo: IPE/USP, 1981.

——. *Minas Gerais: Estruturas populacionais tipicas.* São Paulo: EDEC, 1982.

——, ed. *Economia escravista brasileira.* In *Estudos Economicos,* 13/1. São Paulo: IPE/USP, 1983.

Freitas, Décio. *Os guerrilheiros do imperador.* Rio de Janeiro: Graal, 1978.

Galizza, Diana Soares de. *O declínio da escravidão na Paraiba, 1850–1888.* João Pessoa: Ed. Universitaria/UFPb, 1979.

Hasenbalg, Carlos Alfredo. *Discriminação e desigualdades raciais no Brasil.* Rio de Janeiro: Graal, 1979.

Lapa, José Roberto do Amaral, ed. *Modos de produção e realidade brasileira.* Petropolis: Vozes, 1980.

Luna, Francisco Vidal. *Minas Gerais: Escravos e senhores.* São Paulo: IPE/USP, 1981.

Maestri Fº, Mario José. *O escravo gaucho: resistência e trabalho.* São Paulo: Brasiliense, 1984.

——. *O escravo no Rio Grande do Sul: A charqueada e a gênese do escravismo gaucho.* Porto Alegre: EDUCS/EST, 1984.

Martins, José de Souza. *O cativeiro da terra.* 2d ed. São Paulo: Livraria Editora Ciencias Humanas, 1981.

Mattoso, Katia M. de Queirós. *Testamentos de escravos libertos do século XIX: Uma fonte para o estudo de mentalidades.* Bahia: UFBa, 1979 (Estudos Baianos nº 85).

Mello, João Manoel Cardoso de. *O capitalismo tardio.* 2d ed. São Paulo: Brasiliense, 1982.

Merrick, Thomas W., and Douglas H. Graham. *Population and Economic Development in Brazil, 1800 to the Present.* Baltimore: Johns Hopkins Univ. Press, 1979 (Brazilian Edition, Rio de Janeiro: Zahar, 1981).

Moura, Clovis. *Os quilombos e a rebelião negra.* São Paulo: Brasiliense, 1981.

——. *Brasil: As raizes do protesto negro.* São Paulo: Global, 1983.

Neuhaus, Paulo, ed. *Economia brasiliera: Uma visão historica.* Rio de Janeiro: Campus, 1980.

Novais, Fernando. *Portugal e Brasil na crise do antigo sistema colonial (1777–1808).* São Paulo: HUCITEC, 1979.

Rabello, Elizabeth Darwiche. *As elites na sociedade paulista na segunda metade do século XVIII.* São Paulo: Ed. Comercial Safady, 1980.

Salvador, José Gonçalves. *Os magnatas do tráfico negreiro.* São Paulo: Pioneira/ Edusp, 1981.

Samara, E. de Mesquita, and I. del Nero da Costa. *Demografia historica: Bibliografia brasileira.* São Paulo: IPE/USP/FINEP, 1984.

Santos, Maria Januaria V. *A balaiada e a insurreição de escravos no Maranhão.* São Paulo: Atica, 1983.

Santos, Ronaldo Marcos dos. *Resistência e superação do escravismo na provincia de São Paulo.* São Paulo: IPE/USP, 1980.

Silva, Eduardo. *Barões e escravidão: Três gerações de fazendeiros e a crise da estrutura escravista.* Rio de Janeiro: Nova Fronteira/Pro Memoria/INL, 1984.

INDEX